ENZO
CALZAGHE
A FIGHTING LIFE

WRITTEN WITH
MICHAEL PEARLMAN

GREAT NORTHERN

THIS book is for my soulmate,
Jackie Calzaghe
and the other wonderful women in my life;
my daughters Sonia and Melissa,
my mother Victoria
and Jackie's mother Rebecca Phillips.
And for my hero Guiseppe
and Joe, my best friend.

Great Northern Books
PO Box 213, Ilkley, LS29 9WS
www.greatnorthernbooks.co.uk

ISBN:978-1905080-53-3

Design and layout: David Burrill

Printed in Great Britain by CPI Group (UK) Ltd, Croydon, CR0 4YY

CIP Data
A catalogue for this book is available from the British Library

ABOUT THE AUTHOR: Enzo Calzaghe MBE is the most decorated trainer in the history of British boxing. He was the trainer for his son Joe in all 46 of his professional fights and has also taken Gavin Rees and Enzo Maccarinelli to world titles. He won an unprecedented 17 awards for his efforts including BBC Sports Personality trainer of the year. Enzo is also a keen musician and budding film maker and lives in Pentwynmawr with his wife Jackie.

ABOUT THE CO-AUTHOR: Michael Pearlman has been the boxing and football writer for the *South Wales Argus* since 2003.

During that time he had unlimited access to the Team Calzaghe gym and produced a weekly column with Joe Calzaghe. He has covered the gym's boxers' fights across the UK and in America.

Michael lives with girlfriend Alison in Cardiff and insists writing this book was a doddle in comparison to the agony of supporting Tottenham Hotspur.

Acknowledgements

Thanks to my wife and my kids for allowing me to tell my story honestly, even though there have been some things that might have hurt their feelings or that they'd rather I hadn't disclosed to the world and to Uccio and Rhona, Sergio and all the other people who helped me remember the distant past.

My family's support has carried me through the good times and the bad and I would be lost without them. Particular thanks to Joe for being so helpful and supportive and for lending his perspective.

Barry Cox, Patricia Lennon and Liz Slack at Great Northern Books have allowed me to tell my story and endured a million phone calls and have always been encouraging even when I was driving them mad.

I would like to express gratitude to all the great people I've worked with and met in the boxing world over the years and of course to my friends in both Sardinia and Newbridge. I'm only sorry that with a lifetime of stories to tell I couldn't mention everyone.

Michael Pearlman, who helped me to write the book is a true friend and I can't begin to thank him for taking on a project that many people would have found daunting, trying to translate my multilingual ramblings into the written word! Michael has done a brilliant job and I am so glad he agreed to work with me. It truly has been a pleasure.

I have quoted from a number of newspapers including the *Sun*, the *Daily Mirror*, *Daily Telegraph*, the *Guardian*, the *South Wales Echo*, *Wales on Sunday* and the *South Wales Argus*. Despite writing about my frustration with the Press at times I built up a wonderful rapport with writers such as Kevin Mitchell, Paul Tully, John Francis, Pete Shuttleworth, Pat Sheehan, Steffan Garrero, Mark Staniforth, Steve Bunce, Steve Lillis and Ron Lewis and am grateful to them. Thanks also to Ken Gorman, a man covering Welsh sport for longer than even I've been involved with it!

Michael would like to thank Stephen Rose, Doug Nicholls,

Chris Wathan, Julian Doyle and Alison Sanders for help, advice and in Alison's case, enduring months of loaning Michael to me. Massive appreciation also goes to Richard Coomber for his time and assistance and thorough subediting.

But my gratitude is mainly reserved for Joe's legions of fans that supported us for two decades. Without you this story would never have been told.

CONTENTS

Foreword by

Joe Calzaghe

It has been three years since I retired and the easiest question in the world for me to answer is one I am asked most often. What do I most miss about boxing?

It's not the glory nights, it's not the paydays, it's not the celebrity or the adulation and it certainly isn't the hard work and early starts, crash diets and periods of lengthy starvation. The only thing I truly miss about boxing is my dad. Spending each and every day working with him in the gym was a privilege and that closeness we have, the back and forth and understanding, I miss it more than I ever imagined I would. It might not be the coolest thing to admit, but my dad has probably been my best friend since I was a little kid and he remains so. Being with him every day was by and large a pleasure.

Depression among ex-sport stars is rife it seems and I am not going to lie, I've had some down days myself since I retired at the age of thirty six. I'm financially set for life and I have great kids and hopefully a new career in the acting world. But the happiest I feel these days is after I spend a few hours training with dad.

We will go on a three mile run first, the staple of my training regime since I was a kid. When I was a little boy who was telling everyone he would be a world champion boxer, my dad took it upon himself to nurture that dream in every way he possibly could.

He read dusty old boxing manuals written in the 1950s that he hired from the library and he would use anything in the house that wasn't screwed down as a makeshift accessory to aid my training. A sofa cushion, tea towel, the stairs, everything to him could be put to use to give me an advantage. He'd never go easy on me, but he'd also never ask me to do anything he wouldn't do himself. "Why don't you want to go running in the snow Joe? I am going to," he'd tell me when I just wanted to stay in the warm and watch the television.

Though Paul Williams was officially my first trainer and the guy who gave Dad his opportunity in the boxing world, I have always thought of Dad as my coach.

He had such an amazing aptitude for boxing and I can honestly say that having seen him on the pads so often, Dad would have been a very, very good fighter if he'd have ever taken it up. I am pretty certain he could have boxed professionally, but it's probably lucky he kept all his faculties intact so he could become a great trainer instead even though he never planned to be. By the time Dad and my mum Jackie settled down in Wales to raise my two younger sisters and I my dad had already lived a life with enough drama and incident to fill this whole book!

When I was beginning my boxing dream Dad was on the cusp of a music career and outside of the gym the two of us would spend hours out and about together hitchhiking to gigs and recording sessions, moments that I cherish. Dad was my hero since I was a tiny kid. I remember waiting up on a Saturday night when I was still in primary school until he'd come home from a gig. I would wait and wait until I could hear his god awful winkle-picker-boots on the path coming closer to the house, click, click, click, knowing that in moments we could watch football or boxing together. That was by far the highlight of my week. The anticipation would get my heart thumping.

As teenagers we began to hear these stories from dad's past and it's fantastic to me that finally the world is going to know just what an amazing journey my dad's life has been, even though I think he's going to be quite embarrassed about some of it being public knowledge.

What is certain is that Dad gave up a whole lot to be my trainer and over the years we formed a partnership that was pure poetry, a bond and an understanding that I simply wouldn't have been able to replicate with anyone else.

There were two instances when I questioned whether or not to make a break from being trained by Dad and I thank my lucky stars I never made that move because it would've been a huge, huge mistake.

I have been around boxing gyms my whole life from amateur training camps with the Olympic development squad to grotty, dingy gyms in London or Manchester in search of sparring and I've encountered many, many boxing trainers. Not one of them is anything like Dad. For so long people didn't realise just how talented he was in his own right but he just had an ingrained understanding of the sport that I don't think you could teach. It's in his soul.

I owe everything to my dad. My boxing style, my motivational style, everything about the success I have had is directly related to my dad. If it wasn't for him I would never have got to where I did.

The fact Dad would go on to train three world champions from one small gym in the Gwent valleys shows how much talent he has. As much as anything it's because despite a perception of being a figure of fun, Dad understands how to read people better than anyone I know. That is what marks him out as being exceptionally good at what he does.

For over twenty years Dad managed me through every situation brilliantly. He always knew which buttons to press and when because he knows every ounce of my character. Some days I would turn up and not be in the mood and Dad would take one look at me and before I'd opened my mouth say, "Bugger off home Joe and come back tomorrow." If I was a bit nervous, overly confident, acting complacent or depressed, every range of emotion a boxer could experience my dad understood completely and utterly. Sometimes he would deliberately start an argument with me because he would know that's exactly what I needed at that moment.

He never complained even though people looked at him in a totally negative way for years and years. When I was at my best people said it was because I was so talented and anyone could have got me there and when I experienced poor performances, albeit in world title winning fights, people pointed the finger at Dad and diminished and derided him. He bottled up all that hurt to protect me and make my life as easy as possible.

That even led to a simply horrible time when I wondered if our working relationship was over and done with and I had to face my dad knowing I had let him down and humiliated him in public. But Dad said to me from day one in the gym when I was nine-years-old that he would always be a father first and a trainer second and that never changed. Thanks to his strength of character, straight talking and belief in me we overcame any problems I had and we did it together.

We would have our disagreements and that's probably an understatement actually, but I think that is natural if you are around someone around the clock as we were. It was a unique situation. Any boxer would be familiar with feeling like crap before a fight, worrying about an injury, struggling to make the weight and constantly being dehydrated and that can of course lead to some fiery words with your coach. But imagine if you then have to spend all of Sunday with the bastard because he wants to see his grandkids! We could drive each other mad, but the good times far outweighed the disagreements.

But boy, could we argue. We would have huge explosive rows and the way we spoke to each other turned the air blue as we both have fiery tempers. But we'd have a blast at one another and then it'd be over. An hour later we'd have a kiss and a hug and I'd be back in the gym and we'd have an amazing training session because Dad had wound me up so much.

I think arguably dad's greatest achievements as a trainer didn't even involve me. We relied on one another for so long but by the end of my career he had a thriving gym with great boxers. Those days were the most fun of my career with a stable packed full of talented fighters who loved each other to pieces. No one worked harder in any gym in Britain and I would imagine no one enjoyed themselves more than we did at that time. I was the undisputed super middleweight champion of the world and undefeated yet it was Dad who won the most awards. He thoroughly deserved every one of them and it made me so proud to see his talents celebrated.

I slogged long and hard to get to that stage of my career when I fought two legends in America and it would have been very tempting to carry on beyond that. I could still be boxing today. There was and still is money to be made even though none of the names left to fight really motivated or inspired me. It was Dad who told me to quit and he never changed his stance even though I knew my retirement was a day he dreaded like no other. He was insistent I should never, ever just fight for the money and desperately wanted me to protect my legacy and move on with my life, to find happiness in something else. It was completely selfless advice and he was a major factor in me hanging up my gloves once and for all.

Recently I watched back over some of my old fights on a compilation DVD and I was blown away by some of the camera shots of my dad. The sheer happiness in his face and elation in his eyes when I won filled me with contentment and the best thing of all was that we got to share each and every victory together. I am so thankful for that.

We've always joked in the Calzaghe family that Dad's life would make a great movie and I hope you'll agree with that after you've read what he has to say. But my message to you is that Enzo Calzaghe is completely unique. He doesn't conform to convention in any way imaginable and he is consumed with enthusiasm for life. Dad never rests for a minute, he doesn't sleep too often and he's always taking on new challenges and trying to stay active even though every other man his age who has made good money would probably love the chance to put their feet up and smell the roses.

But that's just not Dad and when I go and see him in our gym, rushing around juggling a million things and enjoying every second of it I pray to God I will have the same life in me at his age... but know full well that I won't. I wish I was more like him.

I am so thrilled Dad is telling his story. He fell into training and yet ended up with three world champions, pitting his wits against the likes of Freddie Roach and coming out on top as people looked on in amazement. He is my hero. He's not just a great father or trainer even though he is both of those. He is an inspirational person and I owe him everything.

Chapter One:

Father Versus Trainer

What sane father would willingly put his child in harm's way, or worse still, actively encourage him to do something that could lead to brain damage or even death?

I have been in the corner for every one of my son Joe Calzaghe's professional fights. Mostly it has been to see him dominate an opponent on the way to winning or defending a world title. But on a couple of occasions I've suffered the agony of seeing him knocked down, watched him try to unscramble his thoughts and regain control of his wobbling legs. That is hard. It's the reason his mother, my wife Jackie, never once watched him fight. She couldn't bear the idea of her baby boy getting hurt inside the ring.

Despite all the safety precautions, boxing is as real as it gets, a combat sport where a single punch can end a career and even worse, a life. It's an inherent danger and yet everyone willingly fights, knowing the risk. No guts no glory. The worst case scenario is clear to every fighter and every trainer and when you stand in the corner shouting instructions you know that ultimately you are powerless to prevent catastrophe. It only takes one tiny mistake in the ring and things can go horribly wrong.

That's a tremendous burden, the kind of thing that leads to sleepless nights or can wake you in a cold sweat. Yet we still do it.

Ahead of the biggest fight of Joe's career I wrestled those demons like never before.

It all started three weeks before Joe and Jeff Lacy were finally going to step into the ring. This was a fight that had been on and off more times than a page three girl's brassiere and for Joe it was a lot more than a super middleweight unification battle. It would be the defining night of his career.

I study boxing, of course I do, and while I had kept my counsel on Lacy, I just didn't rate the guy at all. I thought he was extremely limited, nothing more than a bully. He had one style and when things were going his way he had great power which was too much for virtually everyone else in the division. But I didn't see him getting on top of Joe. I was totally convinced Joe would break his heart and was in for the night he'd always dreamed about. There was just the long-time worry about his brittle hands.

After a career littered with wrist and hand problems Joe had broken his hand in his previous fight. That had forced him out of facing Lacy initially and we had literally wrapped him, or his hand at least, in cotton wool. Thank God Joe's promoter Frank Warren resurrected the fight despite plenty of trash talk about Joe from the USA when he pulled out initially. 'Stay-at-home Joe does it again,' they scoffed. 'Will he ever fight anyone that matters?' The time had come. It was now or never for Joe. Three weeks to go.

We couldn't put it off any longer and decided Joe needed to resume sparring. If the hand got hurt, the hand got hurt. We needed to know one way or the other what we were dealing with.

Well guess what? He had shooting pains in his wrist after landing a shot against the first guy he sparred with. I saw him wince immediately and got him out of the ring pronto. I drove him straight to the train station and off he went to London to get the opinion of a Harley Street specialist. Meanwhile, I paced around the gym, round and round, waiting and hoping.

Joe phoned me hours later and said the doctor's diagnosis was that he had damaged a bone in his left wrist and couldn't throw a punch for a week. He added that the doctor had given him a cortisone injection and was going into more details but I only heard two words. "A week."

I was elated. 'A week! One week! One little, tiny... doesn't matter anyway week. Thank God for that!' I had endured hours worrying that it would be a lot worse than that. The rest of the stuff? We'd just deal with it. We could get injections done, the fight was twenty days away and everything was going to work out. Thank the Lord.

I zoned back in and Joe was still talking. "I'll have to pull out of the fight," he told me through that terrible mobile phone reception static noise you always get on the train. WHAT? "Joe,

Joe, did I just hear you right? Pull out of the fight? Joe, Joe..."

We got disconnected and it was a good job. I couldn't believe my ears. I thought Joe would be as excited as I was but it dawned on me as I stewed on it in the gym that he believed the hype. He believed Jeff Lacy was the best he'd faced, an immense challenge, the super middleweight Mike Tyson. He'd believed the publicity machine and thought that with a lame wrist he could or even would lose. It shocked me that he didn't have as much faith in his own ability as I did, but I wasn't mad at Joe, just obsessed with making him see things my way.

I knew instantly that as soon as he got back, I was going to talk him into taking the fight. As his trainer, it was the only advice I could give him. As a father it was harder. Until then Joe had never had to put his faith in me making a decision like that for him. He knew he could rely on his own skills and abilities and made his own judgements or could listen to Frank Warren his boxing savvy promoter. But he was going to pull out of the fight. That is what he'd just told me. I think he said he wanted me to call Frank there and then. He'd convinced himself he couldn't beat Lacy with a bad hand after he left the doctor's office. He had a broken wing and a broken heart.

As a trainer it was simple but as a father it was a nightmare. If your kid came to you, genuinely feeling ill I am sure you would have no hesitation telling them to stay off school for the day. You want to protect your child, it's instinctive. But my boy wasn't going to school. He was going to fight a guy everyone said was a monster. What sort of a sadistic bastard of a father wouldn't pull his kid out of danger if that is what he wanted?

But I stuck to my first instinct which was that the fight had to go ahead. I truly believed it was the end of the line for Joe if he pulled out again. More importantly than that I had total conviction Joe Calzaghe could beat Jeff Lacy with only one hand. Putting those beliefs together I would have been cheating myself and Joe if I'd have just been a yes man. Telling him it'll all be fine and he should do what he felt right wasn't an option because he couldn't see what this would do to his reputation. I had to trust my gut.

I watched a Lacy DVD again while I waited for Joe to get back to Wales. It only reaffirmed what I already knew. Lacy was overhyped, overrated and over here in three weeks time. It was Joe's destiny to beat him. When he got into Newport Station he phoned for me to pick him up and I started practising what I was going to say on the ride down.

There was no anger in my voice. It was all just passion, bubbling to the surface as I explained how I felt as soon as the passenger door shut.

"You can't pull out. You just can't. You have to take the fight. If you don't, that's it. You'll be a fucking laughing stock. Don't even talk again about not fighting. Get that thought out of your head. I haven't phoned Frank Warren and I am not going to. If you want to tell him you will have to phone him yourself."

"Dad, I'm hurt. I can't use my fucking hand, I can't even hit the bag, let alone Lacy, and I can't possibly fight. My wrist is fucked."

"If you pull out it's over for you, you'll be finished."

"Don't be so stupid, Dad. I'll just fight him in a couple of months. He wants my belt too if you remember?"

"You don't get it, Joe! You won't fight in a couple of months. Can't you see what is happening? If you pull out now you will be finished. People will lose all respect for you. It'll be one time too many. You'll be damaged goods and Lacy won't want to know. He will move on to bigger paydays. You won't ever get a chance like this again. I am telling you if you pull out Lacy will tell you to go fuck yourself. You'll be ruined."

"That's not true. And even if it is, I can't physically fight with one hand. He's too good..."

"No, Joe, he isn't. Don't think that. He is made for you. If you box the way you box he won't be able to touch you. You will out-box him and out-think him from the first round. You will destroy him. It will be the easiest fight you've ever had."

"Are you serious? Have you seen how hard he hits? Did you see the Robin Reid fight?"

I couldn't believe what I was hearing. I yelled at Joe as I'd never yelled at him before.

"Are you serious? Get your head out of your arse and wake up and smell the coffee. He can't touch you. Jeff Lacy is not even in your league, Joe. It doesn't matter you haven't sparred and it won't matter if your hand doesn't heal. You are going to absolutely smash him to pieces. You will annihilate him, Joe, I promise you that, even if you only have one hand. But please, please don't call Frank Warren and pull out. There will be no coming back for you. I am telling you this as your trainer, you must still fight. There is no other option. Pull out if you want, but if you do you might as well retire."

Joe went quiet. I'd given him something to think about and I could sense he was coming round. I prayed I was right and that he would do what was best.

Despite all the anxiety I had over sending him into battle hurt, I still felt in my gut that I was doing the right thing. I convinced Joe to stick with the fight even if as a father it made me feel like a bad guy. I had total conviction that I was doing the right thing and what else could I trust apart from my instincts?

I insisted that if something went wrong we would tell the truth which was that I forced Joe to fight. People would respect him for fighting hurt and the blame would be shifted to me. I would make clear I cajoled Joe to take the fight against his better judgement and I'd have been finished. It was the gamble of a lifetime on my part, but I believed. I just knew he'd beat Jeff Lacy and thought he would do it easily. Sometimes in life, you are forced into making decisions you know will impact everything around you. I had just made one and I felt good about it despite the worrying. It helped that Frank Warren told Joe exactly the same thing when they talked. I had dissuaded Joe from pulling out and Frank was in complete agreement.

But yet, for all that conviction in my decision, there was always that doubt, that nagging little voice in your head, the one that snaps you out of pleasant dreams and haunts you late at night. 'You're going to get your boy hurt, just to try and prove that you're the best. How could you?'

That voice was quietened in the final fortnight before the fight when all the indicators suggested I would be vindicated. In the months leading into battle Lacy had come over for press events and Joe had gone to the States and Joe always seemed more comfortable. In that final two weeks with the media conferences and public workouts, Lacy always had his girlfriend in tow and I made that point to Joe. "He never leaves her side Joe. He's a long way from home and he's scared," I told him.

Once I'd convinced Joe that it wasn't a gamble he got right back on track. He wasn't humouring me or preparing half-heartedly. He agreed to push through the pain barrier and did exactly that. He put the worries about his wrist to one side and it was really at the media briefings that his confidence just grew and grew. Joe had been a world champion for almost ten years and that gave him plenty of experience in reading an opponent. He could see Lacy was out of his depth. Lacy had been told by a million and one people back home that he'd just need to come over and beat an old man. If people tell you something enough, you start to believe it. But now the fight was close, he realised Joe was not a no-hoper old man and I could tell he felt he was in way over his head.

Joe's wrist was manageable by fight night. It was by no means the first time he'd fought hurt and it wouldn't be the last. Joe had never liked me wrapping his hands before a fight so as usual we left it to Frank Warren's matchmaker Dean Powell. He's one of the best in the business and he made sure Joe's hands were as well protected as possible.

By the time we made our way to ringside I knew I had done the right thing. I felt it in my gut and most importantly saw it in Joe's face.

I had convinced him right down to his soul that this was his night. I felt very proud.

We were greeted by a roar, the crowd absolutely electric, something I miss hugely these days in my semi-retirement. I knew that things were about to change for us and it sent my mind spinning across the crazy journey that had brought me to the pinnacle of the great sport of boxing.

That packed arena in Manchester was a far cry from the dark alleys and sinister streets on which I slept as a homeless busker across Europe in my youth, from Holland to Hounslow, Bruges to Bournemouth, Rome to Reigate and Calais to Cardiff.

I heard a line once by the wrestler Dusty Rhodes and it fits my life like a glove. 'I've wined and dined with Kings and Queens and I've slept in alleys eating pork and beans'. Mind you if I had beans to eat when I was homeless I was extremely grateful. Eating any food meant it had been a good day. And I was homeless for a long time. Yet I've also met royalty and gigged with some of the greatest singers.

My journey to becoming the most decorated trainer in British boxing history was far from orthodox. I broke my brothers' hearts by walking out on them and our musical dream just as it seemed to be coming to fruition. I chose Joe over them. To a degree, I think my wonderful daughters Sonia and Melissa and beautiful wife Jackie have felt the same way in their lives. They've gone without attention and company from me because I was so focused on Joe. Hell, Jackie could've divorced me a hundred times over and deservedly so.

I have also been a habitual drug user and a hustler. It hurts me to say these things but to tell my story properly I have to hold my hands up to a lot of things that don't make me or anyone who knows me proud. That's reality, that's how life is, you have to be accountable for everything you do.

My name is Pietro Vincenzo Calzaghe and this is my story.

Chapter Two:

The Italian Bastard Gang

Not only was I lucky to survive my early years, with the doctors warning my parents I was probably going to die, but I was such a strange little kid I wasn't even able to express how scared I was.

I was born in Sardinia as the second child to Guiseppe and Victoria whose relationship wasn't without its difficulties. Financially life was tough and for my father, it was a time of adapting to everyday life after the atrocities of war. For my parents, love meant having to leave their home to start a totally new life.

In a sense Sassari will always be home for the Calzaghe family, if not necessarily for me personally. Overlooking the Sardinian Sea on the north and on the west, it is bounded by the Provinces of Oristano and Nuoro on the south and by the Province of Olbia-Tempio on the east. It's a provincial town which homes nearly 20 per cent of the entire population of Sardinia, but it's also a postcard place with countryside and sea views to die for.

My dad was born and raised in a hamlet named Bancali near Sassari where his father was a builder and he grew up in an environment where physical strength was respected. Even as a teenager my father was a giant figure and the villagers nicknamed him 'the animal' because he was so unbelievably strong. Though he was from a sleepy little village, he never had to worry about his services being in demand and was permanently employed on building sites as anyone in Sassari in the building trade knew him. Dad has hands like shovels and could carry three bags of cement on his back day after day. You can tell he's related to Joe easier than you can to me because neither of them really has a neck, but they both have huge upper body strength and similar work rates.

My father was and still is a stubborn so-and-so and as a teenager he forged documents to enlist in the army under the age for conscription, just because he felt he should fight for his country. Growing up in Britain – as I would – with a father who fought for the enemy in World War II was no picnic but for Dad it was just simple: Italy was at war and he should fight. His reward was a year in a Spanish POW camp where he was lucky to escape with his life. When the war ended he returned to Italy and took a job as a policeman in Torino. It was a natural fit for him due to his size and the respect he commanded and still does to this day. He would tell us kids stories of Italy's leader from the war years, Benito Mussolini, for decades to come. Dad couldn't stand the man and felt he betrayed Italy. Let's leave it at that.

It was working the beat in Torino that he met my mother Victoria and they were quickly married – a family trait – and my older brother Antonio was born as my parents enjoyed being young and in love while Europe was rebuilt from bomb blitz after blitz. Unfortunately their blissful existence wouldn't last because police officers weren't allowed by Italian law to be married until they were twenty-eight at the time and someone shopped my father to the authorities and he was sacked from the force – crazy.

My parents returned to Sassari and I was born in 1949. My birth gave my parents a whole new set of problems. Put very simply, I was an incredibly difficult and very odd little child, totally opposite to Antonio who by all accounts was an angelic boy.

I'd like to think I've got a great work ethic and that I give every task my best effort and commitment but as a child I seemingly couldn't be arsed to do anything! I barely learned to speak and by two-and-a-half years old I had hardly said a word. I could walk, eventually, but I never wanted to and would beg my mother to carry me, to pick me up and never let go. I would throw out my arms and not say a word as I waited to be plucked into the air by my mother or if I was really lucky, my father.

Being strange, quiet and lazy is one thing but I would also harm myself frequently and that was difficult for my mother to deal with. I was a teeny two-year-old loony who couldn't be left alone for ten seconds because I'd be putting myself in danger. The most frequent thing I would do would be to take the light bulbs out of lamps when they were really hot and stick them to my face or put them in my mouth. I got badly burned several times. If I'd done that once you'd think that's not so strange, but it happened dozens of times and I believe my parents were both frantic at how dangerous I was to leave alone, even for a second.

But that was nothing compared to the day my mother used to say was the worst of her life. She came into the front room of our house and I was sat in the corner, not crying but barely moving around or doing anything and she thought I appeared stranger than usual. She could also smell something burning. She came over to pick me up and as she did, to her horror, she realised I was sitting on a steaming hot metal iron. The heat was so intense that it had become completely imbedded onto my inner thighs and was only just a whisker away from burning off my little penis. The fact I didn't cry was even more worrying for my parents. 'What is wrong with this child,' my mother yelled as my uncle Vincenzo was sent to get word to my father.

Dad was hastily called away from the building site and he rushed me to hospital on foot. But even though they gave me good care there my burns were so severe that they got infected and the doctors warned my mum and dad that I possibly wasn't long for this world.

Now I am a parent I can only imagine what they went through. My mother would sit by my bedside for hours on end as I fought the initial infection and stared up at the lights above the hospital bed, still unable or unwilling to communicate. Apparently I didn't even shed a tear. I spent nearly eight weeks in hospital before they discharged me, still heavily bandaged and lucky to be alive. I continued to see the doctors for six months.

Back home, my mother would take me into the sea a lot and she used to say that it was the salt water which was my miracle cure as the wound healed without complication. I think the six months of health care was probably a factor too. And I am very grateful to the doctors who saved me. I've had a few brushes with death in my time, but I've always been very lucky.

So it was by no means plain sailing for Mum and Dad with this little lunatic running around (well not actually running, moving slowly and harming myself to be more accurate) and I have no idea why I was like I was. But I suppose my parents felt a fresh start couldn't do any harm as I wasn't exactly flourishing where I was and like many of their compatriots at the time they began talking about moving to another country where they could earn better money than they could in Italy.

A lot of Italians were moving to the United Kingdom and when I was around three years old the decision was made that we would emigrate to England. That was in 1952 and my father was twenty-six years old with three children as my brother Uccio had just been born. He needed more money and quickly to support his swelling family.

Dad headed to England and a few months later, when he had sent back enough money, we followed on and went to start a new life. My father had found work in London at a brickwork yard and like many other Italian families we gravitated to Bedford, a hive of European immigrants at that time. We lived in rented accommodation in Shakespeare Street but my parents weren't satisfied with their lot. Eventually thanks to them working all hours, we bought a house on Dudley Street, a narrow up and down on a long windy road in Bedford which was this Italian boy's first true home.

My mother gave birth to my sister Alba while we were in England and she is the only Calzaghe sibling born in the UK. Weirdly, she's also the only one who now lives in Sardinia, with the boys all in England or over the Severn Bridge.

You would have thought with four kids and a father who worked all hours my mother would've been at home looking after us, but she was such an amazing woman that simply wasn't enough for her, she had to contribute in every way possible. In order to buy a house, which was my parents' dream, we needed all the money we could get and my mother worked in a mortuary during the day and as a cleaner in the evenings. And yet she always seemed to be home when we needed her. It was some sort of Clarke Kent/Superman thing I think. I was never a latch-key child even though my mother worked two jobs and I used to wonder how she managed to do so much with her day.

It wasn't just Mum and Dad and my brothers and baby sister who moved to Bedford either. As Italians, extended family was very normal and in my family especially the connection was deep. My father's sister Nina married my mother's brother Peppino and they had two sons, Mario and Marco, who were virtually the same age as Antonio and I and they too moved to Bedford to my utter delight just a few weeks after we did.

We all lived very close and of course the Italians stuck together, meaning that as I grew up and reached school age, we were a little unit of kids, staying safer by never going out alone. It was the same with our parents. When Mum and Dad decided to go back to Italy, so did my aunt and uncle. They were always best friends and having them around helped to make Bedford seem more familiar and appealing.

I might have been an odd little Italian child who could barely communicate but I had my brothers Antonio and Uccio and my cousins Mario and Marco. We were a gang who quickly became a target for the local kids, but we would just deal with it together.

It was bloody difficult being an Italian family in the UK in the 1950s because the war created raw feelings. Even though people liked my dad and respected him because he was such a tough worker, Italians really weren't very popular and the local people reminded us of that every day. I completely understand why it happened, but as a kid it was a lot to take.

There can't be many people who remember being called a 'filthy Italian bastard' or a 'greasy wop' at five years old but I can. I am sure my brothers can too, because we kids were getting it daily. I was a tiny boy, about three foot and permanently wearing short trousers. Those trousers were worn to an age where it was decidedly uncool and it was yet another reason I attracted attention. My parents used to get clothes tailor-made for us in Italy. There were no hand-me-downs even though times were tough. My parents expected us to look smart. They were very image conscious and didn't want the local people to look down on them any more than they already did for being Italian.

One upside of being a target was that I learned the laws of the jungle, that's how I see it. I began to find my voice and that was a huge relief to Mum and Dad. I certainly wasn't shy anymore after a couple of years in England. I'd learned the language ok, not bad at all and to be honest I was probably as fluent then as I am now! I've lost count of the number of people I've spoken to who can't understand a word I am saying as an adult. I speak at 100 mph and I was probably never again as good with English as I was as a kid. I revelled in mastering the lingo. I had found my groove a little bit as I felt confident and safe with all my brothers and cousins and we started to get into a lot of trouble that I relished. It was exciting.

Plenty of the strife I've been in during my life has been totally my fault but as kids we were often in fights or just beaten shitless because we were Italian. Nowadays, that wouldn't be ok. If a group of kids were being smashed up just for being different, it would be called bullying and racist and they would be encouraged to tell the teachers at school, or their parents or whoever. But back then the parents of the kids responsible often wouldn't care too much that their sons were beating up the Italian boys.

Bullying will be mentioned again in this book because Joe was bullied at school and to this day it is something he feels very strongly about. He's a patron of a large anti-bullying organisation called LATCH and has raised a lot of money for them. But for me, at the time, I didn't realise I was being bullied. If I'm being truthful, it was entirely normal. Hurtful words just weren't such a big deal in the 1950s I guess, neither was the odd punch out of nowhere from time to time. We understood that was how it was and just dealt with it.

Racist language wasn't seen as being a bad thing. I know that sounds very politically incorrect, but just look at the comedy stars in that time and you'll see what I mean. But I just never understood it. 'You honestly don't like someone just because they were born in another country? But they might be the nicest person you've ever met! I feel sorry for you.' That's how I felt but I wasn't going to let anyone get the better of me without a fight.

We didn't have the option to go running to our parents either. If I had gone and told my dad that me and my brothers were getting beaten up because we were Italian we'd have been beaten up again! That's a bit of a joke, but we would probably have got a backhander for showing such weakness and for not looking after ourselves. My dad absolutely wouldn't stand for that. He expected us to act with honour and to defend ourselves properly if we needed to.

Moaning about having tough days simply wasn't how things worked in the Calzaghe family home and it was frowned upon by my father. He had been raised to solve his own problems and expected us to do the same. Therefore, our little gang, the collective of 'little smelly Italian bastards' as we would be called, took matters into our own hands if we found trouble, sometimes doing ok, sometimes being given a bit of a pasting. By the time I was ten I bet I'd been in one hundred fights with other kids. Not a problem.

To be honest, I've taken quite a few slaps from my dad in my life and it might sound strange, but it's only with fondness that I recall those moments. My father only ever wished for his kids to be good and to show pride in everything they did. He is a man of huge honour and the stories people tell of him back in Sassari make me proud. He had a reputation for dishing out justice when people did bad things in the community and he had a trademark of letting his forehead do the talking rather than his fists. I believe here it's called a Glasgow Kiss. My father will be remembered long after he's gone in Sardinia and people recognise him to be a good person and a man of integrity. That is enough to make any son eternally proud.

There was closeness to the family unit during the 1950s that you don't see so much these days. My dad was a hard, hard man like a lot of men at that time and the mothers were even harder! But we wouldn't need to lock our front door on Dudley Street even though the Calzaghe boys were in regular scraps and my parents would always have friends or the family popping in and out and yes, some of them were British. Don't get the impression everyone in Bedford hated the immigrant families during the fifties. Only some of them...

When I was a child, out on the street you'd be cocky as hell but in the home you didn't say one word back, you were full of fear of getting smacked by your parents. They were teaching you how to live and behave properly. That's the way it was. It was beautiful to me. I loved it. I used to get smacked so many times I knew Dad's moves! Every single way, every time he threw a hand at me I could roll with it and know how to make it hurt less. It was a science. It almost seems comical to look back on it now even if it did sting back then. To be fair, I know for a fact my father never hit any of his kids as hard as he could and he never, ever laid a hand on us unless we had done wrong. It wasn't random or violent it was always about punishment if he was forced to lift his hands to us.

To the age of twenty-one I had to watch out to make sure I didn't get a backhand around my chops from Dad if I had done something wrong. It was always deserved when I got a slap and I don't think Dad ever really enjoyed doing it. By way of comparison, my brother Antonio was good and I can virtually never remember him being punished other than when he was covering for one of his younger brothers. And besides, we had a little gang so whenever we got into trouble, we could rotate it so that the punishment got distributed. I was probably responsible all of the time for getting us into mischief, but I only got a third of the slaps from Dad. That's what brothers are for!

There were a lot of other immigrant families in Bedford back in those days not from Italy, largely from places like Poland and Hungary and you never got trouble with the immigrants, only the English kids. But I managed to make an enemy.

One Hungarian family lived close to us and had two kids, one of whom, a girl called Margaret, was in my class at school. She was a nice girl as I remember. But she had a younger brother who was in Uccio's class and I couldn't stand him. His name was Joe Bugner and he went on to become the European and British heavyweight boxing champion and fought Muhammad Ali for the world title in a fight people remember to this day.

Unfortunately for me Uccio really liked Joe and he'd always be around our house after school because he loved the fact my mother would always give him food. I remember he would play-fight with Uccio a lot and even as a kid he was pretty handy with his fists. We were forever arguing and inevitably one day it flared up into a fight, though it ended with my brother rolling on the floor laughing. I don't remember what it was about, but I remember Joe Bugner knocked me down and jumped on me, screaming in my face that he was going to hurt me. "Stop it", I told him. "Your breath stinks so badly I think you are going to kill me." And it really did, it was like being beaten up by a giant garlic bulb. I hated Joe Bugner back then but of course it was great to follow his career as a professional fighter. I loved telling people I used to fight with him at school when he was making it big in the squared circle. It was a great claim to fame.

I suppose fighting with him was good training for everyday life at school, because that was a battlefield as well, albeit not one where you had any chance of winning. The pain I would experience fighting with other kids was nothing compared to the pain inflicted by the worst bullies of all... the teachers.

School for me was the best and worst experience. I only got to go to school for around seven years but it was incredible to me in some regards. Here you are, kids, and you are put in this environment where everyone wants to be a big shot, to make some kind of impact and be someone. I saw the playground as a battle zone and the social pecking order of a school was incredible to me. I had a kind of vicious circle thing going on as I tried to fit in. I would get a lot of stick on a daily basis. I'd be in the canteen for two minutes and suddenly another kid would tell me I was a "spaghetti-eating faggot," or a "greasy arsehole," and of course I had to react and show I would look after myself. It was the Calzaghe code. I wasn't scared because I was more worried what my father would do if word got back that I acted like a sissy. Turn the other cheek? No way. Not ever. React, give one back, that's how we were taught and it got me in all sorts of bother once I started school. Therefore I was seen as volatile and found it hard to make English friends.

I had a bad attitude really as I was always on edge and looking to make a mark and the teachers, with any excuse, loved to give you a caning. That was my fate so often and school became a series of beatings with all manner of painful classroom objects.

I was the rebellious type and played truant quite a bit, but just about got by without being chucked out. I detested history but I coped with most lessons apart from the one I couldn't abide at all which was music. I would be truant every time we had a music lesson. I hated it and I skipped it even though the school started telling my mother it was happening. So I dodged the lesson knowing I'd get a hiding from my dad. That's how strong the hate was. Influenced by the Sardinian background where most men don't have the time or inclination to play musical instruments, I thought music was a girly activity. How dumb did that turn out to be?

I had one teacher in particular who I think genuinely enjoyed bashing the crap out of students. He was quite senior, maybe a deputy head or something of that manner. Every morning he used to make us line up in the yard at 8.30am, waiting to go into the building, one-by-one in total silence, come rain or shine and even in the freezing cold. If this teacher was still at the school by then I bet he didn't even let the kids talk about the moon landing. He was a total grump. Of course, one day I was talking in line. He was a big guy and I was about ten or eleven years old and didn't see him coming. He slapped me round the head and knocked me out and even now, more than half a century later, I still remember it. I will recall it for the rest of my life. First a thud and then I was coming to and looking at my friends who were too afraid to help me up or talk to me. I could see stars and tried desperately not to start crying my eyes out as I lay prone on the concrete with drops of blood trickling down my face.

I think a lot of people who, like me, are in their fifties or sixties will remember when school was like that. While I never had a problem with my parents disciplining me physically I hated when the teachers did it, which was practically every day. My parents knew me and knew my character. They could assess me properly. These teachers didn't really know me from Adam or Joe bloody Bugner and they were crueller than parents. It was like some of them really relished the violence as if it was the best part for them, being able to really hurt boys half their size and I found it disgusting.

But as things progressed school became easier for me in terms of fighting with other students and the teachers did help with that. I was on the wrong end of a caning so often that I think some of the other kids respected me for it. I was a tough little son of a bitch. More importantly though, school became easier because the older we got the more we all began to realise that none of the bullshit we were fighting about mattered. Italian, Hungarian, English? So what, something else existed that was far more important and a much better thing to do with our time – football.

Once I started playing football at school – morning, noon and night – I had a focus and a passion. I was a good player, very small but quick and with close control and pretty good balance. I was ideally suited to being a winger and after playing for the school team and a couple of local sides I even got asked to play for Bedford County along with my brother Uccio who could and should have gone on to be a professional player. He was absolutely amazing, like Gianfranco Zola, one of my favourites.

I loved the game, the camaraderie, the way you could express yourself with a ball. How you could play with anyone or anything and even a pair of balled-up socks could give you a whole day of entertainment doing keepy-ups around the house. Once I'd had a taste of football nothing else seemed worth doing. It made me very happy.

It was wonderful to be growing up in a house that my family owned, with my brothers and new baby sister Alba but the price to pay was that my parents were always working. Dad was never around because of all the shifts he did and it's my great regret that he has never once seen me play football. I know that would've meant so much to me if he could have done so. I'm pretty sure I don't have the legs to show him what I've got anymore and it upsets me to think about it.

Getting to spend time with our dad was the absolute best thing in the world, an amazing treat. When we were in England though it just didn't happen and that hurt him. He wanted to get to know his children better and couldn't financially do that in England. Whenever he was awake, he was at work, usually sixteen hours a day, six days a week.

Because of buying a house there was no spare money so we never all travelled back to Sassari together. More often than not it would be the case that one parent would go back to visit the family and the rest of us would stay in Bedford. We didn't take holidays. No one did back then. But one summer when we broke up from school it had been agreed that my parents, all the kids and also my aunt and uncle and cousins would travel back to Italy for a one month trip. We ended up staying for the full six weeks of the school holidays and as you can imagine it was the most exciting thing in the world to us. What could possibly be better than a whole summer with our father in the sunshine?

I think that summer was probably the happiest time of my entire life. At the very least, it was the time where I felt the most carefree. It was just absolutely wonderful. Uccio, Antonio and I and my cousins Marco and Mario met a lot of the local kids in town and, of course, the days were taken up with soccer, soccer and more soccer. We couldn't speak Italian, by then we behaved English and it was only the universal language of football that gave us comrades. We went to where there were some kids hanging around, took a football and it really was that easy for us to find company. A few gestures, a few flicks and tricks and we made friends despite only being able to speak the odd word of Italian here and there. While my mum and dad were catching up with the neighbours and Dad was doing some business around town we would be out on the streets playing the beautiful game in a beautiful football-obsessed country.

But that wasn't even the best part. Even though he had a lot of business going on despite being on holiday, my father would make sure that every day the five of us would head to the beach and swim in the sea together in the sizzling afternoon sunshine. It quickly became our holiday tradition with all the immediate family going to the beach. For me this was the ultimate good time. I was spending a portion of every day with my dad when he was totally relaxed and completely happy and I was like a pig in shit. I just wanted more and more and more. I'd never known such joy.

Dad wasn't really apart from us on that trip except for when we were playing football in the mornings. We'd all spend the evenings together around the table with my grandparents, aunties and uncles, cousins, brothers and sister. We would eat meatballs and fresh spaghetti, seafood and wonderful warmed bread and to this day it's the kind of food I love making myself because it evokes fabulous memories. All of the Calzaghe boys are fantastic cooks and my father and brother Sergio have both worked as head chefs professionally.

The trips to the beach every afternoon were the cherry on top. I can see it now if I close my eyes. I was probably eleven years old and would climb on to my dad and his huge shoulders in the sea and he would help me to stand up and then I would dive in, the warm salt water splashing my eyes as I dived down into the blue. I can taste the bubbles and feel the anticipation of going up on his shoulders again. It was a wonderful feeling, among the best moments I've shared with my father who always tried to be affectionate despite not having that sort of upbringing himself.

That feeling was my utopia. If only I could have bottled it I would be a billionaire now. We hopefully all recall those little moments that makes life so very rich. My dad adored his kids and on this trip he got to show us, got to hang out with us and I had never felt closer to him. He was my hero and he wanted to spend time with me. What could be better than that? It was everything I had ever wanted. And that makes it all the stranger that over the next decade I would do nothing but drive Dad to distraction by being what I thought at the time was a free spirit. I would disappoint him time and time again and I know that goes for my mother as well, even more so.

That summer was a watershed for me. It marked the point where I went from being a fairly typical kid to a boy who was about to enter an adult world. I didn't know it then, but Sardinia was about to become something more than a holiday destination and a memory. It was to be our home again.

We returned to the UK for the start of the school year in September 1961 and settled back into life in England, but everyone was thinking about Sardinia. We kids could talk about nothing else. Sardinia had almost infected us. We became absolutely besotted with the place and Mum and Dad yearned for everything they had left behind. We had a good life in Bedford but in order to sustain it my parents were required to work around the clock, almost twenty-four hours a day. My father had managed to do so much manual labour that we could buy a house, he was earning about £26 a week, but he genuinely never got to take a minute for himself. My father is alive and kicking today but I doubt he would've been if we had stayed in England, he'd have worked himself into the ground

So one day, early in 1962, Mum and Dad called me and my brothers to the table, sat us down and asked us what we would think about moving to Sardinia. We were all genuinely stunned but thrilled at the same time. It was exciting for us and we could all tell that Mum and Dad really wanted to go back. It was pretty amazing that they asked us as well. That seemed unnecessary to me, we were just kids but they wanted to make sure we were happy with things. Make it 'our' decision. God bless them.

I was happy and excited but couldn't help feeling a bit of regret because after taking an age to settle in, I was starting to do quite well in school and I did like it overall. But it wasn't to be. My mother, Uccio, Alba and I returned to Sardinia a few weeks later while Dad and Antonio stayed on a while to take care of selling the house. Even though I don't think it was planned, I never went to school again in my life. At the age of twelve I was suddenly in a new country with a language I couldn't speak and was about to be introduced to working life.

I didn't react well at all.

Chapter Three:

Terrible Teen

After becoming 'English' and adjusting to a life where you played cricket and ate fish and chips and had to go to school to be caned by the teachers, we were back to the life I'd once had but could not remember in Sardinia.

For me and my brothers and sister this was the ultimate adventure, but there is a reason why you go to exotic places on holiday and not to live. There are practicalities, difficulties and at that time I was essentially a little English kid and my brother Uccio was too. Even though I was back where I was born, I was again an alien.

We went to Sardinia full of joy and excited that my parents were happy but it soon dawned on me and Uccio especially that this was going to be a terrible idea. In fact, a couple of weeks after we got back to Sardinia, we hated it. It was horrible for us because we were totally out of our comfort zone. We might have been back in our home town, but we felt like outsiders.

My sister was a toddler when we moved back to Sardinia but even she was more adult than I was, she contributed more around the house too. We had moved back into our family home, which was crowded and Uccio and I were miserable as sin almost as soon as we arrived back.

Boy, did I miss school too. I couldn't believe it, I took it for granted and then poof, just like that, it was gone. The local school was Italian and I could barely speak two words of the lingo, so I never went to school again, instead doing a couple of evening classes that were spoken in English. But I had no grasp of Italian culture and life and struggled and I just remember playing football all day long.

However, shortly before I turned thirteen, I had a conversation with my father that was a game-changer, when he basically told me in no uncertain terms I was a man now and needed to start acting like one and it was time for me to get a job. We all needed to pull together because the final Calzaghe sibling, Sergio, was on his way.

I wasn't best pleased but figured I had an advantage because I could spend ages pretending to look for a job, keep Mum and Dad off my back and go and play football. After all, I was going to be a professional soccer player and probably play for Italy and when I did, I would be the main bread-winner in the family. 'You'll thank me later,' I would think when I told my mother, "Yes, I will go to the shop for you and buy milk," when really I was buggering off to meet up with friends to play football. Hours later I'd return without the milk and would get a flea in my ear.

My father didn't come down in the last shower and realised my game within days. We had another chat and we agreed that yes it would be good for me to get a job and then he smiled. "Good Enzo, I am glad you see it that way. I have got you a job and you start tomorrow."

Fuck. This was it, I had no escape. Not only that, the job was in a butcher's and I was worryingly out of my depth. I was just this stringy little kid, not even a teen, and I wasn't ready for the adult environment.

My first morning as a working man was not so bad. I went behind the counter, which I could just about see over, and served the customers, using what little Italian I understood to give them their meat and take their cash. It was pretty simple stuff – sausages, beef joints, check the price list, a smile and I'm a butcher, easy-peasy. But I think I talked too much for the owner's liking and he decided he was going to teach me a lesson by putting me in the back in the afternoon.

"We have a delivery coming in Enzo, you sort it out and carve it for me," he said. That sounded harder than working out change and counting sausages. So, the delivery duly arrives and it's a horse. A fucking horse. Couldn't I start with a rabbit? And the owner of the shop sets me up in this little corner, puts a knife in my hand bigger than my arm, brings me over a horse and tells me, *"fai a pezzi questo cavallo immediatamente,"* carve up this horse immediately. What the fuck are you talking about carve it? It's a horse!

That was me, I couldn't get out of there fast enough and before

I knew it I had run all the way home to Mummy. I was a sobbing, snivelling mess. Bless my mother, as I whimpered incomprehensibly about horses and never eating meat again, she told me I didn't need to go back there if I was so upset. I knew my dad would be disappointed in me and I knew I had let him down, but you try and carve a horse aged twelve and tell me how you get on.

I soon realised that the trick was to stick at a job just long enough to satisfy my father and then get sacked or jack it in to give me a bit of downtime before starting the next job. I reckon that in the first year in Sardinia I must have tried about a baker's dozen of jobs, including working at a bakery. I did my best to follow my dad on to a building site where I was physically useless, worked in cafes and restaurants washing pots and pans, and I fetched drinks in a bar or took people's coats. All sorts of jobs and not one of them stuck for longer than a few weeks. Often I'd be halfway through a game of street football and my mother would suddenly appear screaming, telling me I should've been at work an hour ago.

Thankfully there was always football and that was going well. I had been a county level player for Bedford and once back in Sardinia I was soon asked to join the academy at Torres FC, a club that has produced some great players over the years. Gianfranco Zola started at Torres and brilliantly he had digs with my sister Alba, one of a long line of strong matriarchs in the Calzaghe clan, who as an adult would often have the academy kids living in her family home.

Things were all right, playing football every week and just doing the bare minimum to stay employed long enough to keep out of serious trouble with my dad. You've heard the expression if a job is worth doing, it's worth doing well. Well my motto was that if I had to do a job, I would do a half-arsed job. As far as I was concerned it wasn't worth doing. I had zero interest in work but I was getting by.

Probably the only thing I found less interesting than being a working man was music. That was fine for a while because the music mad member of my family, my uncle Vincenzo, had found his protégé in my brother Uccio who had the voice of an angel.

Vincenzo gigged with various different bands and then started his own roping in Uccio as a singer. It was a perfect fit. They were called the Reindeers and were good. My brother learned guitar and could sing in English and that was oh so cool. He was eleven years old and sang like a rock star. He loved it.

But these musical types are temperamental and that little git Uccio had a massive strop, quit the band and basically told Vincenzo to stick it one day. My uncle was hopping mad about it. My dad wanted them to patch things up but my uncle was having none of it, he was furious with my brother. That was when Dad sat me down and told me that he wanted me to start going to band practice with Vincenzo and the Reindeers. I wasn't really given much of a choice. In fact I wasn't given any choice whatsoever. Now I come to think about it, a lot of my 'discussions' with Dad ended with him essentially just telling me what to do!

On my first day with the band I was given a bass guitar and slowly but surely I started to learn how to play it, and it wasn't so bad. I actually liked learning a new skill and didn't hate the band practice as I expected I would. It was better than having to be at work and my dad cut me slack on that front when I was making Vincenzo so happy. Of course, my younger brother Uccio had to start working. If it wasn't music he had to get a job. But one concern loomed on my horizon – Vincenzo and The Reindeers were booked for a large public show on the island for an Italian public holiday. We were going to be playing in front of a few thousand people.

The day of the gig arrived and I'd never been so nervous. It seemed like every month or so there would be a big festival for one patron Saint or another, Peter, Andrew, all of them, they all seemed to get a festival in Sassari. I was around fifteen by then, settled back into Sardinian life even though I didn't like it and well out of the habit of going to school. A few weeks after picking up a bass guitar for the first time, here we are at this massive outdoor gig with what felt like the whole of Italy coming to watch us. I didn't grow to five foot until I was sixteen or seventeen so I was still tiny, a teenager who looked like a child with little hands trying to act the big man on bass.

We were expected to play about a dozen songs and the problem was I had only learned two, one called "Michelle" and one called "Girl". Would that really be enough to do a whole gig? I figured it would, especially as the band was seven strong and I was just there because I was young, not bad-looking and my uncle figured I would eventually show I had inherited my dad's musical talent, because he is a great singer.

I remember Vincenzo did the singing and we had a female backing singer who sang a solo or two. It was a relaxed sort of set and I was just happy hiding near the back of the stage, throwing myself into the two songs I knew and the rest of the time just miming along and imagining I was George Harrison. The Beatles were beginning to resonate with me and I had started growing my hair to look more like them.

Before the gig I had been shaking like a leaf, but now here we were on stage and it felt good, natural almost and I enjoyed the reaction we were getting. It wasn't spectacular, just polite clapping at the end of each song but that seemed good enough for me. But then I saw Vincenzo eyeing me and my heart sank. 'That bastard is going to make me sing,' I thought to myself. And sure enough he starts beckoning me over.

"Non vengo, non vengo," I told him. "I am not coming." So the wily bastard started playing another song and came to play his guitar right by me. Suddenly, he was jamming it into my back. *"Alla fine di questa canzone, se non inizi a cantare, io e tuo padre ti ammazzeremo,"* he told me with some menace. "At the end of this song if you don't start singing, me and your dad will murder you."

Endure humiliation in front of thousands or being given a beating when I got home? It was a conundrum for sure. I thought for a while and decided to take my bruises like a man. I'm outta here I decided. I opted for the beating, tried to duck off the stage but Vincenzo was wise to it and began pushing me forward by jabbing his guitar in my back. For want of a better phrase, I was fucked. My life was about to be over, I was going to be a laughing stock.

Vincenzo started talking on the microphone, introducing me in Italian and then he pushed me in front of the stick and told me to sing in English. I was shaking like a leaf and when I started singing it dawned on me pretty quickly that I sounded like absolute dog shit. I was even worse than I feared possible. By way of example, my performance that night was worse than my son Joe's on *Strictly Come Dancing*!

I finished the song and unbelievably, the audience liked it. That is almost certainly because I sang in English pretty naturally, rather than because I was good, which I definitely wasn't (I am not being modest) but I didn't care. I loved the attention and the relief was just coursing through me. I felt six foot tall and like I had the biggest nut sack in Italy. After just three minutes of shit singing, I was a rock and roll star in my mind. It was probably the first time much of that audience had heard a song live in English and we did the same number three times and each time the ovation was bigger and bigger.

It wasn't a conscious decision but afterwards, when I had a few sips on a beer and the world and his wife came up to congratulate me, I think a little devil on my shoulder basically decided 'fuck football, this is way more fun'. I had gone from being decoration on a stage to singing the same song three times and I was officially converted to a life of leaving my heart and soul on the stage. Enzo the artist had been born. I was music obsessed from that day to this and within a few hours Uccio was back in the band because he saw how exciting it was. My uncle now got two Calzaghe boys for the price (zero) of one.

I feel so comfortable in the limelight now that everyone probably realises I love being the centre of attention. I act up because of that and doing things like the *Calzaghe Clan* documentary for BBC Wales or the HBO documentaries to promote Joe's biggest fights, were spot on for my character, exactly the attention I crave.

But back then? It was as foreign to me as the Italian language, being given attention and a glimpse of fame and as such I reacted like most people would in that situation: I became a big-headed idiot. 'No mum, I won't be putting the rubbish out today because if no-one has told you, I am a rock god now. I will lie in bed until band practice because even musical geniuses have to sleep sometime.'

In the next couple of years I became a massive egomaniac,

growing my hair and thinking I was the mutt's nuts and that isolated me from the family. Mum and Dad were working hard, my brothers both worked and even Alba who was a kid had taken a part-time job in a hairdresser's sweeping up because it was important for the family. Mum and Dad were saving to buy a corner shop, my dad's big dream on our return to Italy, and everyone in the family was helping him to achieve that ambition except me.

So I gigged in the evening for not much money but in order to keep Dad off my back I needed to make some cash during the day and I began a career that would last a decade hustling on the busy markets in Sassari. I became friends with some gypsy boys and we would hang about on what the locals called *Via Mala*, 'the bad road' where people of ill-repute would hang about and there was plenty of action if you were prepared to leave your morals at the door. I loved it instantly. It was natural to me, haggling and bartering, trading this for that and hanging around with the big drinkers, the workers, mafia-types and the druggies. The stench of marijuana was permanent and curiosity killed the cat eventually as I tried my first illegal substance.

When I was fifteen or so I had my first drag on a spliff and from there I became a smoker of both cigarettes and hash, Moroccan Black and other types and that was the final nail in the coffin of my football career. If I had written a farewell letter it would probably have read: 'Bye-bye Torres FC, I actually won't be available to win the World Cup with Italy. I'll be getting stoned instead as I am a rock and roll god.'

The market scene was full of great characters and it was a life I was so comfortable with, selling anything we could. A lot of the stuff I presume was stolen and a lot of the boys I hung around with were drug dealing, but I never quite went that far. But while I wasn't a drug dealer, it would be a lie if I said I didn't sometimes acquire recreational drugs and move them on, though usually in bulk and normally in exchange for something I was more comfortable selling, like tobacco or moody watches. Maybe you'd be fair to say I was an occasional drug trader, a part-time musician and full-time hustler. I had long hair, had risen to the grand height of about five foot four inches and I felt like I was finding my way.

I was becoming a man even though I knew it wasn't the kind of man my parents really wanted in the house or respected. I was headed down a path that they knew could only lead to ruin.

I would hardly sleep for days on end and then go home and kip for two days solid. My mother would go crazy, throwing wet kitchen towels at me and yelling at me that I needed to get up and was a lazy bastard and a disgrace, but it wasn't enough to get me out of my pit.

I was well into the weed, permanently stoned and then something good happened and my uncle's band (let me tell you, it was never 'our' band, it was his) began getting a bit of radio play locally. We probably recorded six or eight songs to be played on the radio and gigs became much more common, five or six nights a week which was exactly what I wanted. Music was close to being my job, leaving the days free for drugs and alcohol.

I also took up with a second band after answering an advert, a group of very well educated boys who called themselves Boba. They were accomplished musicians who looked the part and it was quite a big honour to play with them and meant that by juggling gigs, I was now playing seven nights a week, sometimes twice a night. The boys in Boba would always have some drinks after a gig and could never understand why I wouldn't stay and drink with them, but they were a lot richer than I was – in the UK you'd call them posh like Coldplay – and I just couldn't get excited about that scene. The minute I finished the gig I was thinking about getting back among my people in my part of town, thinking there was a beer and a spliff and who knows maybe even a young lady's lips for kissing with my name on. The night was full of possibilities now, wasn't it? It was the 60s for goodness sake. Girls were finally on my radar, though I was a slow starter on that front. I thought sitting with or talking to girls in school made you a sissy, so I barely spoke to a female during my time in Bedford. I was a shy kid and had now come out of my shell and I remember having a girlfriend or two, but nothing serious.

My dad hated me staying around on the lower side of the city and my new-found enthusiasm for hanging out with the unemployed, not to mention smoking cigarettes and doing drugs. We lived in an area which was all working people and he didn't approve of me hanging about with what he saw as bums, people too lazy and ignorant to do a proper job. He was probably right, but I was a seventeen year old kid. No-one that age listens to their parents, do they? Fortunately for me, Dad was far too busy to spend his days busting my chops. He was by then running a grocery shop he invested everything in with my mother and it was turning into a nightmare for them. I don't know for certain, but I think people took advantage of the fact Mum and Dad being wonderful people. Although Dad was a hard man, he also believed strongly in a sense of local community and if someone needed bread for the family but was low on cash, Dad took them at their word that they would pay him when they could. But many didn't and it soon adds up. As I understand it, there was also some gentleman who wanted money to 'look after' the shop. If you've ever watched a film directed by Martin Scorsese and starring Robert De Niro you will know what I mean.

It was going to take something big to put a rocket up my arse and make me put some money on the table by getting a job, but seeing my father at that time did exactly that. He had been loving life in the shop at first, it certainly beat humping bricks as he had been doing in England, but he was in a tough spot financially and we literally lived on bread and grapes for what felt like forever. That was breakfast, lunch and dinner. We grew the grapes and just about managed to buy a loaf a day to have with olive oil. Dad was terribly worried.

I don't recall us kids caring a jot because even if it sounds cheesy, we had so much love in our house that it just wasn't a big deal to not have much food and I was doing so many drugs I probably barely noticed. But it hurt my father deeply. It hurt his pride and it angered him that friends would avoid him on the streets because they owed him money. I hate to write this, to admit it, but Dad went into a spiral of depression and for the first time in my life I saw him cry. My father was a mess and it cut me to the core. Ultimately Dad had to shut the shop and take a job making cigarettes on a production line in a factory and it broke my heart and his too.

Desperate for any kind of employment that wasn't in a factory, he registered an interest in working as a clerk for the tourist agency, which was called S.I.T for short, but he got turned down at the interview because he was too old for the position. He was crestfallen because the money was pretty good, but they must have liked him because they asked if he had any sons who could maybe do the job. Dad needed the money so sent his most responsible kid by far, my brother Antonio, to work there, but it didn't stick for him even though he had a great work ethic compared to me. So you guessed it, off I went and I had my first permanent job, working as a clerk when in reality that was only the title, the job description was basically working as a slave for twelve to fourteen hours a day.

I reported to a man who I won't name because of what I think of him. I have never despised a person more in my life. He was a bully and a fascist, a horrible, horrible little man who had no respect for me and no work ethic himself. He insisted on calling me Pietro Vincenzo even though everyone by then knew me as Enzo and would make me do all sorts of chores for him that had zero to do with the actual job. The job might have been fine but this guy made it so that I lived the life of a slave. He abused me verbally and made me run all of his errands and do his job for him. It was disgusting. I used to be permanently knackered because I was gigging in the evening but no longer had the chance to sleep in the day and I felt like I was rotting away in that office with that sadistic bastard. I felt angry at how the system worked. What a contradiction: my dad is cheated by the world even though he's a proud, talented and great man and yet he had to cower down to the bosses to put food on his table. Why was this?

I tried, I genuinely did try because my family was relying on me and I stuck the job out for about a year I think. And I began to get my revenge on the boss by being a conniving little bandit. He was so work-shy he had me lock up for him and do the books and that was too bad for him. I knew where the money was, I knew the combination to the safe and the amount of money in there was recorded by me. Nowadays you would be paid overtime for the outrageous hours I worked but I paid myself overtime. It is one of the more justifiable times I've taken what I felt I was owed. I would give my family all my wages but thought the money I pinched was fair game. It was what I used to call 'arsehole tax' and I spent it on booze and drugs.

Eventually things came to a head and I walked out and never went back after a blazing row with Mr Wanker as I called him to my friends. I knew I was in for it with Mum and Dad and I explained to my dad why I quit, why I hated my boss and to be honest all bosses, because there was no equality, some people had all the money and the rest of us had none. Dad was very good about it. Not so my mother who rightly told me I was a selfish so-and-so who was depriving my family when they most needed my help, but I think a little part of Dad admired that I didn't want to take that shit from an arsehole.

I quickly reverted to my old life and Mum especially worried that I was becoming a lost cause, always drunk, stoned or scamming. I had a group of really close friends for the first time that weren't my brothers, including a kid called Constanzo and another boy, a talented boxer named Aldo. Just before I turned eighteen Aldo and I were selling pegs and other bits and pieces on a market stall and he told me he had an aunt and uncle who lived in Florence. "Why don't we go and visit them?" I asked him. He agreed and off we went. I never said a word to my parents and knew I was in for it. We walked off the market stall just like that. We scrounged a few bucks and got the first boat to Rome. We never left the ferry port and we crossed over to Florence despite our tickets only being valid to Rome. To me it was a massive adventure and just what I needed after rotting in that office for a year. I had never been anywhere apart from Sassari and Bedford so I was willing to get into trouble.

I had essentially done a runner when my family were having a dark time and that shouldn't surprise anyone because I was a self-centred young man. Florence was wondrous to me and when Aldo's uncle asked us if we fancied staying a while and making a few bucks we jumped at the chance. I phoned home and told my parents where I was and knew there would be murder when we got home, but I didn't care. We started hustling big time at the local train station in Florence using street smarts to scam tourists. We would provide them with lira in exchange for foreign currency, only trading with those who had no idea what the lira was worth, fleecing them. We made bundles of money when we found the right mark. If not, we'd just beg for money, literally scraping around for foreign coins and scrounging cigarettes or eating discarded (and perfectly good) food.

With what we had and what Aldo's uncle let us keep, we would buy one of three things, alcohol, marijuana or amphetamines. By then I loved anything that got you high. We could always cadge a fag in a place like Florence and so saved on that expense. Food meant nothing, we ate if we could but that wasn't a problem, I was more than used to getting by on little or no food and that would stand me in good stead later in life.

I wrote home and got a reply from Mum and the gist was, 'Enzo, we love you very much and miss you. When you come home we are going to kill you. Love Mum and Dad.'

We would walk miles every day, pound the streets all day long and after a while I started to become delusional and was hallucinating and had days when I was unsteady on my feet. I was unhealthy as anything and still had a taste for hash as well as all the speed I was taking. It wasn't a good combination, but I couldn't help myself. My life was fun. Weight was falling off me, I had long, lank, greasy hair and I began to look like a street bum, which is basically what I was apart from a couple of hours at night when we slept with a roof over our heads on the floor at Aldo's uncle's house.

Something had to give and after a couple of months we decided to face the music and go back to Sassari. My parents agreed to come and pick me up off the boat and even though I am sure my dad expected to take me home and give me a good smack, when they saw the state of me I think all that anger just turned to concern. I looked half dead and they were very worried about me. We went home and Dad instantly set about making the biggest portion of spaghetti carbonara you have ever seen. I couldn't eat more than a couple of bites before I had to go and be sick, that's how long it had been since I had a proper meal. My parents fed me non-stop for a week or so and I began to return to normal after that. I stopped hallucinating at least.

I went back to gigging with Boba and Vincenzo's band and resorted to type with the boozing and the drug use, carrying on with no job forthcoming. I started to settle in, thinking I had found my place in life but this time my parents were a lot less concerned because they knew what was around the corner and they knew that this time my bad ways couldn't possibly last.

And then the letter arrived and they were happy and I was sad. The fun was over for at least a year. I was conscripted to the army and had to report in a couple of weeks.

Shit.

Chapter Four:

Did James Bond Ever Clean Toilets?

I hear a lot these days that people think our youth are out of control and why don't we go back to National Service? Probably because we don't want the army full of wasters who don't give a shit about being there would be my answer and trust me, I speak from experience.

Getting the letter to tell me I was going to be in the army was like being punched in the stomach, because I couldn't have been less suited to life in the services if I possibly tried. By this point I was typical of the bad youth you see reported in the newspapers in the UK today. I did a lot of drugs and I was permanently living for the moment and not giving a thought to anyone around me or the future. I had been taught right from wrong, I was just temporarily ignoring everything I had been taught.

While both my brothers Antonio and Uccio and sister Alba were all working, I was living with my parents rent free, eating their food and spending my days knocking about on the streets with long hippie hair and pink jeans. I was definitely becoming the black sheep of the Calzaghe family and it hurt my mother greatly.

Football was totally dead to me because I was permanently drunk or stoned, though I was becoming more of an addict of tablets that made you manic rather than marijuana. Weed made me into a slowed-down robot and that wasn't my style, I was a million miles an hour and as such, uppers, amphetamines, were becoming my drug of choice. I hit them hard, all day, every day and then got drunk in the evenings. It was a wonder I could play an instrument come gig time.

I had been a very fit kid but my lifestyle took a toll on that and at the time I was smoking a lot of cigarettes too because, although I idolised the Beatles musically, I fancied myself as the Italian Joe

Cocker and thought the smoking would help give me that gravelly, raspy sound that Cocker had. It didn't. If the army needed someone like me then God help them but there was absolutely nothing I could do once the letter came. Conscription for eighteen year olds was mandatory and my alternative choice was to tell them I didn't want to be in the army and they'd lock me up in prison for a year and throw away the key. Either way, my hedonistic ways were going to be stopped if I liked it or not.

After the letter telling you that you are set for National Service you would then be informed by another letter where you were being assigned, when to report and what area of the military you were headed to. And to my considerable relief I was duly told I was to join the Air Force, which was renowned for being a lot easier than joining the Army. I was sent to Siena in Tuscany, a lovely place but for me my ultimate nightmare as I went to Air Force training. I hated it.

The first day was probably among my most miserable of all. I already had a big problem with authority figures and then this army guy is telling me I have to cut all my hair off, get a buzz cut as they called them. I had been growing my hair for about five years and it was horrible to be forced to chop it off, a real reminder that I didn't matter anymore; I was just a number on a badge, another bloke who didn't want to be there.

Not only did they make us get our heads shaved but there were to be no moustaches either and that was me done, because I have been a moustache man since my early teens and even at the age of eighteen, I was so proud of it, I just couldn't bring myself to shave it off. I had to go to the army barbers for the head shave and when he came to the moustache I was practically in tears. I know that sounds crazy but there you go, it meant a lot to me and I begged the barber to let me keep it. He told me to go and see the Lieutenant and that is exactly what I did. Amazingly he took pity on me and that is why in the new recruit photo, you'll see 499 freshly shaved men and one Enzo Calzaghe with a moustache!

We reported to Centro Addestramento Reclute or CAR for short, which in Italian essentially means boot camp. All we did every day for about three months was march twenty miles in one direction and then march back. That was it, the 'drill' they called it and every day I was assigned to do that. That is the problem if you are a musician and don't have any skills to offer.

The only interesting thing we did in CAR that I remember was when on a drill we were given fake hand grenades and told to practise throwing them. There is a pretty accepted method to throwing a grenade and once we'd been shown how to do it there was a competition with us throwing these fake grenades at a glass bottle. After missing a couple of times, instinct kicked in for me and I started throwing it like I had been taught back in Bedford, throwing over-arm like I was Dennis Lillee. After all I was from cricket country. Wouldn't you know it, I hit the thing and even though I got told off for my method, I did get to teach some of the Italian boys how to play cricket later that week. And if I was ever in a war situation, who cares how you throw the bloody thing as long as it goes where you want? If I'm ever in the trenches I'll quite happily let Darren Gough chuck the grenades.

After training was over we were all assigned to our final destination and I got lucky, because I ended up going to Milan, known as one of the better places, while some of my friends were sent to Trieste which was known to be far more dangerous and quite hostile at the time.

Around two hundred of us headed to Milan and after a general assembly we were asked to raise our hands when they read a list of skills. Guys put their hands up for certain things like a mechanic or labourer until there were only a few of us left and we went up on the stage. Once again, as I did at CIT for Mr Bully I used that total lie of being a really fast typist and fluent in English (a partial truth) and the recruiting officer seemed really impressed. "Pietro Vincenzo," he said to me. "You type, you speak English, I have a feeling you can be very useful to us, very useful indeed." Wow I thought. This is it. No more of this bollocks, he knows what I am all about, he's dead impressed – 'This guy with a moustache,' he's thinking, 'he can speak English, types it, what a useful bloke he will be.' I decided right there on the spot I was going to be a star and that my military misery was over. He probably wants me to be a spy I thought, the James Bond of the Italian military. I knew I was going to make my father proud, I just didn't realise I would do it as a spy. When will they start training me to pilot a plane? I wondered. I bet Signorina Moneypenny has some great assignments for me.

I went to see the list of assignments the following day expecting to find out exactly when I would be learning to fly a plane and begin whatever spy training is offered in the Italian military, so you'll imagine my surprise when I saw I was assigned to 'general duties.' I wonder what general duties is code for? I pondered on that all night. I soon found out. It was code for 'cleaning up other people's shit and making sure the toilets sparkled to military standards on a daily basis.' If you believe in karma, you'll surely think I got exactly what I deserved. My mother would have loved to have seen me scrubbing those toilets every day, as I did for six months.

I hated everything about being there and the worst aspect was it was like a public boarding school in England, every new recruit was bullied by some arsehole that had been there longer. The favourite trick with new boys was to put toilet paper between their toes while they were asleep and set it on fire. They called it the bicycle because of how fast your legs started spinning when the flames started nipping your toes as you woke. Welcome to the forces.

I didn't get on well there, but just as in Bedford, football was my salvation. I went for trials and was picked to represent the Milan Air Force, having scored in the trial game. I was the new right winger for the team and that meant I missed toilet cleaning duty twice a week for training and once a week when we played in a match, normally against other military bases, which was a fantastic result.

I was so integral to the team that once, when we had a weekend of leave and I decided to come back almost twenty four hours late, I was frogmarched straight from the train station to the football pitch because we had a big game to play. We won and I played pretty well and I felt smug, but after the game I was frogmarched again, this time to military prison where I spent three days paying for my tardiness in solitary confinement. That was the worst of the worst. I was hallucinating again but this time not because of drugs, it was the solitude and darkness that sent me to the edge. It was nightmarish. After that I kept my head down until the end of my stint. A dishonourable discharge would've been a disgrace to my family and I had to see it through, as unhappy as I was. For every boy in Italy of that age, it was something that had to be done, a rite of passage.

By all accounts the army was even worse. About six months after I was discharged a friend of mine from the markets was on leave from his tenure in the army and we went for a beer in Sassari. He was so miserable that he begged me to help him, to get him out of it. He had brought with him a cloth and a hammer and right there in the pub he asked me to break his trigger finger so he would be discharged on medical grounds.

I'd heard tales of this happening in the air force but I thought he was winding me up. He wasn't. "No way," I told him. "We'll see," he told me as he went to the bar. And after several drinks on him and a lot of persuading, I agreed. The first time as I tentatively held the hammer I gave him a tap and he kind of grimaced, looked at me like I was useless and it pissed me off. So the next time I hit him harder, but just bruised his hand, damaging a couple of his knuckles. He yelped in pain. Not so cocky now! The third time there was a thud, he yelped and I was relieved. He inspected his hand and looked like he was about to cry because I'd broken the wrong finger, I took out the middle digit instead. The next time I smashed his finger with that hammer and I heard the bone crunch, thankfully on the correct finger. We attracted quite a crowd who were gasping and laughing at us. But my friend never had to return to the army, he was discharged early. I know it sounds like I've been watching too much of the *Godfather*, but that's exactly how it happened and my pal was by no means the only kid who deliberately broke a bone to get out of the army. I bet it still happens today in some countries which still have mandatory military service.

Still my family were struggling financially but they had some luck with the fact my brothers Uccio and Antonio had landed jobs working in a hotel. They quickly got me in and I went for my first day and was shocked because everyone was really unhappy, there was no camaraderie among the workforce.

"What's going on?" I asked my brother Uccio. "Why is everyone so fucking miserable?"

"Enzo, you don't understand, the boss, he gives us no rights; it's like working in a war camp. We can't use the facilities even in the evenings when everything shuts."

I never really wanted a job in the first place so like the cocksure little toe-rag I was, I marched down to the director's office to tell him where he could stick his job. I was living a much better lifestyle at the time and I was fit and strong, had just turned nineteen and was ready to tell him to shove it because I had re-convinced myself I was going to be a professional footballer after my great season in the forces.

So I knocked on his door, told him I quit and when he asked why I told him all the employees hated him. "Why can't they swim in the pool when it closes? Why don't we get to use the tennis court when it closes? You are a nasty man so I can't work for you."

He was genuinely taken aback and seemed quite hurt by my words. After not saying anything for what felt like ages, he sighed. "You are right, Enzo. Tell the workers they can use the pool and play tennis in the evenings."

I walked out feeling ten feet tall, grabbed Uccio and legged it to the swimming pool. I stripped to my under crackers and dived in. "What the fuck are you doing Enzo?" he screamed at me. I explained to him what had happened and more than ever before, I was my kid brother's hero.

My friend Constanzo was back from the army and he too was in need of some work so I went to see my mate the director who had really been very kind to me since the day I stood up to him. I guess he was the sort who respected you if you fought for your rights, in my eyes a rarity among bosses. He agreed to take Constanzo on and he joined me in the kitchen as a pot washer. So I was working with my best friends, Constanzo and my brother Uccio and life was good. As jobs went this was a decent one and with everyone working in the house money wasn't so tight and my parents were happy I was pulling my weight.

It should surprise no-one that I was silently dreaming of a way out of work though and vowed that it was time I made my mark on the world. I began plotting to leave Sardinia for good and imagined arriving back a millionaire to a fanfare, maybe with a parade in my honour. I have always been a dreamer and at that age, with no education to speak of, options were very limited for me and while I had been with the army, the Reindeers had got by just fine without me so I wasn't gigging at all regularly. And maybe I wasn't going to be a professional footballer.

Two weeks after Constanzo joined the hotel staff the pair of us did a bunk and broke my family's heart all over again. It pains me to think how much I upset my poor mother over the years as a young carefree hippie.

It all happened in one day. I woke up and just decided that was the day I was going to get out of Sassari and see the world, but I didn't want to go on my own. I was street smart but I'd done the army solo and if I was going to go out and rule the world, I'd need a companion. I knew my parents couldn't cope if Uccio left and besides that, he was only a year or so away from conscription to the army so I decided I would have to get Constanzo on side.

"How are you finding the job Constanzo?" I asked him, just after lunch when I knew he'd be hot, bothered and pissed off because we were rushed off our feet.

"It's too fucking hot, Enzo," he told me.

I made my move. I told him we should get out of there, quit on the spot and make ourselves into international playboys, go around Europe and turn into superstar musicians or get top class jobs and earn a fortune. I had a whole big speech worked out, but he cut me off early doors. "Fine, let's go, I've already had my wages, I'll meet you at the bus stop." And with that he chucked off his apron and left the hotel. I was now committed, my new life was about to begin.

Unfortunately I hadn't been paid in advance and had to go and see the director and after he'd been kinder to me than to virtually any other employee, he was understandably furious when I told him I was quitting on the spot and I wanted paying there and then.

"You fucking cheeky little shit, how dare you talk to me like this," he bellowed at me. I didn't back down and I remember he just kept shouting and ranting at me and ended up throwing my wages at my face. "Get out of my hotel and don't come back, you're not welcome here anymore," he told me as I didn't let the door hit me on the bum on the way out. I was home free and dashed back to the house to complete my great escape.

Every one of the Calzaghe Clan was in town working and that meant the door was locked and no-one was in. so I had to climb up our drain pipe and squeeze through a window to get into the house. We all had passports and I grabbed mine, threw on a couple of shirts and my guitar and got ready to roll, knowing that I was about to embark on the total unknown. It was an awesome feeling.

I left a note for my parents telling them that I loved them but that I had to do this, I wasn't making them proud and in my own way I wanted to do just that. I thought I needed to go out and make something of myself and that the next time they saw me, they wouldn't believe their eyes. As it was that prediction turned out to be exactly the truth, but in the total opposite way than I intended. When I next saw my parents again I certainly shocked them, of that I can promise you.

So I left the house, met Constanzo and just like that my life in Sardinia was over. I would return many, many times but never again was it really home.

It seemed logical to us to head first to Rome, a city neither of us had been to – though I'd been in the ferry port – and we caught the ferry (or rather we stowed away in some bloke's car on the boat) from Olbia to Civitavecchia and slowly made our way to Rome, taking in the sights and buzzing about the possibilities.

The idea of Rome was very romantic to me and when we arrived we were both blown away with the place. It was somewhere that was talked about a lot when I was a kid and suddenly there I was. I felt like I could have been in Australia or on Mars, figuratively I was a million miles away from home.

We gravitated to the hippy area, around the Spanish Steps between the Piazza di Spagna and Piazza Trinità dei Monti. That became one of our first homes from home and certainly wouldn't be our last across Europe. We loved the hustle and bustle of the market style and for a long time things were beautiful for Constanzo and I. If we had a cigarette, we shared it. A sandwich, shared. We played music and we drank, had some laughs and more times than not found somewhere safe to crash if the mood took us to sleep, which rarely was a problem. We did Rome for a couple of weeks and then started vaguely thinking about a route for our odyssey and it was essentially a case of where shall we go next? The action sounded like it was in Amsterdam for a couple of hippie guys and so off we went, not at any great pace, thumbing our way across borders and stopping off in all manner of places on the way to the Dutch capital.

We went to France and of course tried Paris. Fuck that. It might be the city of love or whatever but the Parisians had no love for us, busking was a bust there and hitchhiking was even harder and we just didn't take to it. We largely spent our time near the Saint Michel Bridge which was not a particularly fun experience. A lot of people congregated there at night and the police could get quite heavy so we didn't stay long in Paris before we were thumbing our way out of there.

We moved on to Belgium which was a cracking hitchhiking country, lovely people and from what I remember we spent quite a long time in Brussels and some time in Antwerp. It was in Belgium I decided I was definitely going back to England on this trip and the reason was simple... it was the chips. One bite of a chip in Belgium and it took me right back to my childhood, the taste was amazing and that became a new secret mission for me.

But our immediate destination was Amsterdam and when we eventually arrived it was a match made in heaven. Accommodation was totally out of the question for us because we had no money so for many nights we slept in Dam Square which happened to have a large tunnel nearby. At night, I swear, it was insane with homeless people queuing up in a civilised manner to get in this tunnel and sleep rough, like you all had your own bed space lined up in rows. Some people would probably find that quite terrifying but for us it was just becoming normal. I can honestly say I was never frightened sleeping rough and I did it hundreds of times. Could it get hard? Absolutely. And I did crave a bed at times, of course I did. But we could either eat or buy drugs and drink alcohol or save to sleep in a hostel. That wasn't a hard choice to make. A warm bed and food – who needs it?

The red-light district was another home from home and we started to become very savvy, knowing where we could steal fags and food. We met some other hippies who became companions and I thought we were having the time of our lives.

Unfortunately I developed this massive abscess in my mouth that just got worse and worse, more and more swollen and clearly needed medical attention. I couldn't even eat it was so painful. But of course, I had no money for a dentist. I needed at least a couple of days' work and eventually got a lead from a girl named Janette who was a friend of Erika who was dating Constanzo. I remember her sending me off with Constanzo, handing me an address and saying, "they will sort you out, Peter." For some reason everyone we met in Holland liked to call me Peter because of the Pietro part of my name.

We walked into this office somewhere in the centre of Amsterdam and what was strange was there was a room with a bed in it. The guy asked us if we wanted to be in movies. Within an hour, we had signed a contract (with fake names) that meant we were now officially stars of the adult film industry and would be starting our new careers the very next day with some apparently beautiful women. We both talked excitedly about how brilliant it would be, but I think we both probably knew that when push came to shove, we were going to bottle it. Thankfully the guy did give me a little bit of pocket money to go to a dentist saying he needed me looking less like the elephant man.

I turned up and the dentist asked for payment, I told him what I had and he said that was only half what he charged. I begged him to do what he could and so he removed the abscess and spared himself the expense by not administering an anaesthetic. I screamed bloody murder and eventually passed out and woke up in the waiting room. Didn't that bloody dentist know I was about to become a famous porno star?

I am either ashamed or proud, depending on your perspective, to confirm that we did bottle it and never went back to the porn studio. It is my sincere hope that guy we signed the deal with isn't going to read this book and hold me to my contract because I don't think anyone wants to see that.

One particular morning much like any other Constanzo woke in that tunnel, turned to me and said me he was going to the shop which was ten minutes down the road. Outside the shop was a cigarette machine and we knew how to operate it without paying. So off he went and an hour later he wasn't back, same story two, three, four hours more while I was still sleeping off a heavy night.

I was already paranoid from the drugs I was taking, and when he hadn't come back by lunchtime I feared the worst. Something had happened and I went looking for him in a bit of a panic. Constanzo and I had been like brothers for probably six months or more and I knew something had to have gone wrong because we were basically never apart. I headed to the red-light district and managed to find Erika, who was his (sort of) girlfriend. She hadn't seen him. We spent the next couple of days looking for Constanzo before one of Erika's friends said she had seen him leaving the city and that is when it hit me. He had done a bunk. I was absolutely devastated.

It got a lot worse too because I found out sometime later that when he got home he told everyone – and word got back to my parents – that he had to leave because I had basically gone mental and was smoked and coked out of my mind 24/7. I think he even said I was doing heroin. That was complete bollocks and in my opinion he just missed home and wanted an excuse for bottling it and not having the balls to tell me he had had enough. It was a coward's way out. But I'm not mad and not sad when I look back on it and I see him now in Sardinia and there is not a problem whatsoever. If he had told me his intentions I might have gone home with him and then I would never have met the love of my life. Everything happens for a reason I think.

But right then? I was penniless, homeless and totally alone in a foreign country and I felt like my best friend had betrayed me. And things only got worse in the next couple of weeks.

That girl Erika, a German girl from Lubeck asked me if I fancied going with her to her hometown as she felt the pull of home too and with no plan and very little enthusiasm for anything, I agreed. We hitchhiked for four days through Dresden and places like that, usually on large lorries and she would tell me about her family and how much she wanted me to meet them. But, as we approached her house, she changed quickly and started acting all distant and moody – something I would experience later with Joe before a fight – and shortly before we arrived she had a change of heart and told me her parents wouldn't approve of me. If only they knew what she was up to in Holland! She ended up going into the house without me and I skulked around in the yard. In the dead of night when her parents had gone to sleep she sneaked me in and banished me to this tiny little attic room.

I lived in that attic without going out the house for ten days. Like a hippie, druggie version of Anne Frank. It was like military prison all over again. She brought me food and I used the toilet if her parents were out but I was just up there, being quiet as a mouse and hardly moving. I just looked out of the window and wondered where the fuck it had all gone wrong and caught up on six months of missed sleep.

I missed my home and I missed my parents, my brothers and sister, my family, my old life. But I couldn't go back because I was the same fuck up I had been when I left.

Thankfully, on the tenth day Erika had a blazing row with her parents and wanted to sneak away and we did a runner in the dead of night. My legs were completely done in by being in the confines of the attic and hardly eating. I was so weak I could barely move, let alone run. It took a day until I stopped limping like a war veteran. We moved on and headed back to Amsterdam and it was pretty likely we would just settle back into our normal life there, being bums and sleeping rough, doing what we could for a buck. But things rarely turn out as we expect, do they? Less than two weeks later I was fleeing Amsterdam fearing for my life and being chased by some heavy duty guys working for a homosexual mobster. And that is what put me on the path to Jackie, my kids, boxing, Wales and my whole life as it is today. Well, that and a bottle of whisky.

I did warn you this was no ordinary story, didn't I?

Chapter Five:

Homeward Bound, I Wish I Was

Erika and I were just friends, two misfits, but with Constanzo ditching me and the fact I was immature meant that I didn't really like being on my own all the time. By this point I was drug free because the experience of hardly being able to walk in Germany had shaken me up and I was starting to take seriously the need to go back to Italy as a big success story. I'd called home and heard all the shit Constanzo had said about me and I was determined to prove the lies wrong in a big way. Luckily Uccio was back in Sardinia from the army and he fought my corner and told everyone it was a pack of lies. He's always been my biggest supporter and my best friend.

So we pitched up in Amsterdam and managed to find some really good accommodation with a couple of school teachers we had met the first time around. They were nice people, quite middle-class and I can't really recall why they were happy to have these two malnourished hippies staying with them, but they were and so we cracked on with our Amsterdam life.

They had a son, about eighteen years old, also with that long hippie hair and look and we hit it off really quickly. I forget his name but he was a typical Flemish-looking kid and used to call me 'Peter Man.' This kid was pretty pleased to have us staying and he said to me one day, "Peter Man, why don't you come to work with me today?" So I thought ok, I could use something to do and in any case, maybe there would be work for me too. When he told me he worked as a bouncer at a strip club in the red-light district I was completely swayed. That sounded great to me especially as we were going to hit a party or two after his shift. What could be better?

I went with him and just hung around this exceptionally seedy place and waited until the middle of the night when it shut and we were done. I was pretty tired but my new amigo wanted me to go and meet some other friends and we took a taxi even though we were only going five minutes down the road to a pretty sleazy hotel in the red-light district.

We entered a very dark lounge room. There were only guys in there and they looked absolutely menacing. As soon as we arrived I knew I was in way over my head. I could feel that in the pit of my stomach. It was one night I wish I had been stoned out of my mind. It was very late, very dark and these guys were definitely crooks. I was uncomfortable, scared even. Luckily after nipping off to another room for a bit my friend came back and said we were going to go and visit another party with some other associates of his. We jumped into a cab and he asked me if I could hold some things for him.

He gave me a large envelope of cash and a big bag of five-hundred dextroamphetamine pills that we knew as Dexys Midnight Runners because they kept you running all night long. Back then, they were a drug of choice. They even had a band named after them and I can't hear "Come on Eileen" without thinking of this story. We got there and found only four guests at the so-called party. In fact, there were as many bouncers as guests because every corner of the room had a massive guy working security. I didn't like this one bit. Then a huge middle-aged guy came in, a massive bloke with a big bald head. He went straight over to my mate and started playing with his hair and then within a few seconds was kissing him on the mouth and touching his body.

It sounds bad now to admit, but at the time I freaked out. I had never known any gay people in Sardinia and I didn't know what to say or do. I panicked, pure and simple and when I excused myself to go to the toilet I absolutely legged it away from there, I ran from the house as fast as I possibly could and never looked back. I had no idea what the fuck was going on. I ran and I ran for an hour and was in a right state. I had gone over the top maybe as I stood my ground with people who I thought were gangsters and yet two guys kissing sent me into a spin. But there was a bigger problem, much bigger. I had a big envelope of cash in my pocket and lots of amphetamines.

What the fuck was I going to do? I quickly got back to where we were staying and grabbed my stuff and then ran a block or two away and jumped into the biggest bush I could find. I figured those guys were going to come looking for me pretty fast and if they found me it wouldn't be pretty. My best chance was to wait until daylight and then get the hell out of Amsterdam. I left the pills at the digs but I kept the cash. I figured if I was going to be beaten to death, I might as well have something to show for it. I left Erika without so much a as a goodbye. She'd have done the same thing.

The second the sun came up I sprinted for the main road and the first lorry to stop for me was going to Rotterdam. "Fine," I told him, "I'll ride the whole way with you." I didn't really have a plan, but I still hadn't visited the UK on my travels and ever since Belgium my heart had been pulling me in that direction, so I hitched to Rotterdam and then to the Hook of Holland, a giant port largely used by fishermen and trawlers.

I was there for a while trying to sort my head out and work out where to go and I decided on Bournemouth because my auntie and uncle Nina and Peppino who had moved with us to Bedford had returned to the UK. I heard from Uccio that they were running a restaurant and I believed Antonio my brother was also somewhere in Bournemouth. That sounded good to me. Plus, for once, I had a bit of cash in my pocket after stealing from the gay mafia guy.

I started talking to a captain of a boat and telling him my tales and he took a shine to me and said I could get a lift with him to England. He owned a tomato boat and said I could stow on and help him out. I think I gave him a black stone gem ring that I had as collateral. It wasn't worth too much. That's how it was, how I arrived in England as a stowaway on a tomato boat. What would the *Daily Mail* say?

I recall it was a long thin trawler and we set off in the night and the sea was rough from minute one. Before long I was puking my guts up frequently. The captain said he'd let me into a trade secret for getting your sea legs and I will happily share that with you now. He took me to the back of the boat that us tomato-boat fishermen call the stern and gave me a can of lager. He told me to drink it and I did and then he gave me another, and another and another and so on. I stopped being sick and I wasn't sick again on the trip. Next time you feel sea-sick go to the back of the boat and crack open a can or six. It works, I swear.

We arrived in Whitstable and over the course of the next couple of weeks I fell in love with England all over again. It was beautiful: the hills, the grass, the smell – I loved it. It was like I was back home, doing what I should be doing. I felt like I was on the right path for the first time in a long time and I was right.

They stamped my passport in Whitstable and gave me a stay for a month or two and I headed to London initially because I felt like I should, I had to see it I guess. I was told I could stay with some friends of friends from my Amsterdam days and headed to their place in Streatham Hill. It was a massive hashish factory with loads and loads of the stuff, people stoned out of their brains and I wasn't having it, not anymore. I slept one night on the floor, felt unwelcome and left the next morning after helping them to cut the stuff the night before, my last real experience with wacky baccy.

I walked around London for a couple of days and slept rough and then began heading for Bournemouth. I didn't even bother hitching really. I just walked, miles and miles each and every day and I loved it. I was so free-spirited. One day I would go slower, one day faster, the next day just stay where I was and do some busking as I still had my guitar. If I could eat then wonderful and if I couldn't then I would eat the next day. I had a destination and that made me feel comfortable.

I went to Brighton, stopped in a few other places too and slowly made my way to the Dorset coast and made a beeline for Bournemouth. My brother had been working in a hotel between Bournemouth and Poole and my aunt and uncle were running a place called the Double-O-Egg Cafe which went on to become a very popular punk hangout in the 1970s. The Sex Pistols went there a lot I believe and loads of the other big punk acts too.

I got to Bournemouth one evening and stupidly I figured it would be like Sassari where everyone knows everyone. I was so naive. As I get to the city limits I start saying to people, "Hello there. Do you know Antonio Calzaghe?" You can imagine the looks people gave me, this Italian hippie wearing three jackets, with a guitar on his back and holes in his shoes, who probably looked like he hadn't had a wash in a week (and hadn't!) You know they say that real men don't ask for directions? What a load of bollocks that is. I've been asking directions my whole life. I love stopping and talking to people. Meeting your fellow man is a good thing, I have always believed that. Why look at a map when you can make a new friend? But in hindsight, expecting to find my brother that way wasn't the brightest idea I ever had.

So I carried on, asking everyone in Bournemouth and then something strange happened. I saw a man about fifty yards away coming towards me in a hurry. Forty yards. He looks familiar. Thirty yards. Are you kidding me? Twenty yards. My heart is pounding out of my chest. Ten yards. "ANTONIO!" I screamed. It was my brother, right there in front of me. What were the chances?

I'll never forget the joy, the wonderful reunion we had. Those special words he uttered that will stay with me forever.

"Enzo, I can't stop. I am taking a girl to the theatre. See you."

I kid you not. My brother didn't even stop to have a conversation with me. I couldn't believe it and I spent the next two hours walking around cursing Antonio, swearing in Italian and English about what a *bastardo* he was. I have always been able to swear fluently in Italian. It came in useful when I shouted at the officials during fights.

Around midnight a student who was about the six-hundredth person I'd stopped, pointed me in the direction of the Double-O-Egg. However, as I arrived my uncle was packing up a car he had rented because they were moving back to Sardinia.

This was just too unbelievable to be true. All that time pissing about in Amsterdam and such places and now the home I assumed I would have in the UK wasn't going to be there anymore. I was shit out of luck. I don't think my aunt and uncle liked what they saw when they looked at me and I remember my auntie especially begging me to go back to Sardinia with them. When that didn't work, my uncle Peppino swore blue murder at me. "*sali su questa cazzo di macchina*," get in the fucking car.

In the end I had to be honest with them and admit that I was too ashamed to go back to Sardinia. I was more of a mess than when I left. They took pity on me, delayed their trip and stayed the night so I had a bed for the evening and the next morning phoned the new guy who was running the cafe and convinced him to give me a job for a couple of weeks. I wouldn't get paid but I could live in the restaurant and eat there if I worked as a waiter. Antonio helped me to sort it out after his date at the theatre and I reported for duty for my latest career. It took me about a day-and-a-half to get into trouble.

It all started as most situations like these do with a couple of attractive young girls. They came in from Bristol and stayed for a long time as I did my thing and flirted with them and ignored the rest of the customers. Obviously as they had about four hot drinks each on the house, I believe they were enjoying the chat and the banter. Unfortunately though, they were soon joined in the cafe by four guys who had had a bit to drink and were getting aggressive. Soon they were touching the girls inappropriately and I stepped in and asked them to leave. You can probably guess the two-word reply I received.

I decided this was going to end badly and I had lost quite a lot of my English by then so I just beckoned the biggest of the four of them to come outside with me. I muttered at him in Italian. I figured if I dropped the big boy then the others would leave the place too, it was how I had been taught by my father. One-on-one combat was best; dropping the head into their chest usually got the job done. Unlike my boy I have generally always been a very dirty fighter.

In this instance my best plans were out of the window because the guy came out with all his mates and I was ready for a proper pasting.

I started swinging punches like a windmill and darting in and out of these four guys. A couple of minutes passed in a blur with me running and running, swinging and swinging. I hadn't been hit and I hadn't laid a finger on any of them. It was ridiculous, like choreography from a Bruce Lee movie. I was going berserk but I needed an escape and the manager of the restaurant demanded I went back in and I happily went!

I thought that was the last of it but this man called Phil, who ate in the cafe every day, had other ideas. He was a big guy and as I came back he passed me on the way out and said, "I'll sort it." The lads saw him coming and didn't back away and I was amazed to see this one bloke holding his ground to the point the four punks backed down and drove off. Even then Phil chased after the car and grabbed one of them by the throat through the window. He came back in, sat down and grinned at me and said: "It's sorted," with his cockney accent that I found hilarious.

It took me a second and then I realised something was very different about Phil. When he left the restaurant he had front teeth! The little punk took a swing at him through the window and knocked his teeth out. Normal guys would be bothered but Phil thought it funny. He was a nutter and I knew then we would be good friends and so it proved.

I wasn't very happy in Bournemouth even with all the chips I could eat. The big family reunion hadn't worked out as I'd hoped and I decided that even though I hadn't achieved anything like I planned, perhaps I had to accept my parents were right about me and I was a bum. I vowed to go back to Sardinia and start again because even though I felt like a failure I really missed my family. As much as I could make them miserable and they didn't respect my lifestyle, we loved each other.

I needed funds quickly so like the world's most ungrateful little bugger I started taking cash from the till and more than my share of the waiters' tips from the Double-O-Egg and within a few days had enough for a ferry to Italy. I hitched to Southampton that same night and got on a boat to Le Havre. I met some people on the way and when we arrived in France, we agreed to try and hitch together and what little money we had, we pooled together to buy a bottle of Vat 69 Whisky. It was forty percent proof and it changed my life forever.

My plan was to hitch overnight to Dijon and then just keep hitching towards Italy and when we got into a lorry headed to Dijon we carried on drinking. We arrived at the bus depot in the dead of night and while the others went off to look for a hostel, I had no money, was pissed out of my head and simply crashed out on the street. I remember being poked during the night, but I didn't have anything to steal by that stage so I slept right through it.

Turns out the person doing the poking was a policeman and once he found out I had just been in Britain and had time left on my visa, he decided maybe her Majesty and the rest of the UK would like me back. He put me on the opposite side of the road while I was asleep. So when I woke I thumbed a lorry, got in and fell asleep and duly woke up back in sodding Le Havre! I was dejected and confused, and craving familiarity I went back to Bournemouth and even though the Double-O-Egg's books were probably balanced for the first time since I had arrived, they kindly took me back. They obviously didn't work out I'd been sticking my fingers in the till.

I got a bit of money in my pocket and decided to move again to see more of Britain before my visa ran out and Phil told me he'd give me a lift to Southampton train station. When we got there he noticed a train to Cardiff where he'd once lived and started telling me about the place and I just thought, why not? I had barely even heard of Wales let alone thought about going there but it just seemed like a bit of an adventure and if I was going to go home to Sardinia, maybe it would be my last adventure like this.

I've seen before people quote me as saying at the time (you'll find this quote on Wikipedia): "Sod going home, let's give Cardiff a go," and to be honest, even though I can't remember if those were the words I uttered, it certainly sounds about right! I had such a relaxed attitude to everything and just decided to up sticks to Cardiff with only my guitar and this cockney guy called Phil for company. I hadn't made my fame and fortune yet, maybe I would in Cardiff.

He told me we could kip for free at the Salvation Army when we arrived. But for whatever reason, he was allowed in and I was not. So I spent my first night in Cardiff sleeping in a phone box opposite the bus station on St Mary's Street in the city centre. I could take you there now and certainly until recently, that phone box was still there. I stayed there a few nights before I was moved on by the police and I ended up sheltering under a bridge in Tiger Bay at night with a couple of other homeless people. By this stage I had been travelling for over a year and I was cold, tired and down in the dumps. I just needed a little cash and I would go back to Italy.

So Phil and I sat down and looked in the paper at job

opportunities and saw there was a restaurant that needed staff. When we arrived they told us they had just filled their last vacancy but luckily the people there sent us down to this Wimpy bar and told us they might have some work instead. We arrived and suddenly on first sight I wasn't tired, I wasn't hungry and I wasn't desperate to leave the UK. I was in love.

It was like a thunderbolt. From the very first second I saw this amazing-looking girl pouring coffee, I knew I had found everything I was looking for. I had found my soulmate. If that sounds mad, so be it.

It's fair to say Jackie did not feel the same way. In fact, if you ask her, as I did when I started talking about this passage of my life for the book, she reminded me that she thought I was "a total and utter idiot." Love at first sight for me, complete and utter indifference from Jackie. I thought she was simply amazing. She had long hair right down to her backside, stunning features and pencilled-on eyebrows. I was a hippie at heart and I saw a kindred spirit.

She saw what many people see when they look at me now which is a scruffy Italian who can't really be taken too seriously. I forgot all about the fact I was there to ask for work and sat down and ordered a coffee, then a tea, then a coffee, then another tea. I was doing everything I could to make sure this beautiful woman would come and serve us. Before long another girl came over to take our order and made clear Jackie wanted me to know that I should "piss off."

It wasn't exactly going as I had planned. I thought I was hot stuff, I look back on photographs of the time and I think I had a touch of the Errol Flynn about me, maybe Douglas Fairbanks Jr, but certainly I rated myself as a Casanova type. She wasn't having a bit of it though. I begged the new waitress to ask her friend Jackie if she'd go out with me tonight. A minute later and with a broad smile, she returned. "I asked her," she said. "She says you should get knotted."

If I wasn't such a persistent bastard that might have been that, but that night when Phil returned to the Salvation Army I went back to that Wimpy. I thought at the very least, the lovely Jackie might let me walk her home. I had a big black coat on, my guitar around my shoulders and these bloody shoes with holes in them and I figured that as flattery had got me nowhere, I'd try a bit of stalking!

Jackie wasn't impressed to see me, but eventually she relented and let me walk her home, though we barely spoke. Then the next night I waited again and this time she had a burger in her hand and she offered it to me. It was a first sign of affection or at least pity. Progress. At that point I hadn't had a meal in three or four days and had been taking food out of the rubbish bins in Cardiff, so I was more than grateful. I wolfed it down and that broke the ice a little bit and she let me cadge a couple of cigarettes as well.

She told me to come to the Wimpy the next day about a job and warned me that even though her boss was a total arsehole, they might just have something for me as one of the pot washers hadn't been showing up. And sure enough, I was pretty much hired on the spot.

As I had settled, my mate Phil buggered off never to be seen by me again but I wasn't too bothered. I spent every second of the day with Jackie and I'd won her round, we were totally love-struck with one another in a matter of days. I do owe Phil though. He played his part in me getting to where I was meant to be.

I lasted all of a couple of weeks before I started plotting my way out of my working life, as was the norm, but not as a way to leave Jackie. I wanted her with me. Now I had a bigger dream than just returning home a success. I had fallen in love and moved in with Jackie into a house share she had in Cardiff. I wanted to marry this girl. It sounds crazy, but within a week we were talking about marriage and I asked Jackie to come to Sardinia with me. She said yes to Sardinia but claims she was the one who proposed marriage to me. We've been arguing about it for over forty years. Who proposed to who? We had this magic chemistry between us and still do and it felt totally natural to us to get engaged after a couple of weeks together.

We agreed to give the Wimpy the swerve and both quit, though once again I had to get my money, just like when I had fled Italy in the first place. The manager was a big guy, always boasting about martial arts belts and such like and when I asked him for the money he said he'd buy my guitar off me or I could sod off without a pound in my pocket.

I thought he was just another bully boss and argued my case but he ended up pushing me out of the office and eventually with the help of a waiter, out of the building. I started screaming and shouting, ranting and raving and he came out looking all smug with four waiters around him outside the front of the restaurant. He didn't have my guitar which I clung to for dear life, so he wouldn't pay me the money I was owed.

What happened next was like a dream. We advanced on one another and even though he had back-up, it escalated quickly into a fight between the two of us. I only knew one way to scrap and that was like a street fighter, as I'd learned in Bedford and Sardinia where not backing down was a necessity. I got a butt in and it's fair to say that it was me who got the better of things. When I looked up, two of the waiters had gone into the restaurant and a second later came back with carving knives and I had to leg it, only just managing to retrieve my guitar. I was supposed to work for free at the Double-O-Egg and paid myself and at the Wimpy I never saw a penny of the money I was actually owed. That's karma for you. To this day that is the last time I was in a fight that didn't involve boxing pads.

Even without my wages I had the ultimate prize and I was going to marry the woman of my dreams. I had always believed in fate and do to this day. All those trials and tribulations were meant to lead me to Jackie. There were so many 'what ifs' along the way to us meeting, I believe in my heart that it was written in the stars for us, we were meant to be.

I was only twenty at the time and Jackie was seventeen so it wasn't as simple as just getting married, we needed permission from Jackie's elders and it was with a lot of trepidation I set off to meet her mother. Tragically, her father had passed away when Jackie was only nine, he worked down the coal mines his whole life and died prematurely from an illness related to that, as many others did too. Jackie doesn't like to talk about it but I thought her father looked very distinguished in the pictures, a David Niven sort. He was only forty when he died in what was a very different era in terms of workplace health and safety.

I was incredibly nervous when I met Jackie's mother, Rebecca

Phillips, a wonderful, wonderful woman who made me feel welcome and part of the family from the first seconds of meeting her. I wish I could say the same about when my folks met Jackie, but it was totally different unfortunately. I don't think Rebecca intended to give us her blessing, but we really hit it off and by the time we left I could tell she was actually quite excited about her daughter getting married, even if she was only seventeen. I didn't need to try and impress Rebecca. I guess she could see in me just how much I loved her daughter.

A couple of days later I met Jackie's two uncles named Ivor and John and they also gave me their blessing to wed Jackie, so we were all set. Being raised a Catholic, I just figured it was a case of waiting for a church, I'd never even heard of a Registry Office, I had no idea what that meant, but that is what Jackie wanted and within a week-and-a-half after sorting out the necessary paperwork etc, we were ready to get hitched.

Jackie was bright, clever, funny, sarcastic, full of gumption and I couldn't wait to be married to her. The problem I had was I still didn't really have two beans to rub together and couldn't afford a suit. But I promised Jackie I would sort it out before the big day. With a few hours to spare, I scrounged a couple of quid to get a haircut at this barbershop run by an Italian guy and thank the lord, when I told him my predicament he lent me a jacket and a nice shirt for the afternoon. Hallelujah, brother, let's get married!

We had a very small, quick and incredibly cheap ceremony and then being the old romantic I was I whisked Jackie off to a different Wimpy bar to celebrate our nuptials. Between the two of us we had enough money to split one Knickerbocker Glory and to us that was quite posh and a sign that Mr and Mrs Calzaghe were on their way up.

We saved a little bit of cash and with it we headed to Sardinia to build a new life together shortly after getting married. My voyage across Europe was finished.

Even on the journey things started to go wrong. We had some of our luggage pinched on the ferry on the way over there and the thieves broke our suitcase so I had to find something to keep our remaining few possessions in. The only thing I could lay my hands on at the time was a chicken basket and so that was what I used.

I had promised my family I am going to travel to Europe and come home a big success story, a millionaire and this was what I was reduced to.

Meanwhile, I'd not told my parents what I'd been up to. They had heard rumours I'm doing coke, heroin and all sorts while I was away. I'd then got married, not told them and called them up one day and said, "I am coming home now."

Was I a millionaire? No. Was I clean, presentable and looking well? No. Was I on my own, as they expected? No. I was married to a girl who though she looked Italian, couldn't speak a word of the language. But did we at least look like a well-to-do couple? No. I arrived off the boat clutching a chicken basket full of our gear and introduced a wife they didn't know existed. I think my parents felt humiliated.

Living in Sardinia never ever worked for us, not for a second. My parents weren't too keen on Jackie and I was too immature to be married and definitely too immature to be a father. That was going to be a big problem because during our nine-month stint in Sardinia I got Jackie pregnant. Joe was on the way.

My parents grudgingly accepted the marriage but were never really receptive to it or positive. They looked at Jackie like she was a little child. She was seventeen and as feisty and spunky as they came but she just didn't hit it off with my dad and especially my mum to begin with. They looked at her like they looked at Alba or even Sergio, just a kid. They were still bemused and not really very amused that they had a daughter-in-law and we all had to adjust to us moving back into the family home. Antonio was still in England but the rest of the family were all squeezed under one roof.

It wasn't exactly the Ritz Hotel for two newly-weds and looking back now, I appreciate Jackie was never happy there. She was independent and the language barrier denied her that side of her personality. She wasn't made to feel welcome and I don't know how she stuck it for so long, only love can make you do such things.

On the other hand, I was loving it, it was a perfect situation for me as I had a trophy wife on my arm and I was back, the wanderer had returned and before long I was back into my old habits, working on the markets hustling, hanging around with undesirables and gigging. A couple of local bands had come looking for me when I returned and it was like slipping on a pair of comfortable shoes, I was back to a year ago and the only difference was I now had a wife and was soon to find out I had a kid on the way. I didn't cheat on Jackie but I didn't act like a husband either. Sometimes I would get drunk in the mornings, I was still work-shy and she deserved so much better.

My father is a very wise man and I think he could see that my marriage had no chance with me running back to Mummy and Daddy with a new wife and gently encouraged us to find our own place to live. At the time I felt rejected by him, but looking back I can see it was entirely selfless on his part. He was doing what was best for both of us and arranged a nice little place for us in Sassari, though it was close to the prison. It was a one-bedroom apartment with a little kitchen and for the first time in what felt like months Jackie seemed genuinely happy. She'd had a run-in or two with my mother Victoria, so this was great for her, she was the queen of our little castle.

But how much could she take? I was back in the music scene in a big way and all that goes with that. The coming in at all hours, the drugs, the alcohol, it wasn't fair on Jackie. She had had enough and after about six months of toughing it out every day she told me, "I want to go back, Enzo. When can we go back?"

When we found out Joe was on the way I eventually had to concede. Not even I was selfish enough to keep my pregnant wife in a country she wasn't happy in and Jackie ground me down and convinced me she'd leave for the UK with or without me. She was nostalgic for home, didn't feel respected and it was uncomfortable for her. My marriage was rocky really as we fought like cats and dogs. It was constant, a very volatile relationship and I didn't really want to go back to Wales straight away and Jackie didn't want to be in Sardinia, so we compromised and moved instead to Bournemouth, an area I was familiar with and where Antonio lived. My brother was great and hooked us up with some work in a hotel where we could stay called the Harbour Heights and we both worked as kitchen porters. We took work as casuals in all those hotels around the Sandbanks area and it was a good time, apart from when we fought.

Jackie never caved in, something that hasn't changed, and she was always right, or thought so, whenever we argued. In one of the hotels she was a chambermaid and I was a waiter and I remember taking some coffee to a secretary and maybe having a tiny little flirt. I went back into the kitchen area which had swinging doors like the saloon at the OK Corral and kicked them open and as I did – BANG – I got a big open hand right across the face. I dropped the tray and had to pay for the damages. That was bad news for me and Jackie but as I'm sure you've guessed it was her who belted me. It was just her way. We still laugh about that and I think she'd still do the same thing to me now.

When the summer ended the work dried up in Bournemouth and we went to stay with one of Jackie's sisters in Finchley in London. We started looking for somewhere to live and found a place on St Marks Road near Ladbroke Grove and both got jobs. I was working in a nails and screw factory near Liverpool Street and Jackie, who was trained as a secretary, landed a great job, working for Twentieth Century Fox. She was giving birth in a few months and we needed every penny we could get.

What I found baffling was all the forms I had to fill out working in England. Social security, staff numbers, all this stuff, it meant nothing to me. I had gone from being a lazy guy to a workhorse, absolutely flogging myself to put money in the bank (although at the time I didn't trust banks and would hide money all over the flat). I worked in the factory until 4pm and then went to work as a waiter in a hotel until about 8pm, mainly doing teas and coffees and then serving dinner. After that I would get a tube to Piccadilly to do my third job of the day, working in a bar called the Latin Quarter, which I believe is long gone now. I would get a taxi home about 3am and fall into bed shattered knowing that five hours later it would all begin again.

The change in my attitude was totally down to the fact I was days away from becoming a dad. Jackie stopped at Twentieth Century Fox and I was absolutely shitting myself about becoming a father. And in typical fashion I made the worst start you can.

I had started playing football with a bunch of boys near Wormwood Scrubs and after a game we had a few drinks. One became two, two became three and before I knew it I was crashed out on someone's floor. When Jackie finally managed to locate me the next day she was already at Hammersmith Hospital in labour and by the time I managed to get down there Joe had been born. I have had to live with that. I missed his birth. When I arrived on the ward, I could tell none of the nurses even believed I was the father. Joe was the spit of his mother and even though I am a small guy and Jackie was little too, Joe weighed in at 10lbs 6oz. He was huge. He never did have it easy on the scales!

Joe was born in the same hospital as Lennox Lewis and on the same ward as Frank Bruno. Sorry to shatter the illusions of anyone who thought Joe was Welsh born, but trust me when I tell you that in his heart he is Welsh to his core, even though technically he is English.

All my relatives were desperate to see baby Joe. In my heart I felt my parents and family saw me as a black sheep and I felt like the failure of the family. But how could I be a failure when I produced this beautiful, happy, healthy son? He was my pride and joy and I wanted to show him off. So we headed to Sardinia for a holiday, though in my mind, there was no time limit on coming back. I was sick of London and hard work. But before we even arrived it nearly ended in disaster.

Weeks after Joe was born we went from Dover to Calais and then caught a train that would eventually stop in Genoa from where we'd get the ferry to Sardinia. We had an hour stop in Paris, got off the train to stretch our legs and then I had to go and get supplies for Jackie. I put them both back on the train and off I went to a shop. When I came back and there was no sign of Jackie or little Joe in our seats.

I was frantic, absolutely manic. I must have the wrong train, I thought. But I ran to the front and it definitely said Genoa. I found the ticket conductor and I was screaming and shouting, fearing the worst had happened and that someone had taken them. I began running up and down the platform like a mad man. I would just have to search all the trains. I pegged it around the station here, there and everywhere and still there was no sign of them. I ran to another platform, jumped on to a train to Czechoslovakia that left about two minutes later and to my utter amazement, sitting there as calm as day were Jackie and Joe.

"Get off the fucking train," I screamed as it started chugging into life. Jackie scooped up Joe and I went mental. "What the fuck are you doing? You scared me half to death! You were ninety seconds away from Czechoslovakia, Jackie," I screamed at her feeling like my head was going to explode. "Enzo, you put us on that train," she replied, dead calm. And she was right. In my haste to get to the shop, I put them back on the wrong train. I dare not even think about what could have happened.

Eventually we made our way back to Sardinia on the right trains and boats and all together and it was a much more pleasant experience than when I took my new wife there a few months earlier. Mum and Dad were thrilled to be grandparents and seemed happy for us to stay as long as we wanted. I was sick to death of working so hard and an extended vacation carrying my boy around and showing him off to anyone who knew me appealed. We had a huge party to welcome Joe into the Calzaghe clan, everyone was made up for us and we all celebrated in Bancali where my grandfather had a farm.

There was a little farmhouse next door, a very small bungalow and Jackie and I stayed there for our entire stay so we'd have some privacy. There wasn't a cot or anything for the baby and please don't ring the social services, but Joe slept in a big drawer with a blanket in it. He was like a little Borrower.

I was determined not to make the same mistakes as before and steered clear of the markets, the drugs and the temptations, but I still managed to royally piss Jackie off. I started hanging around with a friend of mine who I still see to this day. His name is Sergio Russo, a dentist who at the time was a qualified football referee. One day he invited me to the other side of Sardinia for a semi-pro match he was refereeing and off we went. I enjoyed it and then we got some excellent hospitality afterwards. I hadn't done much boozing since Joe was born but cut loose that night and paid a heavy price. We returned in the early hours and just as I was walking towards the front door a window was flung open and Joe's pram was launched at me along with several expletives from Jackie. It hit me on the shoulder and that pain was nothing compared to the ear-bashing that accompanied it.

Jackie was right though, I still wasn't putting her and the baby first. I thought her love was unconditional, but all these selfish acts and stupid choices were mounting up.

One of my mother's brothers, Mario, had a small building firm and I started working there. Mario died at only fifty-two, but he didn't half pack a lot into his years because he had eleven children and two of them represented Italy in wrestling at the Olympics. That side of my family was renowned for wrestling prowess but it just never appealed to me as a sport. I started working as a labourer for Mario and he was great to work with. My uncle was a typical small Sardinian man who was very rugged and extremely proud of his eleven children. I was doing back-breaking labour every day and coming home to a wife who thought we were only on holiday and was thoroughly miserable as the days went on. Bancali is an extremely remote place and Jackie was bored out of her mind with absolutely no adults to converse with. She only had baby Joe and childish Enzo. After a little while, enough was enough. I realised I couldn't force Sardinia on Jackie anymore – she loves it now and drags me there sometimes – and I never tried again. I knew living in Italy simply wasn't an option. I agreed we could head back to the UK and this time we were going to go back to Wales, back to where Jackie felt most comfortable.

So we returned to her mother's house in Markham and I felt about as comfortable there as Jackie did in Sardinia. At least in Sardinia no-one called Jackie a 'dirty Italian bastard.' The people in Markham hated my guts and I felt like a pathetic loser because I was living in my mother-in-law's house. I felt emasculated, miserable and could only really enjoy myself when I was playing with the baby.

I worked nights in a cider factory in Hereford but I was still most interested in having a drink, drifting and being carefree even though I was now responsible for a family. I needed to find a role in the community and I desperately needed some allies and within a few months I got halfway. I got the call I was praying for and my best buddy came back into my life when Uccio came to Wales after jacking in his job. Ucc was desperate to spend time with me and the feeling was mutual. I needed him more than ever and I bullshitted him that Markham was great and the people really liked me! So he arrived, full of hope, Italian as pizza and with an accent even harder to understand than mine.

"People fucking hated us from the minute I arrived in Markham. They didn't like us because we were Italian, hated us because we didn't apologise for being Italian and were constantly suspicious of us. I think they thought we were going to shag their wives and girlfriends and in my case, they weren't always wrong!" Uccio Calzaghe.

It was amazing having Uccio over. He was rarely around because he had more girlfriends at that time than we had hot dinners, but it did mean I had a comrade and we started playing music together and drinking together when he wasn't out shagging. Uccio loved Jackie from the minute they met in Sardinia. He loved her attitude and the fact she didn't take any nonsense, they got on brilliantly and always have done, so she was fine with him being around a lot of the time.

One night was particularly memorable when the terrible twosome, my cousins Mario and Marco pitched up for a weekend. Uccio and I took the boys into Cardiff for a night out and we went for a meal first at an Italian restaurant owned by the father of Giorgio Chinaglia, who became a famous Italian international footballer and, at the time, played for Swansea. We had a few beers and when it came time to pay the bill Marco went to the toilet and didn't come back. Two minutes later Mario pulled the same trick and then Uccio bolted out of the door. I sat there like a mug wondering what was happening until it dawned on me those three toerags had contrived to do a runner without tipping me off. I had very little cash on me so I had to do the same, but I'd sat there so long it was pretty obvious what I was going to pull. I carefully and deliberately counted out the money I had, barely enough to pay for my own meal but I put it in a pile on the table. Then all I could do was run. When I eventually made my break half a dozen chefs and waiters chased me into the street with meat cleavers! Only my tricky winger's pace kept me alive that day!

The next night they stitched me up again. We went for food I had never heard of called curry and I told the waiter I would have roast chicken as I didn't recognise anything on the menu. He asked me if I wanted it hot and I told him, "Of course, as hot as it comes," because I didn't know why he would think I'd want cold chicken in a restaurant. Of course he meant spicy, my cousins knew that and egged on the waiter and the first bite of that chicken practically blew my head off!

One evening Uccio and I were drinking in the local boozer where we had to be wary because people eyeballed us all the time and were absolutely vile towards us. But that night we were approached nervously by a local man. "Good evening gentlemen, my name is Wynford and I am forming a local football team," he said to us as Uccio and I relaxed. Usually when someone approached us it was far less cordial. "Would you be interested in playing?" he asked. It was a game-changing conversation. We were golden from then on. We went to trials that Sunday and the following week was to be our first game for Markham. The only complication was that despite only being in the country for weeks Uccio was getting married and we had to go to the ceremony in Cardiff the night before the game. Jackie and I went along, we all had a little do, and then we all woke with the hangover from hell.

We had completely forgotten that Uccio and I were supposed to be playing against Tredegar Town and by the time we dashed back to Markham our side was 2-0 down approaching half time. Once again we were as popular as head lice. Anyway, to cut what has become one of my favourite stories to bore the grandchildren with short, I came on at half time and 25 minutes later we were 5-2 up and I had scored all five goals. We won 7-2 and suddenly, since Uccio and I were the best players on the team, we were no longer social lepers in Markham. Even our big defender Albert Pearce who I remember never took to us, smiled after that game, especially as he scored an own goal in the first half! I played regularly after that and again football had helped me to adapt to the culture of where I was living just as it had done in Sardinia and in the Air Force.

Once life became a bit easier, once I had proved I could fit in, I started getting restless and was thinking about where we would go next. That was how my mind worked. Jackie had different ideas. She put our names down for a council house and eventually a place became available in Pentwynmawr. It was on a brand new estate but many of the private houses hadn't been sold so the council had to take them on instead. It was a four-bedroom detached house and Jackie ensured we got in first and snapped it up. We had our own home for the first time and we loved it so much we still live there today, four decades on.

Why does a guy with a bit of money still live in a council house? Simple. Because I like the area, the people and because having a big house just to show off isn't me. We've never thought about moving and certainly Joe becoming a successful millionaire wasn't going to change our minds. I am sure if his mother asked him he'd buy us a posh house in London tomorrow. But that's just not us.

I found a job I loved too, maybe for the very first time, and began working on the buses as a conductor. It suited me down to the ground. I would chat to people all day every day and honestly thought about it as a permanent career. When they sacked me I was training to become a bus driver and it was a vocation I thought would be my future. I did it for around four years and things were beautiful in the Calzaghe household from my perspective at least. My son was growing into a little man and we had our first daughter Sonia with another, Melissa, on the way.

We weren't exactly wealthy, I made a pittance on the buses, but we were rich with love and had a happy home. When I couldn't afford to put bread on the table, I'm not going to lie, I would take bread to put on the table. But by and large I was becoming quite a different man from the one who had been such a shit husband to Jackie in the early days.

But I worked a lot of weekends so the football fell by the wayside and music started to again consume me now that I had Uccio to play with. Gigging was becoming more and more what I wanted to do with my time. I should've been more concerned about the three young kids I had at home who had all been born within three-and-a-half years of each other, but the penny still hadn't dropped for me.

I wanted to be a rock and roll star and nearly became one. And the price of that dream was coming within a whisker of losing everything that really mattered.

Chapter Six:

Married to the Music and Killing Dreams

Before there was boxing there was music. My dream, my life's work, my reason for getting out of bed in the morning was to perform and make people happy.

I've always been a dreamer and I love those lyrics by John Lennon. That's my philosophy to a tee. I was a restless soul and always lacked concentration. Why stay in one place? It just wasn't me. Only meeting the love of my life ever put an anchor on my backside. If it wasn't for Jackie and the family, I'd probably never have owned a home in my life. Working on the buses, fun as it was, it wasn't enough for the great Enzo Calzaghe. I was destined for better, wasn't I? In my mind, since my uncle Vincenzo had stuck his guitar in my back and forced me to the front of the stage in Sardinia, since I had received those cheers and that applause, I had been a rock and roll star in waiting.

Sure, my glittering career had largely been playing gigs in pubs and busking, but confidence as a musician is in your heart. You look at the true legends, the Beatles, Joe Cocker and the king, Elvis Pressley, and they just have 'it.' It wouldn't matter if you were watching the Beatles in the Cavern Club in Liverpool playing to a hundred people or Dodger Stadium in front of eighty thousand. You would definitely know you were watching something special. Why? Because they knew they were special too. They carried themselves in a way that was exceptional. The Calzaghe boys had that confidence. Did we have that talent? Not a chance. But we had charisma, I think people who watch us play for fun now would say that we still have that and we believed we were brilliant and audiences responded to that.

Uccio and I formed a band called Burgundy with some local guys and we played some good gigs. By this time I guess Joe was about seven and boxing wasn't his big thing yet, he still loved his football and dreamt of being a professional. I was the main singer in Burgundy and Uccio played guitar and also sang. Burgundy was really just an opportunity to make some money and Uccio and I figured as we were always writing songs we should perform and get paid. We joined up with a guy called Steve Love who I taught to play bass and another guy who we called Tubbs. That was the band. We got a good name in the local area and after a while we got involved with an agent from Newport who gave us what I would describe as a semi-contract and he booked us on a tour of Scotland with twelve gigs over two weeks. I agreed to go without a second thought about Jackie and the kids.

I thought nothing of it. I didn't realise at the time this was all taking a toll on my marriage. I was just being myself and letting people down like I always seemed to. We bought a van off a dodgy fella for a pittance and the four of us went to Scotland with a new guitarist named Nigel Brown and our mate Dai Evans as a roadie.

We lasted about two hundred miles and the tour started to blow a fuse. The bloody van had a broken piston. None of us had a bean to spend on parts so we were in trouble and drove all the way up to Scotland losing gear capacity as we went. Four gears, down to three, eventually we crawled along the motorway doing about twenty-eight miles an hour in second gear. It was a nightmare and it took us about fifteen hours to get to Falkirk which was our base. There were lots of bands all based in this same hostel for the tour and one of them was called Vanity Fair. We'd heard of them so that only reaffirmed our view that we were the dog's bollocks. We thought we were stars and we turned up for our first gig in matching white suits from a charity shop that made us look like a very cheesy cabaret act.

Our first gig was in a place called the El Paso club in an area of Glasgow noted for its gangs. It was as rough as arseholes. We finished our set about 11pm and were having a pint when around a dozen coppers smashed their way into the club and beat the shit out of some rowdy punters. We were astonished, but the proprietor assured us that was a quiet night for the El Paso club.

I couldn't understand a word of the Scottish accent and when people asked me where I was from, at first I answered England. After I saw the looks I got and following that first night police brawl, I quickly realised Italy was a much safer answer in Scotland than England.

We ploughed on receiving pretty indifferent, middle of the road reactions from our audience. Our luck turned a bit at a gig all the way up in Wick. The alternator packed in on the way up and the van finally broke down, but fortunately for us we stopped about a hundred yards away from a forestry outpost with a couple of machines there. We stole about four or five parts from these machines and Dai patched the van up and we were on our way again. I should say sorry to the people we stole from. We were absolute chancers and it still took us nearly nine hours to get there, but at least we had a van in semi-working order for a few days.

On the last night of the tour we were in Inverness and by the time we arrived, late and covered in oil after spending most of the day under that bastard van, we didn't get to assess the place at all and during our first few numbers there was nothing but silence. It soon got nastier. We were playing stuff like Simon and Garfunkel, but there wasn't so much as a clap and that turned to boos, jeers, abuse and a few things thrown. They were turning on us big time. We had a little interval and wondered what the fuck was going on. I went for a shit and some Scottish guy started banging on the door of the bog telling us to play some fucking rock music. The penny dropped. We were like Westlife at a Motorhead gig.

"We are going to have to rock this place or they will lynch us," I told the boys and Nigel Brown, who was a rock freak anyway, told us to roll up our sleeves, push the amp up and put the guitars into overdrive. We went back on and I was throwing my arms around like Pete Townshend and we just jammed. We played loud and they loved it, we totally won them around. It would have been a fitting way to cap our little tour, but of course what came next was a long drive back in the poxy van.

It packed up around Newcastle for the final time and we'd practically rolled there. It was never getting back to Wales. We had to hire a car to tow the van back home. But when you factor in a hire car, our boozing and everything else we ended up coming back slightly out of pocket on the tour. I pissed off for two weeks and lost my family money. Was it any wonder Jackie was getting so despondent about me? She was slogging her guts out at home and I acted like I didn't give a fuck about anything. I should have seen the signs that she resented all this stuff I was getting up to, especially as I also had a day job that I was neglecting and jeopardising.

Right after we got back from Scotland I met a guy named Paul Williams who lived on our housing estate. Paul was a quiet guy and we just bumped into each other when Joe was starting to become more and more interested in boxing. The timing was perfect. I was keen on Joe boxing because he started having real problems with bullies at school. This wasn't like it was for me, he wasn't different to the other kids and he didn't have a little army of Italian bastards who could watch his back. It worried us. Joe was getting more and more down and the boxing had been something he was desperate to do for a little while. I had got him some rolled up carpet that he used as a punchbag and little Joe was obsessed. He must have seen Rocky about a hundred times. He told me he wanted to be just like Sugar Ray 'Lemon'.

Paul told me he ran a boxing gym on Mondays, Wednesdays and Fridays and I was welcome to take Joe along. So Joe and I ran down there on a Monday and straight away I found it amazing.

Newbridge Amateur Boxing Club was really only a little blue shack but it felt special to me from the moment I set foot in the place. There was something I couldn't quite put my finger on but I felt very comfortable watching the guys doing pad work, skipping, hammering the heavy bag and working their socks off. Joe was only nine and looked tiny in his little tracksuit and I could tell it was quite intimidating for him; he was a little kid in quite an adult environment.

The gym was right by the Welfare Ground where Newbridge RFC still plays to this day. It was a little dump but became my home from home until the council demolished it many years later. I began hanging around the gym more and more. Meanwhile, Burgundy were getting booked five or six nights a week in south Wales and we even went into a studio in Treorchy owned by a friend of mine named Gwynford. He had a little four track studio and we recorded three or four songs there and sent them off to *Melody Maker* magazine which had a competition run by a group called the Barron Knights, who had gigged with the Beatles and

Rolling Stones in the sixties. Funnily enough I would lose touch with Gwynford and didn't see him again for twenty-five years. I bumped into him in a record shop in Pontypool a couple of years ago and raced over to him to say hello. He remembered me but asked why I was wearing a Team Calzaghe jumper. He had no idea what my surname was or who my son was from back in the day, it was all a mystery to him.

So we sent off this recording and to our utter astonishment the magazine got in touch. They were very businesslike and basically told us that the Barron Knights didn't love the band but they really loved our songs, particularly one Uccio and I wrote called "Natasha". Pete Langford from the Knights rang personally and asked us to meet him and we went to Leyton Buzzard near Milton Keynes and they treated us fantastically. They said they really liked what Uccio and I were doing and they would be interested in recording with us and maybe using our songs too. It was dreamland but they didn't rate Burgundy, they only wanted the Calzaghes. This is the point in a Hollywood film you'd have a heart-to-heart with the band, break up but then get back together and make it to the top anyway, but we split there and then, called it a day and there were absolutely no hard feelings.

Fortunately around this time my brother Sergio arrived in Wales after his national service and the three of us fronted a new band named Foreign Legion with some musicians recommended to us by Pete Langford. Sergio wanted to get to know his big brothers better and set about getting a qualification as a chef. But his great voice and guitar playing was a big asset to us and it was an exciting time. We picked the name Foreign Legion because it was us, the three Italian brothers and I think we only ever had one British guy in our years together. We were a seven-piece group of overseas musicians. We had a Ukrainian keyboard player, a Spanish bass guitarist and then a Polish guitarist, but always an English drummer.

In the meantime Uccio and I were commuting to Milton Keynes where the Barron Knights were based, hitchhiking almost on a daily basis and not working a day job as there simply wasn't the time. My family were back to living hand-to-mouth and Jackie resented it, but didn't want to tell me I couldn't follow my dream, especially as we seemed to be moving in the right direction.

We were working in a studio owned by a nice man named Nigel Pegrum who was in Steeleye Span and in the Small Faces at one stage. He's now a big producer in Australia. The Barron Knights were putting a fair amount of time and money into us, they liked us and the more I heard them talk about "Natasha" potentially being a number one song, the less I thought about home and what my actions meant for my family. When Joe wasn't training or in school he would tag along with me anyway, so at least I wasn't neglecting him. He loved it and trust me when I tell you, the pair of us could write a book on hitchhiking.

That was the way things were for the best part of about three years until the Barron Knights asked Uccio and I to move up to Milton Keynes. The commute was a killer and Uccio didn't fancy it anymore. He was between marriages at the time so he moved to Milton Keynes, renting a house and waiting on a council home to buy up there. He put both of our names down for a council house but I really didn't like my chances of convincing Jackie. I knew she'd hate the idea of leaving Wales. It took me two months, but eventually she relented and said she would do it for me and we'd have a new life and a new house in Milton Keynes.

We got the nod for houses on a new estate and Uccio and I went up on a coach, splashing out on transport because it was a special occasion as we went to collect the keys of our new homes. Jackie barely said a word as I left our family home in Wales but we got to the office as planned and Uccio picked up his keys and then an official came and tapped me on the shoulder and asked for a quiet word. He had a letter from one Jackie Calzaghe stating that under no circumstances was he to give the Calzaghe family a council house because only one Calzaghe would be moving to Milton Keynes... me. She was refusing to give up her current residence and there was nothing that the office could do, I was no longer eligible for a council home.

I was absolutely fuming, shaking with rage. The way I saw it Jackie had just crushed my dreams by being selfish and going back on her word. I returned to Wales absolutely gutted and stormed back to the house. How could she do it to me? We had the row to end all rows and quite a few home truths came out.

Jackie told me that music was always my dream, not hers or the family's and I was a selfish prick because I was letting down my kids. I should have been putting food on the table and shoes on their feet, not worrying whether Pete Langford and the boys liked my chords or lyrics. So not only did I not move to Milton Keynes but I also lost Uccio and Sergio who did go down there. Uccio really relished the fresh start. It was exactly the right thing for him but what could I do? I wasn't about to walk out on my family.

Once again I was hitching to Milton Keynes three or four times a week and hardly ever seeing the kids. I would hitch from Newbridge to Newport, get on to the M4, get dropped off at the services at Swindon if I could and then hook a lift towards Milton Keynes. I was brilliant at it. Arguably I've never been better at anything than I was at hitchhiking. I was rarely bringing money home with me though and Jackie was getting more than upset, she'd go days on end not talking to me but I figured it would all be worth it when we made it big.

The Barron Knights were finding us a good amount of gigs and we'd written over thirty different songs and had plenty of material. We played a couple of shows at the Apollo Victoria and supported some big names at the time, bands like Steeleye Span, Bucks Fizz, Q Tips and even once that Welsh dame herself, Shirley Bassey. It was no big deal to us because we felt we were on the cusp and believed we would be huge ourselves. We never got star struck. We'd started hanging out with Paul Young who at the time was in Q Tips and I had millions of stories and a pocket full of dreams. But Jackie just wasn't interested as she wanted a husband not a bloke who popped back from time to time with tales of gigs and stories from the road, smelling of beer and looking like he never slept.

One day I came back and Jackie said when the kids had gone to bed she wanted to talk to me. She'd barely said two words to me for days so I figured it was good news. What did I say about being a dreamer? The conversation floored me. Jackie very calmly told me that marriage doesn't last forever if you don't look after it and cherish it. "I know you won't like this Enzo, but I have to tell you this. I don't love you anymore and I don't want to be married to you. I want a divorce." That was the moment the dagger pierced my heart. Where I was from, marriage was forever. You got married and you were together until one of you dropped dead. Divorce wasn't in my dictionary.

Of course I wouldn't accept it, not for a minute. I thought this was just anger talking and I could talk her round. Even though this was years in the making, in my mind it was just some stupid nonsense that would pass. I soon realised it wasn't. She was dead serious about wanting a divorce. I got down on my knees, I begged her to give me another chance, I pleaded and I poured my heart out and cried a lot. But I never offered to stop chasing the dream with my music. I couldn't see the bigger picture at the time.

What followed was the most miserable time of my life. Jackie wanted nothing to do with me. To keep things normal for the kids, I could come and go from the house, but I felt empty inside, starved of the attention and affection from Jackie that I had come to rely on so heavily. I cracked on with my music and essentially moved out of our home and crashed with Uccio and Sergio in Milton Keynes during the week. I would ring a payphone down the road from our house at an arranged time to speak to the girls Sonia and Mel, and Joe would often come and visit for a couple of days and hang out with his uncles. Joe was becoming a good amateur boxer with Paul Williams as his trainer. I was still all about the music.

Foreign Legion signed a publishing deal so at least I was making a penny or two but we still didn't have a recording contract even though there was more and more buzz about the band. I was trying to patch up my marriage but I couldn't chase two dreams and we had a massive gig coming up, a showcase the Barron Knights had put on at the Craufurd Arms in Milton Keynes and there were a lot of record label guys there. We looked the business, played a great set and Pete Langford came bounding over to us afterwards.

"They loved you," he told us. "They thought you were great, everyone thought you were great. EMI are interested in you and we've already had an offer for you guys to go to America and do a tour."

America? Fuck me, this was really happening. All that dedication, all those hours commuting to Milton Keynes and suddenly we had an offer to go to America and looked like we were going to get a recording deal afterwards. I was going to be the singer in a professional band. We had a hell of a celebration and the next day I got on a bus and went back to Wales to tell Jackie the news, to tell the kids the news. Dad was off to America on tour. I started thinking about the adventure, the promise of the road, the opportunities that were ahead of us and it took me back to life on the road in Europe, living day-to-day without a care in the world.

And then I had what I can only describe as a panic attack. I could barely breathe or focus. My soul spoke to me, almost voices in my head. Is that really what I wanted? The hangovers? Being stoned out of my mind? Hoovering up drugs? It sent a shiver down my spine, if I am honest when I thought about the bright lights of America. It was one of those 'moment of clarity' incidents they talk about. I got off that bus and I had a different mindset. After a decade of pissing away an amazing life I had woken up. If I went to America I would almost definitely be powerless to avoid divorce. The kids wouldn't see me for six months and Joe had some big amateur fights coming up. I also had a separate court case approaching for driving off without paying at a petrol station and I was a mess, my hair was falling out in clumps because of the stress and now I had this opportunity to get away from it all. But I couldn't feel it in my heart like Uccio and Sergio could.

When I got back home I walked to the payphone down the street from our house and called Uccio. The gist of the conversation was pretty simple. I wasn't going to America, I wasn't signing a recording deal and I wouldn't be coming back to Milton Keynes to do any recording. I was done, finished. I was quitting the band and quitting any attempt at a career as a professional musician. I told him I was going to try to be a boxing trainer and try to save my marriage.

I felt like a complete bastard. Of course I did. The Barron Knights and their friends had been so generous and kind to us and Sergio and Uccio were massively excited, I was letting them all down and Uccio told me in no uncertain terms he thought I was the biggest arsehole on the planet. But I didn't want to be divorced and never see my kids. I didn't want to end up visiting them once a month and watch Jackie move on with her life. The divorce case finally woke me up and I fought all the way. Every meeting with a solicitor, a mediator, every meddling bastard who sent me letters from a court house or a solicitor's office, I just ignored them. I told Jackie I had quit the band and I moved back into the house even though nothing had changed in her eyes. We lived together even though we weren't really together. She was willing to do that for the sake of the children.

I hid behind the catholic religion as a means to fight the divorce and even though I thought I was being romantic in fighting Jackie every step of the way, I realise now that really I was just hurting her more and more.

Strangely I didn't hit the booze even though I was utterly depressed. I started getting very fit, throwing myself into running and exercise and was spending more and more time focusing on Joe's blossoming amateur career. If I needed money I would hitch to London first thing, do a day of busking and then hitch back with a bit of change in my pocket and put some food on the table for once. Jackie still wouldn't talk to me much, but I hung on in there.

I got myself a car for nothing from a man who knew a man so I could get to places easier to play a bit of music for a shilling or two and I made Joe my unofficial roadie. At that point we were spending almost 24/7 together as he was finishing up with school and doing his exams. I am ashamed to say my marriage hiatus and life on the road trying to be a musician lasted years, not months. And even though Jackie and I were enduring a very frosty relationship, we had never fully parted in all that time.

But then Joe suffered a massive blow in his career prospects when he was fifteen, he hurt his wrist sparring in Cwmbran and I had to take him to the Royal Gwent Hospital. The doctor X-rayed it and said Joe had extensive tissue damage that would leave his wrist in chronic pain. And then almost casually told him: "I don't think you'll be able to box again." Joe didn't even get upset. It was like he'd been in a traffic accident. He was in absolute shock and I found it tough to find the words to help him through that dark time. But I'll get to that.

There was very little I could say or do to make him feel better and it was fortunate that around that time my dad got in touch and said the family were hiring a restaurant for the summer in Sardinia and would we like to go over? I jumped at the chance as did Joe, but Jackie didn't want to come and the girls decided to stay with her. It wasn't choosing sides it was simply them being there for their mother.

The lease of the restaurant was six months and with Uccio and Sergio back to square one because I'd walked out on the band, they decided to come along too so all the Calzaghe boys, minus my brother Antonio who had a family and his own life, headed home to Sardinia. We scraped together five grand or so and spent the summer all working together, cooking the food, waiting tables, having some laughs and it was fantastic. Joe was just a gopher really but far too lazy to contribute. He'd stopped boxing without wanting to and he wasn't interested in washing pots, he enjoyed making friends, laying on the beach and catching the eye of some of the girls around the resort. He was a teenage kid who had hated school for the most part and he was as happy as a pig in the proverbial. We ate like absolute kings, Dad was always cooking up something amazing and I could tell my parents were thrilled having us all around.

My daughter Mel came and visited for a month and I seem to remember she was there one night when we had a massive BBQ with loads of the family in the restaurant drinking and having a great time. It was a stress-free life, a simple life, a happy life and I started to realise I probably shouldn't go back for everyone's sake.

We didn't even know if Joe would box again and I had made Jackie miserable. Who the fuck did I think I was? I had been a shit husband and now I wouldn't even grant her a divorce and make her a happy woman. I had to do the right thing and started mentally preparing to sign the divorce papers and move back to Sardinia. I would sit on the beach, gaze at the water and feel full of regret from wrecking my family life. Maybe I could open a restaurant with Uccio, something like that. Maybe I'd even give music another go. If only I hadn't fucked everything up.

A couple of days later, and as if by magic, Jackie called me. She's never been one for beating around the bush and she told me she wanted me to come home. In her words, she wanted to give it another go. Being away for so long had made her realise she still loved me and didn't want to be apart from me and she appreciated that I didn't go to America. She just wanted me to treat her right, the very least she deserved, but she no longer wanted a divorce, she said she'd rip up the papers. I was shell-shocked. Finally I had decided to let her go and that I was being cruel to her by not granting her a divorce, and now this. I was so panicked I virtually put the phone down on her!

I talked with Dad and Uccio the next day and asked for their advice and they both told me to do what was in my heart. They were both thrilled because they knew I loved Jackie and that I had been a lousy husband and she was right to have been so upset for so long. I guess also for Uccio, if I got my life with Jackie back on track, it meant he hadn't been denied that American tour and recording deal for nothing.

I called Jackie, told her I was coming home as soon as we finished the lease and that I would never let her down again. It was amazing. As soon as I stopped fighting her, the tide turned and her view on me softened. But I was too stupid and ignorant to see I should have taken that approach all along. I treated it like one big game where I couldn't quit or give up and it wasn't fair.

I returned home with exactly the same money as I went out with, because I drank my share of the profits as did my brothers. We laid out £5000 between us, got that back and never saw a penny more. I would be lying if I said that Jackie and I haven't really had a cross word since those times, but not massively. Since nearly splitting up, we've barely been apart for more than a night or two, apart from when Joe boxed in America.

I returned home to my one true love and things were really starting to get moving for me. It was about to become all about the boxing. But first we need to rewind a little.

Chapter Seven:

I Think Your Boy Might Be Special

If I could only use one word to describe my son Joe and his ability to box, it would be easy... magic. Watching Joe box has always been magical, his talent is unique, so special and so complete. To this day I don't really see what weaknesses he had. He stopped fewer fighters in his thirties than he did in the early days, got accused of 'slapping' opponents, but he did that over a thousand times in a fight. He didn't lose his power as much as have to adjust because his hands were so brittle. Joe battled injury throughout his whole career, including the amateurs.

I had done some boxing training as a kid but there was nothing to suggest from my genes that we would have a fighting prodigy on our hands. But from childhood Joe was fascinated by the sport and around eight or nine years old he began begging me to let him box. He loved big fights, loved *Rocky* and began shadow-boxing incessantly to the point where whenever we visited Sardinia his grandmother Victoria would tell him off for doing it.

I could only ignore this passion for so long and got him some little gloves and would roll up carpet for him to use as a punchbag when he was still just a little boy in stature. That made way for a Sugar Ray Leonard speedball. I would wrap teatowels around my hands in the house and use them as pads and would spar with Joe. For about twenty years I was Joe's main sparring partner and he would tell you the same thing. It sounds ridiculous but it just worked: I would try to make difficult angles for Joe to aim at and would just paw at him sometimes to keep him on his toes. That worked for us for a quarter of a century.

I suppose there is one observation I could make about Joe as a kid that maybe has some resonance when I look at Britain today. Because of the way Joe was raised as a child, he always had exceptional, and I do mean exceptional, capacity in his lungs and

Mum,
Antonio,
Uccio, Enzo
(left to right).
This is one of
my most
treasured
pictures.

Family shot. Mum, Victoria,
Antonio, Dad Guiseppe, me,
Uccio and Alba. Taken in 1959
and my most prized possession.
You can see how smart Mum and
Dad dressed us kids even though
we were poor.

Mum and Dad. I cherish the photographs I have of the two of them.

Uccio and I with our first band Boba. The glory days!

Enzo bottom right – same as in the Joe footie team pic, I find that amazing.

Pentwynmawr U10s or 12s, about 1979-80. Joe Bottom right.

Joe in Wales ABA vest.

Amateur Joe. I regret missing so many of his fights at this point in his career.

With Alba, my sister at her home in Sardinia. The only Calzaghe sibling born in the UK, Alba is also the only one who now lives in Italy.

Dad comes to visit his young great-grandsons. It's always great to have Dad over, but boy, do we all miss my mother.

Game changer: Joe and Joe. Everything in boxing felt more serious and important when Joe became a father. It was no longer just about him pursuing his dreams.

Joe with baby Connor.

My girls: Jackie, Sonia and Mel.

Jackie and I become grandparents for the first time with baby Joe.

Sonia's marriage to David. Watching your kids get married is one of life's great honours.

Me with Vincenzo, my uncle and the man responsible for my musical obsession.

Dad, Uccio, me and Sergio. This is the last picture of Uccio before his accident that changed our lives. We always tried to go away together to Sardinia.

Leisure time in the 1980s. I think we can conclude I'm enjoying the game more than Joe is.

With my father at his house in Sardinia. You can see that it is covered in memorabilia from Joe's career.

Foreign Legion. As you can see, posing and acting like stars came very naturally to us!

Uccio, Sergio and I pay tribute to John Lennon at his memorial in Central Park. As I've explained, the Beatles are my ultimate heroes.

The family hit the streets of New York for Joe's fight with Roy Jones. In the middle is the lesser spotted Antonio Calzaghe!

With Dad in 2010. I think we both look pretty good for our respective ages. Must be the olive oil...

Chip off the old block. Joe Junior and Connor.

Doing a public workout with Joe in Cardiff. He HATED this sort of thing.

The boys: Paul Samuels, Joe, Byron Pryce, Bradley Price, A.N. Other, Gavin Rees (all back row). I truly love those boys and they've gone on to do me proud.

The boys. Left to right: Bradley Pryce, Gavin Rees, Kerry Hope and Nathan Clevery in Sardinia. I've taken young boxers there to fight for many, many years. This was probably my best crop of talent though.

Joe on the scales at Madison Square Garden. It was never a joyous moment for Joe when he weighed-in, but doing it at light heavyweight in a beautiful venue like that certainly helped.

Moments after my flashpoint with Bernard Hopkins at a press conference in Las Vegas he flashes a grin and defuses a tense situation. I was ready to explode.

Joe after beating Bernard Hopkins. Taken by Joe's son Connor.
I think the emotion is pretty clear.

Frank Warren, Enzo, Joe, Dean Powell, Brian Coleman and Frank Black after Joe
beat Bernard Hopkins. We were a great team.

his muscles to do physical exercise. We ran everywhere, usually together, or he was out with his mates playing football or chasing rabbits. He had a working-class upbringing in the 1980s before computer games and *Big Brother* on the television ruled the world and turned everyone fat and lazy.

Joe was dedicated from day one when he first went to the boxing gym and with his God-given talent and the advantage of being so physically capable, he could push himself harder and further than other boxers. It was like he was winning before he even set foot in a gym.

When we finally went to the gym, when Joe had his first taste of it, people were blown away. After his very first session, Paul Williams asked me where he had boxed before and told me he thought Joe seemed like a special talent. His assistant at the time described Joe as an 'open class' kid, meaning he seemed like he already boxed at a regional or national level. To that point, he'd only ever boxed a speedball and my sweaty palms wrapped in tea towels. At nine years old, people looked at Joe and thought he could turn pro or box at the Olympics.

I can't begin to explain what a dump the gym was in most people's eyes. It leaked constantly, was freezing cold most of the year, boiling hot in the summer months and you could barely swing a cat in there. When it was demolished few people were upset, including Joe. Me? I loved the place. I was impressed from the first second I stepped in there and it might have been a dump, but it became my dump and I have wonderful memories of my years there.

Paul Williams opened three days a week and generally Joe and I would be there every time he opened up and sometimes quite a long time before it. Within a couple of weeks Paul started showing me the basics and I became an assistant, helping not only Joe but other kids and watching how the adults went about their training. It was all new to me and I was genuinely fascinated. Anytime I wasn't in Milton Keynes I tried to be in a boxing gym, learning a new craft.

It's not quite on the scale of missing his birth, but missing Joe make his amateur debut is a regret of mine. I was gigging and he understood but I still didn't like it especially as he lost and probably needed his dad with him. Many years later I would be in the corner when Joe's son Joe Jr won his first amateur bout and that is a nice feeling, it cleanses the soul a little bit. Joe lost to a kid called Chris Stock from Newport by majority decision and by all accounts, he went to the corner of the ring and cried his eyes out until Paul finished shouting at the judges and went and got him. That was Paul all over. He had a very nice nature about him. Joe never had a great affinity for Paul or his training methods but I can't really do anything but praise him. I was never paid a penny but Paul was the greatest boss I ever had. He taught me the ropes and gave me an opportunity.

Paul never tried to curb me or my instincts and never got territorial about things. He knew I was working with Joe far more than three times a week but never discouraged it. I would give my view to the kids in the gym and he accepted that too. I could never understand why kids were taught to throw two-punches on the bag. I would get Joe to throw four, five, six punches at a time and to me that made perfect sense. Punches in bunches were surely going to do more damage? I always looked at boxing like music, the combinations were the verses and two punches were for the chorus, bang, bang... fight over.

Joe lost four of five times in that first year or two as an amateur but by his calculations he only lost eleven times in around one hundred and ten amateur fights, which sounds about right. He was merely finding his feet and it was difficult because inside the ring Joe was like a different person. He had a tough time of it at school and was naturally a quiet, shy, introverted kind of character, which made me think he must've belonged to the milk man because neither of his parents were shrinking violets. The bullying at school left him suspicious and cautious and he only really came out of his shell when boxing. And I guess he overcompensated because he was constantly being warned by referees in the early days for showboating.

The more I think about it, the more I discuss it with Joe, the more I begin to realise the impact bullying had on his life. I've been almost dismissive of bullying in regards to myself, in focusing on how I didn't really get affected by the racist stuff directed towards me and my brothers, but with time I've come to realise it was a vital ingredient in Joe's success, the morons who picked on him at school fuelled the fire, made him even more determined to prove to everyone that he was going all the way to the top.

It's that classic cliché of the teacher asking you what you want to be when you grow up and laughing at you when you say world champion boxer or England footballer or whatever. But that was Joe. He was certain by the time he was a teenager he wanted to box professionally and when other kids were hanging around outside shops tasting a cigarette for the first time or throwing rocks at things, Joe was running around, with his old man shouting at him that he had to increase his lung capacity. He was incredibly shy too and it all combined to make him an easy target. He had his mates, but he was dealing with stuff his mother and I had no idea about.

It all came to a head one day when a large group of boys on bikes were gathered outside our house on a Saturday morning. I am sketchy on the date, but I'd suggest Joe was around fourteen years old and very much boxing-obsessed. I saw them outside and told Joe his mates were here and they must want him to go out and play. He was completely ashen-faced and mumbled something about not wanting to go out. His mother was encouraging him to go and then the penny dropped for me. I think Jackie and I had both feared for some months that something wasn't right with Joe at school. Finally I could work out what the problem was – he was being bullied. I lost my rag in a big way and I'd like you to show me a father who would've been any different. "Are these kids your friends Joe or are they your enemies?" I asked him. He wouldn't even look at me and his lips trembled and that said everything.

I marched out of the house and went straight up to the kid who was clearly the ringleader and did the same thing I had always been taught to do when in such a situation. I told this kid that we should settle this between ourselves. And then I looked at the others and said, "And after him we can all settle this one-on-one." Unsurprisingly, like the little punks that they were, all those kids scarpered. Joe finally admitted to Jackie and me that he had been experiencing bullying for months and it was very upsetting to hear. I was desperate that Joe change schools but he decided to stick it out and I think after that the situation improved, but he still wasn't happy and kept his head down. His focus became more and more on boxing to the point where, in all honesty, he had no plans to do anything else.

One of the early fights I missed that really set Joe on his way was when he won a Gwent title. I was thrilled. It was his very first success, his first accolade and I was insanely proud. My boy had a little medal, a huge smile and he was going to box for a Welsh title which he also won. This was still a couple of years before my marriage meltdown got its redemption and I was in Milton Keynes a lot of the time, but Uccio, Sergio and I made it to the Assembly Rooms in Derby to watch Joe in the final of the ABAs.

The Assembly Rooms had seen many greats get their start over the years and in 1985 Joe Calzaghe arrived and won there for the first time. Joe boxed at 36kg for the Junior A schoolboy championship and he was superb, his first massive fight resulting in his first champion performance. He fought a boy called Ian Raby and overwhelmed him from the first bell, leaving him in a heap after thirty-five seconds. All the Welsh boys thought it was very difficult to beat the English and Joe did it with consummate ease. He was making a real name for himself.

He was headed on the right path and totally obsessed, training twice a day, turning our house into one large gym to train in and working religiously on his fitness. Even if I was in Milton Keynes and only back for a couple of hours in Wales, Joe and I would still go running absolutely every day. Come rain, shine or snow, we'd do four miles a day at least, a tradition that carried on until he retired. I am known by many nicknames but I have always been known around Newbridge as 'the running man.'

Joe was becoming more assured in the ring and wouldn't let anyone take liberties with him, he had a full-on war in an exhibition match with Robbie Regan and the fight ended up getting thrown out and both of them were told off. But Joe was starting to stand up for himself.

I was finding my feet as a trainer too. I had no formal training, but I was accepted by Paul and his pals and they let me do my thing in the gym. Joe has been dismissive of Paul in the past but that simply isn't fair because he wouldn't have had a boxing career without Paul Williams. I truly believe that is a fact.

A problem I had and still do is I never knew about nutrition. I grew up in an environment where rich food and plenty of it was how it should be and I never meddled with my fighters' diets. Looking back now, I can appreciate that as a teenager Joe had some terrible eating habits. He would have to starve himself to shed weight and would then binge on junk food, burgers and cakes, the full works. It was a battle for Joe to make weight and always has been. 36kg, 40kg, 51kg, 57kg, wherever Joe was in his life, all the way to being the best super middleweight to lace up a glove, he struggled to make weight and relied on crash dieting.

But his fitness compensated. I became a tough taskmaster on him during his teenage years because he was developing that rebellious, anti-boss streak that I'd had and wanted to do other things than box. Joe wanted to listen to music or hang about like other kids are able to do. But I'd make him run in the snow or do another ten minutes of skipping even when he would say that he didn't want to. "You'll never be a champion unless you..." was one of my catchphrases.

Every year the competitions would roll around and Joe and I were always together, training or on the road, thumbing it to and from Milton Keynes. When I left Foreign Legion and Jackie took me back, I even got a job to try and impress her, canvassing door-to-door for Trafalgar Home Improvements and I was quite good at it. A little charm went a long way and I set up appointments for the salesmen. I was encouraged to become a salesman myself, but I didn't like the idea of the extra hours. The job I did finished at 3pm and that gave me time to go to the gym with Joe in the afternoon.

We kept going back to the Assembly Rooms year-on-year and Joe kept winning and it was nice for him to enjoy all this success because despite being a great little player, he seemed to get constantly overlooked for the local football teams because, I think, managers thought he was too flash. If you've seen him play in those games for UNICEF at Old Trafford, you'll know he's a decent player. We both love football and pretty much every other sport that comes on the television. Joe has been my best mate since he was a little boy and our shared interests and love for each other meant we were always together.

After the trip to Sardinia and being reunited with Jackie, I was able to invest more time in being a proper father to Sonia and Mel, which was great. They suffered far more than Joe when I was back and forwards to Milton Keynes and yet they never stopped adoring their dad. It was wonderful to be playing a proper role in watching them grow up in to the wonderful women and mothers they are today.

I would take Joe training anywhere I could at this point. He was working with me and Paul Williams, and I also took him to St Josephs in Newport to work with a former champion fighter called Steve Sims. If we were all in the house watching TV together, what was to stop Joe doing 50 press-ups? I would sometimes dump Joe at a gym, hitch to Milton Keynes and be back and pick him up about ten hours later when he was so exhausted he could barely stand. He said this was his dream and I pushed him as hard as I could towards it.

People couldn't understand why I was constantly out and about gigging or in the gym with Joe and always so active, but I didn't understand how they lived their lives either. Who wants be a couch potato watching *Crossroads* or *Coronation Street*? I couldn't fathom it. I didn't care what Ena Sharples was getting up to or Benny bloody Hawkins for that matter. I was 24/7 music and boxing and then when I quit the band, boxing became my life and I was dedicated around the clock to improving my skills as a trainer and Joe's as a fighter.

In 1989 Joe came back from the Gaelic Games as a winner and with fights in Wales basically having run-out for the time being, it was hard to keep his feet on the ground. I got him sparring against some older boys which turned out badly as one day he went to Cwmbran and hurt his wrist. As I've explained, the doctor essentially wrote off his whole career and it was a tough time for both of us. Joe's dreams were in the pan with my marriage and that was when we went for that trip to Sardinia.

Once we returned I was especially focused on him. Marriage was good, life was good and I wanted Joe to be happy. He came back a little earlier than I did and it was clear we had more to worry about than just his wrist. His attitude stank all of a sudden on my return.

Considering the good news about Jackie and me, I expected things to be easy, but they weren't. Joe was becoming a typical teenager and had discovered drink and would often come home drunk off his skull and end up puking in the toilet. I was losing the battle in getting him to even focus on boxing, let alone start to do it again properly. Joe was becoming a disgrace, a total state and what was worst of all, he reminded me exactly of myself when I was that age. I even had to pick him up from the police station one night after he'd puked all over the side of a road. I let him have it. Thankfully, the scare of the police, the acceptance that he was going nowhere, my shouting, whatever it was, meant the penny dropped and he upped his game.

He got back into training and we were both fixed on one thing that would make all the sacrifices worthwhile – the Barcelona Olympics in 1992. We were very tentative with his wrist but things seemed alright. That meant Joe was going to be a prime candidate for a medal and although Paul mentioned the idea of turning pro once or twice, Joe and I wouldn't consider it until after the Olympics. Although he wasn't especially muscular, he was tall, lean and about eleven stone walking around, so we made the decision he'd box as a welterweight at 10st 11lb. Joe lost in the final of the Welsh championships when he was seventeen in a close one to Michael Smyth who was an older and stronger kid but was nevertheless selected for the European junior youth championships in Prague, the trip famous for producing the last defeat of Joe's entire twenty-five year career. Joe had been disappointed to lose to Smyth but considering how soon it was after his long layoff, I was satisfied with his progress.

Joe was part of a three-man Welsh team and he travelled with the other fighters, Barry Kelly and Michael Griffiths and the Welsh trainers, which didn't include Paul or me. It was all expenses paid for Joe and they told us it would £1000 each if we wanted to go. "It's a bit steep Enzo," Paul told me. "About £999 more than I've got," I replied. But the mind started whirring and I really didn't want to miss it. I'd missed enough. So I convinced Paul that it'd be a great adventure if we hitchhiked our way there.

We visited the Czech Embassy in London and I had a right old giggle as the man at the embassy told me I didn't need any papers because I had an Italian ID card as Paul filled out form after form. He should've been the one laughing.

We thumbed our way across France towards Dresden and in a couple of days were on the train to Czechoslovakia. Guards came on to check our credentials and of course, it wasn't ok to have an Italian ID card, no passport and no visa. I was forcefully removed by soldiers armed with machine guns and I absolute shit myself. This wasn't a bit of aggro in a pub in Gwent. This was armed guards in the Eastern Bloc. I was taken to a holding cell at the main train station in Prague and several officers tried to interrogate me in Czech before realising I didn't speak a word. Paul was waiting at the station in the meantime and eventually, about two hours later, a guy in broken English established I was a boxing trainer and was here for the championships. Thank God, he was an amateur fighter himself. He stamped me for four days. Paul roared with laughter when we caught up.

We had nowhere to stay but had a few quid for a hotel as our travelling costs had been negligible. We checked out the first hotel we saw which was actually incredibly plush and enquired as to the cost of a twin room. The price was in Czech Koruna of course but it didn't take us long to work out they wanted about two quid per night. You had to laugh when the Welsh ABA officials charged a grand for the trip and our hotel was far nicer than where they were staying with the boys.

The hospitality in Prague was top notch and I always loved travelling for Joe's boxing, it felt a little bit like the old days when I moved around so freely only this time I had a purpose and wasn't in a perpetual drug haze. Paul and I enjoyed a couple of fantastic nights drinking with the locals at our hotel.

Joe beat a Hungarian kid first up but he couldn't get used to wearing the head-guard they used over there, he was too wary of the judges who were notorious and over the course of the tournament I think he psyched himself out a little bit. In fairness, four of the judges were ordered out of the tournament for their crazy decisions and Joe was robbed against a boy named Adrian Opreda in my opinion. Opreda just landed a tap every now and again and would hold Joe and twist his head-guard around because he knew it was annoying him. Despite winning the second and third round clearly, Joe lost the verdict and then wasn't sent to Peru for the world juniors as a result which aggravated me, but our problems with the top brass of Welsh boxing were only just beginning.

It wasn't the only delicate situation we had. Paul came out and asked Joe to turn pro and said he'd manage him. It was something Paul had been thinking about for a while and it stung him when Joe said no. But Joe never thought of Paul as his coach, it was always me and I don't think Joe ever properly believed Paul knew what was best. A short time later Paul came to see me, explained he wanted to retire and basically handed me the keys to the boxing gym and disappeared from our lives and neither Joe nor I have seen him since. He'd had enough of boxing, but I am sure he is proud of all Joe achieved and he deserves credit for it too. I am really glad to have this chance to explain my gratitude towards him.

But the reality is that I was now well out of my comfort zone. Small it might be, dank and smelly too, but running the gym in my eyes was a big responsibility and more than anyone had ever been willing to give me before. And at first I found it incredibly hard, people deserted me and I was all alone.

But in the short term, the Olympics were what it was all about and things were looking on course. Since losing to Smyth the year before Joe had grown physically and was prepared for the seniors and we entered the senior ABA at welterweight expecting to win it. Joe came up against a guy called Trevor French who was a Marine and tough as old boots. But Joe overwhelmed him, stopped him and in my eyes had cemented himself as the one to watch for Barcelona.

Joe began training regularly with the other hopefuls for the Olympics down in Crystal Palace and would regularly spar with Robin Reid, who he looked to be in competition with to go and other guys like Richie Woodhall. Both would have big fight with Joe as professionals. Joe hurt a knuckle against a kid called Andrew Gerrard and I phoned Ray Allen, the chairman of the Welsh ABA, and told him I needed to pull Joe out of an upcoming international with Norway at Newport. Ray loved Joe but seemed utterly determined he boxed. Maybe he knew something I didn't. He even told me Joe would win with one hand. But I wasn't having that, I pulled Joe out of the fight and little did I know what a big decision that was. The Welsh ABA had to nominate the boxers to go to Crystal Palace to be assessed for the Olympic team and they stated that only one boxer in each category would be put forward.

I remember it as if it were yesterday. It was Monday morning, about 8am, the phone rang and it was John Francis, a sports reporter on the local paper, the *South Wales Argus*.

"Enzo, I am sorry to bother you, but is it true that Joe hasn't been shortlisted for the Olympics?"

"What! No it's not true, John. You've got totally the wrong end of the stick, don't be so fucking stupid," I told him, and I believed it too. "Joe has just come back from Crystal Palace, there is no problem."

But I was worried for sure. Anyone from South Wales could tell you news and gossip round these parts spreads like wildfire and I trusted John Francis. If he'd heard that, something was up. There have been a few instances where I've heard about a fight or something first through the *Argus* boxing writer. I called Ray Allen and told him what John had told me and he confirmed it. "Joe's not on the list Enzo, I am sorry. He isn't going to the Olympics."

They had nominated a kid called Matthew Turner at light middleweight and that was that. They had decided Joe was too big for his boots after I pulled him out of the Norway fight and hadn't done enough for the Wales ABA. They saw him as a flashy fighter who was constantly complaining about injury. Ray more or less confirmed they were trying to teach Joe a lesson and this comment in Joe's autobiography, from Terry Smith, the secretary of the Welsh ABA at the time, confirms it.

"Joe was very rarely available for Wales when it came to international boxing. There was always some excuse or another. That was probably the root cause of it. In 1992 for the first time, boxers who wanted to compete in the Olympics had to qualify for the tournament proper. Under the old system where we could send

ten or eleven boxers and it was up to Great Britain to determine the team, Joe would certainly have gone. From 1992 you had to qualify to go to the Olympics and that is up to the Welsh ABA to pick the boxers to send. Because Joe may not have been supporting us at the time, somebody said, 'Well why should we send him?' It costs a lot of money and I don't remember much fuss at the time about Joe not going because he was just never available for Wales... Somebody has to pay for you to go to the ABA Championships and we were funding all that, but when it came to Joe boxing for us against other nations you'll find that he was very thin on the ground."

I was raging. Absolutely apoplectic, I wanted to physically hurt someone. A bunch of stiffs in a pub had sat around and decided to kill Joe's Olympic dream.

That was their attitude and I did all I could to try and change it. It was so short-sighted. To this day I don't understand how they let malice cloud their judgement. What was better for them? Matthew Turner failing to get through qualifying for Barcelona or Joe winning a gold medal and coming back the poster boy for Welsh sport? It was such a golden chance – pun intended – for the Welsh ABA to look great and they chucked it away to prove a point to an eighteen year old kid. I had some reassurance from Ray that he'd do what he could over the course of some frantic calls and I confronted Terry Smith in a pub, but I was largely just working at getting Joe another chance. I begged for a box-off, any time and any place, but they weren't having it. At the next meeting they rubber stamped the list and that was that.

Turner got smashed by Robin Reid in the qualifiers and Reid went on to win bronze in Barcelona even though he lost to a guy Joe would have devoured before breakfast. Joe was the British welterweight ABA champion, had won three ABA titles and countless other titles and Reid has nowhere near the same kind of CV. Watching it on television made me feel sick, I don't mind admitting that. I felt nothing but anger.

It got even more frustrating when Joe won a second ABA senior title at light middleweight soon after the Olympics, smashing up Dean Francis en route to beating Glenn Catley in the final. The coach for the British Olympic squad, Ian Irwin, watched and he told me he thought it was utterly crazy that Joe hadn't been put forward to be in his squad. That made me sad.

My father had been watching from ringside that night during a holiday visit to Wales and that at least made me smile. Joe's grandfather loves watching him box, he loves the sport and ever since Joe turned eighteen I have taken kids over to Sardinia every couple of years to compete against the local boys. It was very special when Joe first boxed in Sardinia, an emotional night for the Calzaghe family and one I remember with great fondness.

I've made no secret of how important the approval of my family was to me – still is to me – and the pride in my fathers' eyes watching Joe box was amazing. It meant the world to the family, Joe knew that and even as a teenager he was able to rise to the challenge and produce one of his greatest ever amateur performances. That spoke volumes to me. It's like with footballers being good 'big game' players. This was Joe's equivalent of playing against Man United and he stepped up big time. Is it any wonder I think he'd have won gold in Barcelona?

He was fighting no bum either. He went in against a kid called Paolo DiMasso, a bronze medal winner at the world juniors and a seven-time national champion. He came into the ring wearing sunglasses like a rock star and I remember telling Joe he would need them when he smashed the kid up!

Joe was outstanding, firing punches with an incredible regularity, throwing combinations left, right and centre. Bah-bah-bah, he'd throw a combination. Bah-bah-bah-bah, step to the side, more unanswered shots. It was poetry in motion and while DiMasso was big enough to take it without going down, he had his heart broken for three rounds and couldn't get out of there fast enough. That was essentially the end of Joe getting decent fights in Italy because word spread and no-one would touch him after that. He was perceived as being simply too good.

I remember my uncle Rino presented Joe with a big trophy and we had a brilliant celebration. It was a wonderful occasion. And it was equally beautiful going back in September 2011 with a group of kids, this time including Joe's son Joe Jr. He's still in his infancy as a boxer but he was a winner too and his dad was there to cheer him on, as was mine. You can't buy that kind of feeling.

It took me years to get over the Olympic disappointment and reliving it now just underlines to me how much resentment I still have about it. Joe was denied his dream. But, as is his way, he's turned the whole thing into a positive. Joe's belief is that his career, his amazing professional career, was largely built on a fear of losing and a fear of not being the best. We were always building him up, other than when he faced Chris Eubank, almost all of Joe's defining fights came in the final quarter of his days in the ring. Joe was the epitome of a hungry fighter – literally before fights when he was starving himself – but all the time, 24/7 in terms of his attitude and desire. It's his belief that if he'd won a medal at Barcelona and come back a superstar like Audley Harrison, Amir Khan or James DeGale, he might have lost that hunger and desire. He would have had a huge profile, an opportunity to make instant millions and reckons he might have got a big head and lost focus. Do I think that? Do I heck.

He didn't have it in him to cut corners or to not put the hard work in, to risk losing. I have no doubt the adult Joe would have cried in the ring if he'd lost just as he did as a young boy when he lost for the first time in the amateurs. He just didn't have losing as an option in his head. Maybe he'd have been retired sooner though. If everything had come quickly to Joe, he'd have had very little left to prove in his thirties. As it was, retirement at thirty-one like David Haye was never an option for him. The Olympic disappointment spurred him on and I am thankful for that. But I'll never believe it was right and I will never believe it was for the best.

Joe started to ask about turning professional after winning the ABAs again but we hung on for a year because I had seen in a book that no-one since the 1920s had won three senior ABA titles at different weight categories. Joe was ready to fight at middleweight and it seemed like an absolutely ideal move to make. In 1993 he beat Darren Dorrington in the senior ABA final with one hand as he had another broken knuckle in his right hand. There was just nothing left for him to prove as an amateur after that.

Joe was definitely ready for the big leagues, but I wasn't sure if I was. That might also have been one of the reasons we delayed turning pro for a year. I was finding my feet with training, but the rest? It was all a mystery to me. I knew absolutely nothing about professional boxing. What did I know about managers or promoters? Purses and prizes? I was in over my head.

I had been toiling a little bit, running the gym myself and I feared I was holding Joe back. I talked to Steve 'Sammy' Sims and a Cardiff trainer called Carl Winstone about training and managing Joe, but he didn't want to stop working with me even though he's always been fond of Sammy. We were in this together, at least for the time being, but I was losing heart a little bit with how hard everything was. I had soured on the sport because of the Olympic bullshit and had no idea about how professional boxing worked.

It wasn't just Joe relying on me either. By then I had some open class boys of my own too. Two lads in particular were absolute quality. Gavin Rees and Bradley Pryce were cracking fighters who I was certain could make it as professionals even though at the time they were just two little shrimps still at primary school. They were belters and if I could keep them focused and on the right track they were ready to go far. They did go far, but I didn't always keep them on the right track.

But was I going to be up to it all? I felt like I was sinking without a trace and worried I couldn't get them to where they wanted to be. Paul's gym seemed to have lots of support from the community, business partners and people who could and would provide sponsorship. They vanished with Paul. It was a hard time, a scary time really because I felt responsible for all those boxers.

But I should have had more faith. Within a few months Joe was boxing at the Cardiff Arms Park on the undercard of one of the biggest fights of the whole year and one of the top rugby players in the country had helped to transform things at the Newbridge Amateur Boxing Club.

We were on our way and it was a hell of a journey.

Chapter Eight:

Cracking the Boxing World

The two things that most resonate today when I think back on that tinpot shed that was the Newbridge Boxing Club are the smell and the climate. Clad in tin sheet and therefore achieving temperatures that magnified the weather outside, it was sweltering in the summer and beyond freezing in the winter. It had that smell to it which I now realise is similar in all gyms. The smell of sweat from some of the hardest working fighters I've ever known and the musty stench from the wet leather punch bags and nooks and crannies that never, ever saw a cleaning brush. The gym was so small it was something of a health hazard. Unless you were as small as Gavin Rees, you risked damaging your elbows on the metal walls every time you used the heavy bag.

We had more than a few spots that would spring leaks and we were all constantly tripping over buckets I had to put out to stop it turning into a swimming pool. The only thing I could do when we had a leak that exceeded what a bucket could hold was put down sawdust which would get in your throat and sometimes sting your eyes when the heart was pumping and battle had commenced. During the Great Storm of 1987 we had to close up and hope for the best, so perilous was the gym when the rain lashed down. I feared we'd never see it again as it floated gently down the river by which it sat.

The toilets were a health hazard and there was no shower. The main room simply wasn't an adequate size and it was by no means big enough for a proper ring. Besides that, I couldn't afford one. We had a raised area, not brilliantly assembled, which I filled with stacked carpet that I nailed to the floor. It was the only thing I could do to stop the boxers slipping all over the place. We had rope around the carpet, held up by broom sticks that would collapse all the time.

When they finally demolished the place in 2002, they barely had to tap it and the floorboards came apart. I was crestfallen.

From the day I took the keys from Paul Williams it became my temple. I'd idealised the gym, I'd romanticised it, but in reality knocking it down was the best thing that could've happened to us. The famed Team Calzaghe stable couldn't have achieved their potential in the old gym and almost no-one else mourned its passing.

Joe was straining at the leash to turn professional after the anger subsided over the Olympics and it was only a matter of time before a promoter got in touch. If I'd had one ounce of common sense or savvy I would have listened to what he had to say and then rung the office of every top promoter in the country. I was having a tough time running the gym for a couple of reasons and it never occurred to me to open an auction for the right to let my son do what he was destined to be great at.

Financially it was hard for me because everyone who'd been associated with the gym when Paul was in charge suddenly didn't want to know and walked away. It was just me, myself and I. It was a stressful period. I also found it tough to adjust to being in one place all the time. There's no way of getting away from that fact. I loved Joe, loved the boxing and most of all family life, but I wasn't used to having an anchor in my arse. For the first time since being a teenager I would wake up and know exactly what that day would bring as it was all scheduled. That felt so alien.

We had few supporters, but I remember one fantastic guy who really made a huge impression on the Calzaghe family. He inspired me to make a success of the gym and was one of the only people on the planet who loved the place as much as I did. His name was Fred Taylor and he was one of the men responsible for building the old boxing club. He was hugely respected in the local boxing, and especially the rugby, community, and a huge supporter of the place. He loved to watch Joe's progress and he would sit for hours on end watching him train. It touched my heart. Such was the affection that grew up between us all, Joe was a pall-bearer at Fred's funeral. Sadly, the likes of Fred were a minority. I put a jar out for 'subs' for the guys who used the gym. Unfortunately, and by their own admission, I think Gavin Rees and Bradley Pryce pinched more out of the jar than most people put in it! They were teenagers and the sound of the ice cream van was just too tempting.

The final notable incident of Joe's amateur career was when Nicky Piper, the then European champion from Cardiff came down to spar with Joe around the time he fought Nigel Benn in a world title eliminator. Nicky had a Mercedes, nice clothes and carried himself like a champion. He was a fine boxer and his trainer Charlie Pearson asked if Joe could do eight rounds, which I knew wasn't a problem. Nicky stiffed Joe a couple of times in the first round with the other boys watching on and the third time he tried it Joe sidestepped him and dropped him with a massive left hand. Nicky was fuming and the sparring ended there and then. But if Joe was doing that to a world title contender before he'd thrown a professional punch, he was clearly ready for the big leagues.

So when a talent scout watched Joe win his third and final senior ABA title and we were requested to have a meeting with promoter Mickey Duff that was good enough for me. Naively we didn't even try to negotiate with Mickey. I didn't have a clue about valuation, sign-on fees, percentages of profits, all these fundamentals that are part and parcel of modern contracts. Back then if you talked to me about agents I would've thought you meant Roger Moore or Sean Connery playing James Bond. Mickey was really keen that we sign with him and even though Joe was relying on my better judgement it never popped into my head to stall and see what else was out there. Mickey had been a big time player without question and he'd guided several fighters to world titles over a number of years. Guys like John Conteh, Alan Minter and Lloyd Honeyghan had all been promoted by Mickey and at one time he was part of a core group of promoters that pretty much reigned over British boxing.

And I bet he never had an easier negotiation in his whole career than with this idiot.

I didn't negotiate for Joe to get a signing-on fee, but he got a loan set against future earnings and a contract with a flat rate per week irrespective of his fights. We aren't talking thousands here, we are talking hundreds. Had we got a proper negotiator on our team, I have no doubt Joe could've earned more money with or without Mickey Duff. Eventually we renegotiated a better deal with Mickey when we were in the game and our eyes were opened as to how useless I'd been when making the deal. But I have no doubt I cost Joe money. I fucked up, pure and simple.

One thing I think that helped to persuade us Mickey was the man was the glowing terms in which he spoke about Joe when we signed. He called him the best amateur to come out of the UK in ten years and that was great to hear, especially as Mickey had a promotional deal with Naseem Hamed at the time. I don't have an ounce of doubt to this day that Mickey genuinely rated Joe as a massive prospect and a future world champion. I can't blame him for the fact we got a lousy deal. That was entirely down to me not knowing how to play the game.

I thought Mickey was the biggest and best name out there and I was a little bit in awe of him I think. He'd associated with Terry Lawless and Jarvis Astaire for many years and we spent a great deal of time with Mickey and Terry especially. Mickey would sometimes take liberties. I would quite often be requested to drive him here, there and everywhere and he was very old school in his outlook, he wanted Joe to serve his apprenticeship before challenging for the biggest honours. He also had a terrible sense of organisation with the small details which could be most aggravating. He once got me to pick him up from a hotel after a press conference to take him across London to where he was staying. That would've been all well and good, but Mickey was staying in the hotel I originally collected him from and three hours later on the other side of London without a map and with the language in my shit car turning bluer by the minute, he realised his mistake. That was typical.

I knew when we signed with Mickey that there were a lot of rumours that it was only a matter of time until Joe moved on from working with me and that I wouldn't be able to hack it in professional boxing, but that only fuelled the fire. I was extremely determined. And it made me feel more secure that someone like Mickey Duff, who had seen everything in boxing, never questioned my involvement. I didn't ever formulate an amateur or a professional manner of training, I just taught the way I taught. Deep down I always expected that sooner or later Joe would move on from me. Part of me wasn't even devastated by that thought because perhaps then I could go back to playing more gigs.

I was regularly working the corner for Joe, Paul Samuels who turned professional, Gavin Rees, Bradley Pryce and Bradley's brothers Delroy and Byron in the amateurs and I was learning by doing, even though both Joe and Paul broke my nose sparring. That was fine with me. I expected things to be tough. But Mickey asked if Joe could double up on his training so I sent him to Newport where Sammy Sims was running the St Josephs gym that is now enjoying great success under Tony Borg.

I expected that would be that, really. Joe was doing more and more work in Newport and I suspected my gym would be amateur only. Joe didn't argue when I explained that to him but six weeks later he turned up at our place – he'd moved out into his own house by then – and said he wanted to return and didn't want to be trained by anyone else. He looked nervous. "Joe, are you just saying this because I'm your dad?" I asked him. Ridiculously, I got angry and we had a row. "For fuck's sake, don't throw your career away because you're loyal to your dad." Joe was understandably annoyed. Being a boxer had been his dream since he was nine and he wouldn't jeopardise his ambitions. "I swear to you that being my dad has absolutely nothing to do with it," he replied. "I think you are the best trainer around and I'm not telling you again!"

I never wanted Joe to feel I depended on him and people perceiving me that way was/is one of my main insecurities. Years later that would pour out of me in a blazing row with Bernard Hopkins that is captured on YouTube. But I also wanted to know, needed to know, that if Joe and I were working together it was because he believed in my talents as I did in his. I never felt insecure about our working relationship again after that heart-to-heart. It wouldn't be the last time Joe would nearly split from my gym, but it was the last time I worried he wouldn't know how to tell me.

Joe had boxed in the very best ABA venues like York Hall and the Assembly Rooms, but his professional debut was to be at an unforgettable venue, the Cardiff Arms Park. At the time that was the epicentre of sport in Wales and it was a huge night of boxing too as the main event featured Lennox Lewis clashing with Frank

Bruno for a world title, at the time the biggest British fight out there. I've always found huge domestic battles to be compelling and this was no different, it was a massive stage for Joe and a fantastic occasion.

One thing I couldn't believe was that Jackie refused point blank to come and watch. She was a typical Welsh girl, raised in the Gwent valleys in a rugby-obsessed nation and knew what it meant to be performing at the Arms Park, but she just wasn't interested in seeing Joe fighting, potentially taking punishment and getting hurt. That never changed. Joe's mother couldn't bring herself to see a glove touch his skin and didn't attend a single one of his forty-six professional fights over the years. She did, many years later, let him talk her into appearing on *Family Fortunes* on ITV in 2010. So the Calzaghe clan have been out in public all together at least once.

Joe fought Paul Hanlon on October 1, 1993, in his professional debut and even though I'd dreamed of a packed house, the only places in Cardiff that were packed when Joe came out were the pubs. Nonetheless, Paul was no match for Joe and it was all over in the first round. Joe says he doesn't remember much about the fight and I don't remember a thing, but Paul Hanlon described Joe as being something very special. The Birmingham factory worker is probably better known for fighting Joe than anything else he did in boxing.

For Joe it was a dream night but it was one that created an issue for me. Basically I got sidelined and it hurt like hell. The reality of it was worse than I imagined. Terry Lawless acted as Joe's cornerman, he obviously didn't have faith in me and I let him crack on with it. I was the bucket man and my role was to stand back and pass Terry the sponge. It hurt my pride immensely but I didn't want to rock the boat on Joe's big night so I bit my tongue, my lips, my whole bloody mouth really and let Terry take charge. That's why the fight is a blur. I was enraged, embarrassed and proud and nervous all at the same time. I was almost overcome with emotion. For the whole fight my mouth was dry and palms sweaty and the experience was a haze. But I vowed I wouldn't let it ever happen again.

When Joe next fought, another fight that didn't last a round against Paul Mason, I knew what I was going to do. On the way into the ring I sidled up to Terry and spelled it out loud and clear. "You get back and don't stand on the fucking apron, you pass me the fucking sponge because I am Joe's trainer, not you," I bellowed at him. It had to be addressed because if nothing else, Joe needed to know I believed in myself as he believed in me. It began our chapter as professionals, Joe generally knocking out everyone Terry and Mickey put in front of him with a minimum of effort required.

We were learning the ropes together, but I would absorb stuff I saw other trainers do on fight nights and that most certainly includes Terry Lawless. It was only a matter of principle that saw me scream at him. He was a very nice man who taught me a lot and is missed by the sport.

Joe carried on blasting out opponents, winning seven of his first nine fights inside a round and the other two just after the bell rang for round two. I tailored his training around working to his strengths and never tried to change what made him so exciting. The only down point of that year was another World Cup rolling around and Italy again being disappointed when we lost the final to Brazil on penalties with the brilliant Roberto Baggio missing his kick. I watched that match at home with Joe and it was brutal for us. England didn't even qualify and Diana Ross made more of a splash in the opening ceremony than them. I've mentioned before my identity crisis when it comes to being Italian, English or Welsh, but when it comes to football, I'm Forza Italia.

It wasn't the matchmakers' fault that Joe wasn't getting rounds, he was going in with guys like Karl Barwise, Spencer Alton and Trevor Ambrose who were durable fighters expected to give him a good test. He was simply relentless and needed a far bigger stage than one round undercard demolition jobs. After about eighteen months Joe was beginning to become disillusioned with Mickey and his old school way of building a fighter up. Joe wanted to be contesting titles and was growing impatient.

The only way to get him rounds was to put him in with a cruiserweight and a big bruiser from Manchester named Bobbi Joe Edwards was just the ticket. He was a big, squat guy with a hard head, plenty of power and half a stone on Joe. He took Joe eight rounds, not winning many if any of them but giving Joe valuable ring experience. That's ironic because Joe never went the distance again until he fought Chris Eubank who just so happens to be Bobbi Joe Edwards' cousin. That I felt was a defining test and showed Joe was ready to step up in class, but amazingly he had another dozen fights and a new promoter before the big chance came to finally challenge for a world title.

Back in Newbridge in the shack of my dreams, things had improved markedly thanks to some rugby boys. It sounds made-up, being that half the world probably associates Wales with rugby, but it was genuinely the support of several local players that helped me turn Newbridge Boxing Club into a success so that people took us seriously.

It had been killing me financially to run the place and I barely had time to set up gigs for the evenings and was too knackered anyway, as I was in the gym seven days a week. But that paid off. One Sunday there was a knock at the door of the gym and Byron Hayward was standing there. He was the Newbridge full-back, very popular locally and he asked me if I would train him in boxing, something he'd enjoyed as a kid. I thought it'd be great for the place to have a really dedicated sporting star like him around and on first inspection I was very impressed. He was a tidy fighter, the fundamentals came naturally to him and he worked hard, turned up on time and was very coachable with a great physique.

After a couple of weeks I asked him where he wanted to take the boxing and he said he preferred it to rugby and would like to make it his career. I told him I'd make him a world champion in two years! He laughed at me and asked if maybe in the meantime I could help him get a boxing license. Two years later he'd been in twenty-one amateur fights and didn't lose a single one. He was a very good prospect, a good banger with a great attitude and a lot of humility.

I convinced him to enter the Welsh ABAs at light middleweight only months after he started with me because he had wonderful natural fitness levels and even though it was a matter of weeks away, I knew he stood a good chance to win it. Sure enough Byron got to the final against a boy named Clayton Smith who I had seen before and I knew he was capable. I also knew Byron's style meant he was going to get knocked down sooner rather than later and I warned him of that before the Clayton fight. He looked gutted, like I'd lost faith in him, but the truth was I just wanted him to be expecting it, because then I could tell him what to do if it happened.

And it did. Sure enough in the very first round, down went Byron. But like I said, he was a clever kid. I'd prepared him properly and he listened to every word: he took a knee, caught his breath and took his time getting up and was ready to fight on. Clayton was down not thirty seconds later after a monster Hayward hook and then twice more before the referee stopped it and announced Byron as champion. "I told you, I told you it would be all right if you went down," I said as I hugged him. "What are you talking about? I told you. I never go down," he replied. The poor bastard got hit so hard he didn't even remember it! The way he reacted was purely instinctive so I wasn't quite the genius I thought, but it just shows how good his boxing instincts were. Byron was a very good ambassador for our gym and had the potential certainly to be a good pro. I figured the rugby background was a benefit really, a good publicity tool for him and so I contacted Mickey Duff and asked if he'd maybe like to sign Byron to a deal and have him turn pro.

Just before he was due to sign the deal Byron played for his old club Newport RFC when they were a few players short for a friendly match against Cross Keys. He was fully focused on boxing by then, but it became a massive turning point for him. He damaged his neck at the end of the match and that was that really. He needed six months to heal and the boxing deal with Mickey Duff went away. I begged him not to get downhearted when the doctor advised against boxing and he decided he would give the rugby another go. He was so dedicated to getting fit again and it was no surprise to me when a few years later, he was plucked from relative obscurity by new Wales coach Graham Henry and picked for his country. He deserved to play on that stage as he didn't get to box at the top level, but he helped breathe new life into our place and I will always be grateful. He is a man I admire a great deal.

Several of Byron's rugby mates would come to the gym to train more casually including the renowned coach Kingsley Jones and others from Newport and Newbridge RFC. I felt like it gave us some extra credibility and these rugby lads had a tremendous influence on the kids as well. I liked the vibe they created and was feeling very much at home for the first time, the king of the castle with professional and amateur fighters ready to dominate boxing if given the opportunity.

Therein was the problem. The opportunities just weren't coming for Joe and sooner or later something was going to have to give. He wasn't a wet-behind-the-ears teenager anymore, Joe was twenty four years old and like most people that age he wanted more, more, more, now, now, now. He won three more fights by stoppage in 1995 before finally landing a British title shot against Stephen Wilson. To me that was a foregone conclusion and I think by that stage rather than it being a massive thrill, Joe probably thought he was already too good to be fighting for a British title. He was right, but it wasn't the way to look at things. He won easily.

Joe had a tiny scare in his second defence, when he got caught hard for the first time in his career by a guy named Anthony Brooks, but that was nothing compared to what was lined up next as Joe was to be matched with unbeaten Londoner Mark Delaney. Mickey Duff didn't win the purse bid and Joe had to fight in Delaney's back garden in Brentwood, Essex. I remember Joe was booed out of the building, but he came out beaming, because this was the big stage he craved. To date it was by far his biggest test.

Joe stuck to a game plan and saw out the danger of the first couple of rounds, because only adrenalin could save Delaney who had been brilliantly managed and protected to have a record that was far better than his talents merited. In fact, just by sizing Delaney up Joe made a big impact, dropping him twice in the first round before finishing him off in the fifth. The fight was on the television too, albeit at nearly midnight on ITV, but still, that was tremendous progress. The whole bill was built around Joe's big night and he fought brilliantly.

But then it was the same old story. That fight showed how far Joe had come yet his next two opponents were Warren Stowe and

Pat Lawlor. Neither had a high profile and the TV companies didn't show either fight and so things came to a head with Mickey Duff. As far as Joe was concerned, enough was enough. He'd knocked them both out in two rounds and hadn't needed to sweat. He said he wanted to leave Mickey and I told him straight that I would support him, especially when Mickey told me that Joe wasn't even next in line for a world title fight out of his stable, as another boxer he had named Henry Wharton was ahead of him. Enough of this, we decided. We saw a solicitor who advised that as Mickey had never shown us a fight contract, we had a good case to leave him.

As it was we ended up paying Mickey to leave, such is the boxing world. Apparently we owed him several grand, but we paid it and parted ways with no real bad feeling, just a sense that he couldn't take Joe where he wanted to go, or certainly not fast enough. So we moved on, Mickey got his money and Joe was free to negotiate with whoever he wanted. But once again we didn't really play the field, only this time it was because I think Joe had already made his mind up about what he wanted to do. He wanted to go with Frank Warren. We'd been on Frank's shows and Joe talked to people in the business and everyone told him the same thing, "Sign with Frank".

Frank was the biggest name at the time out of the British promoters and he'd recently taken his stable over to Sky television. "You want to be on Sky, that's where all the money is," Joe was being told by every boxer at every show across the country. Sooner or later, he was going to make that happen. We went and talked with Frank who knew Joe was unhappy and we agreed a deal that meant much more money for Joe and that was fantastic but by no means the biggest motive in joining his stable.

"I'll get you a world title shot after three fights if you keep winning," Frank promised Joe. And that's exactly what he did. We joined Frank's stable in late 1996 with Joe's record at 19-0 and Joe never fought for another promoter again. Frank really rated Joe, had the best mind in the business and stayed true to his word and after three fights, got Joe what he had always dreamed of.

"I was unhappy with Mickey Duff's handling of my career for a

*long time and every time I boxed on a Frank Warren bill it felt
more exciting. There was more atmosphere and with his Sky TV
deal his fighters were earning good money. I was determined to
sign for him. Like dad I don't blame Mickey Duff because we
negotiated the bum deal. I don't blame dad for it either, we were
both just naive about how boxing worked at that time."* Joe
Calzaghe

My boy was about to fight for a world title and it was absolutely
thrilling. Rumour had it that Joe was being lined up to fight the
only other guy in boxing who struck me as a contender to Joe for
the title of Celtic Warrior. Of course I mean Steve Collins and
what a fight that was going to be. I believed Joe could beat
Collins, but also thought it'd be bloody difficult and a great test
for him.

As ever, things didn't work out as they were expected to.

Chapter Nine:

World Champion

The prospect of Joe fighting Steve Collins excited me. As far as I was concerned Collins had proved himself to be the man in a brilliant British super middleweight division at that time.

Unfortunately, Joe arrived in the world too late in terms of his peers. Jackie and I should have got busy earlier! It's a shame Joe didn't get to fight Nigel Benn or Henry Wharton or Michael Watson. Watson was a tremendously brave and talented fighter who sadly saw his career and almost his life cut short in the ring in 1991 in a fight with Chris Eubank at Tottenham's football ground, White Hart Lane. He was winning until a devastating late uppercut almost cost him his life. Watson's plight and the worry and anxiety his family must have felt always struck a chord with me, there at the back of my mind each and every time Joe or any of my fighters got in the ring. Imagine if Joe gets badly hurt, what on earth am I going to say to Jackie? That's the kind of thing that can creep into your mind. It's why my fighters are never allowed to cut corners in training and why I'd never have hesitated to throw in the towel if it was appropriate. But even if you do everything right, take every precaution, there is always that tiny risk of tragedy. Michael Watson is one such example and as a trainer, that's something you have to deal with. As a father/trainer, it fills you with dread in your stomach. Tragedy is an overused word in sport, but sometimes it's a painfully appropriate word in boxing.

Joe against Steve Collins was a fight I knew everyone would want to see. Now we were talking, that was exactly the kind of warrior I dreamed Joe would get to fight, I thought it'd be absolutely tremendous. Collins defended his WBO title seven times, beat Chris Eubank twice and Nigel Benn twice. He was a real demon in the ring and a front-foot fighting tough guy who I thought would be a brilliant foe for Joe. Collins was part of that era that had enthralled Joe in his amateur days and he was one of the three fighters, along with Nigel Benn and Chris Eubank who would put super middleweight boxing in the UK on the map.

Finally, the fight was made. It was all set and Joe was beyond confident of beating Steve Collins. I never needed to say a word to reassure him. He had been out with pals in a bar in Newport when Collins fought Craig Cummings a few months earlier. We knew Joe was a mandatory defence for the winner and Cummings had really troubled Collins, even putting him down in the first round. Watching that in a pub fuelled by a few beers and his mates' encouragement, Joe had been totally convinced he'd beat up Steve Collins. It all seemed meant to be, fated in Joe's favour that his big chance had arrived just as Frank Warren promised it would.

Two weeks before the fight was due to take place Joe was at my house picking at some steamed vegetables while the rest of us ate dinner. It was the night of the Boxing Writers' Awards dinner and while we ate the phone rang a couple of times. When we eventually answered it, was a reporter asking if we'd heard about Steve Collins retiring. Joe and I raced to the front room to look on Ceefax and sure enough there it was. Collins had made his announcement at the dinner. He was done. We read the story in silence and Joe turned to me and sighed. We presumed at that moment his world title opportunity had gone.

I have heard a number of second-hand accounts of why Steve Collins pulled out of the fight and I think by putting them all together you get a pretty clear picture. Steve was desperate to fight Roy Jones Jr, but just as Joe would for many years, he found Jones very difficult to pin down and negotiate with. In the meantime Joe was a mandatory defence that he had to take first. Joe was too young, too dangerous and not a big enough name really for Steve to contemplate fighting before Roy Jones. There were apparently (according to Steve Collins) further issues that he had received doctors' advice to give up the sport. It was rumoured that he suffered a knockdown in sparring. That's certainly what Collins says and he seems a man of honour, someone I have no desire or reason to question. If that's his word on it then so be it. I always put it down to Steve Collins being a smart guy who knew when enough was enough. Medical advice said he should quit, so that's what his brain was telling him and in my opinion Steve's heart was telling him not to fight Joe too.

"No disrespect but at the end of my career Joe was just another in a long list of contenders, I was concentrating on fighting Roy Jones, he was the only fight I wanted. I'd openly challenged him, been to his home but it just wasn't going to happen. It was on and off. I'd had two big pay days and I just didn't have the heart for it anymore. There was nowhere else for me to go. If Joe had come around five years earlier it would have happened, it would've been him with me, him with Chris Eubank and Nigel Benn." Steve Collins, Time of Our Lives, Sky Sports.

Frank Warren confirmed the news the day after the dinner and told us not to worry, that there would still be a world title fight and it would still be a huge night up in Sheffield with Joe headlining the show and we sat tight and waited for confirmation of a new opponent.

All the talk in the papers was that it would be Chris Eubank and that worried me. Eubank was a larger than life character who had been there, done it and dominated. He'd had two famous draws with Nigel Benn and lost two close ones to Steve Collins, but I felt he had more left in the tank than the Irishman and more ring savvy for certain. I knew Collins' machismo meant that he would fight in a certain way against Joe but at two weeks' notice I couldn't quite put my finger on what the strategy should be for Eubank. He had more of an aura about him and from the moment the new fight was announced he began to play mind games that worked on me but thankfully not on Joe.

The press promotion with him was an absolute ordeal in comparison to other fights and I'd never known anything like it. This was a massive chance for Eubank to return to the spotlight and one he'd been craving. He had a massive deal with Sky TV and I think he'd become burned out heading into the Collins fights. Every couple of months he'd been in the ring and he became stale. But by the time he got the nod to face Joe at around two weeks' notice he'd fought only twice in two years. He was fresher, hungrier and more dangerous than Collins and watching him operate ahead of the fight was quite an experience and quite an unsettling one at that.

I also knew it would be difficult because Joe's view of Eubank was more than just one of respect; he had been a big Eubank fan. It'd maybe be stretching the point to say Joe idolised Chris Eubank, but without a doubt I think there wasn't an active boxer who had made a bigger impression on Joe as an amateur. He was transfixed whenever he fought on television. The fight with Eubank represented the only time in Joe's career when I felt it was possible he could become awestruck and let the occasion beat him. I don't really want to admit it, but I think Joe had a little bit of fear about facing the former champion, he knew he was stepping in against the real deal.

Joe was also putting immense pressure on himself. He had married a local girl named Mandy the year after he turned professional and his first son (and my first grandchild) Joe Jr was a little baby who needed nappies and everything else that cost lots of money. Joe didn't have two pennies to rub together from his early fights and he was heaping pressure on himself in regards to winning a world title. It was a boyhood dream for sure, but the financial reality was that Joe needed to get to that level. He had nothing to fall back on. If he couldn't make a success of his boxing career, who knows what he would have done instead? I'd set him up in many jobs when he left school but he generally never lasted more than a day or two. Now doesn't that sound familiar?

From the very first meeting Eubank did his best to get into Joe's head with a mixture of intensity and comedy that I found quite baffling. At a press briefing outside a London hotel for a photo opportunity and interviews, Chris kept us waiting then rode up on a Harley Davidson, wearing jodhpurs, a flashy silk shirt and a leather jacket. It was the very first press event we did with him and it was a bit of a pantomime. You have certain expectations from a talker like Chris and he didn't disappoint us. He stopped to talk with the reporters, the photographers, fans, the doormen of the hotel and passers-by who didn't even care who he was and then sauntered up to Joe and asked him, "And you are?" It was classic really, but I remember at the time staying quiet as I seethed with rage. 'How dare he?' I thought, but I didn't want to convey my anger. Joe as ever just took it in his stride and laughed; firing back he was the guy "who would kick Eubank's ass in the ring." "You have a good record, but you've never been in the trenches," Eubank carried on. "I've been there and that's where I am going to take you."

Joe laughed off the taunts but they resonated with me and struck fear in me because I knew that his words were true. Eubank in my opinion was never a great entertainer in the ring for all his flash and showmanship outside of it, but he had an absolutely iron chin and I felt the fight would most likely go the distance. He was definitely capable of taking Joe to the trenches. Joe had been sparking people out left, right and centre and all but one of his fights had been over in less than six minutes. If it became a full on war, I was worried the experienced ring general might be able to win it with mind games. The event was huge. Eubank was coming for his world title that he'd lost to Collins and it would be a strong bill with a highly vocal crowd in Sheffield, which is a wonderful city for live sport. Chris Eubank was used to the big stage. Joe wasn't.

As a trainer I've never overly concerned myself with watching fight after fight of the upcoming opponent because I think after a while you can drive yourself mad overanalysing. You end up barking too many instructions at your fighter and putting too much doubt in his mind. Probably the reason I stopped doing that was after the Chris Eubank experience. When I found out Collins was out and Eubank was in I got a huge pile of VHS videos and watched him religiously, morning, noon and night and even if I didn't convey it to Joe, I was panicking a bit. This guy was the business in my mind.

Come fight night the bad vibes continued from me. It was our first taste of a big bill and I got everything wrong in terms of the preparation. We arrived too early at the arena and worked too much on the pads to pass what was a nervous few hours. Joe was expending far too much energy. He'd been too restless to eat properly and build up his strength. He hadn't slept very well either and seemed quiet and distant which worried me. I overcompensated in response and was a bundle of nerves and I could tell I was really annoying Joe. Paul Samuels worked with me in the corner that night and the pair of us were trying to get Joe going, but I think we were just aggravating him. He wanted us to fuck off but I didn't want to leave him on his own. I remember the feeling of adrenalin was incredible but I didn't know how to release it, so I was becoming more and more het up with my heart pounding. I didn't drink enough water and the dehydration made me feel giddy when the officials finally knocked on the door and said those two little words that always precede the drama. "It's time."

As Joe made his entrance to the ring in the middle of the night I felt like I had an animal far bigger than a butterfly fluttering in my stomach. I believed in Joe completely and with all my heart, but I felt it was going to be a very close fight and when the crowd roared for Eubank as Tina Turner told the world he was 'Simply The Best', I felt sick. I was really worried that this night was going to go horribly wrong and that everyone would blame me. It was my only night in boxing where I was plagued with doubt.

Within fifteen seconds of the opening bell, that fear melted away at least until the end of the round. Joe caught Eubank flush on his face after a flurry and even though he was up in a flash, Eubank had been knocked on his backside and had to take a count. It was a result of a planned strategy that saw Joe sprint out of his corner at the opening bell and the fans responded big time. They were shocked to see Eubank put down even though Joe had twenty-one knockouts in twenty two fights. "Good shot," Eubank mouthed back as Joe set a pace in the first round that the older man didn't like.

But too much energy was expended trying to end the fight there and then as Joe threw too many wild shots. He was a lot more drained than I would have wished even after the first round. By the end of the third Eubank was landing lots of shots to the body and I felt was starting to bully his way back into the fight, standing his ground and smiling, not posing, but he looked settled and was grinning from ear to ear. Joe was blowing hard.

However, this was to be the night where Joe's superior fitness and conditioning – something he's dedicated his whole life to – paid off. Joe wouldn't let Eubank impose himself even though he had to dig deeper than ever before. A great fifth round set the tone for the middle of the fight with the greater volume and accuracy of punches coming from Joe. But Eubank kept coming. Joe was winning the fight but he was doing so in very physically demanding rounds, thanks to his fitness and bravery. It was becoming the kind of fight everyone said Eubank needed to make it to win, yet it was Joe who stood defiantly, winning round after round. He proved his chin, his power, his style. He dominated Eubank until a nervous last couple of rounds when I think he was fighting on fumes and I was concerned again. As much as anything the atmosphere and the pressure were draining for Joe. He ate some massive shots in the final two sessions of the fight and afterwards he had the battle scars of someone who had been in a war, his right eye closing and swelling while Eubank looked like he'd stepped out of a salon at the post-fight press conference, suited and booted, monocle and all.

That didn't matter when that chime went to indicate ten seconds to go in the final round. I held my breath as the Sheffield crowd went nuts. Two big shots by Eubank – pa! pa! – as Joe stepped forward and held, knowing he was seconds away from fulfilling his childhood dream. Again Eubank got forward, firing two in the ribs and one to the chin as Joe swayed against the ropes, his legs unsteady, pa! pa! pa! Joe had been taken to his limits just as Eubank warned. But he held on, figuratively and literally as the final bell sounded. The crowd stood and roared their appreciation.

I charged into the ring and hugged Joe tightly knowing full well that he was so exhausted he could barely stand. I also knew he'd done it and didn't need to hear the judges' scores read out to celebrate. It was a truly wonderful feeling. I clutched my son, told him how proud I was and it seemed like only a second or two passed before Michael Buffer and that famous voice of his was delivering the news Joe had waited a lifetime for: "The winner and... NEW... world champion... Jo-o-o-o-o-e Ca-a-a-a-alzagh-e-e-e!"

What I couldn't appreciate at the time was what a fantastic fight it had been and how much Joe had proved himself on a big stage. It still blows my mind that it took another ten years for the general public to accept Joe as the best of the best we had. I loved the way Steve Bunce wrote about it. I have a wall full of photographs in my gym, but just a handful of newspapers from Joe's greatest ever nights. That is a regret of mine, but Steve's is one of my favourites.

"It was quite simply one of the finest fights in British boxing history... Every second was fought with little or no regard for the outcome of the next round. They stood with their toes touching and unleashed punches in wild round after wild round. There was a look in Eubank's eyes that was missing in many of his last championship fights and, as each failed right uppercut missed and Calzaghe blocked some that were on target, it was still impossible to rule out a Eubank win. But on Saturday Calzaghe fought like a veteran and not a novice with twenty two easy wins including ten in the first round. The exchanges in most of the rounds were reminiscent of boxing's most brutal and memorable encounters. As punches connected, there were gasps from the ringside area and a constant roar of appreciation from the capacity crowd. Calzaghe can do whatever Frank Warren, the show's promoter, wants because against Eubank he became a true fighter the hard way, the old-fashioned way, by surviving tremendous adversity to win."
Steve Bunce, *Daily Telegraph*.

He had certainly done it the hard way, in my opinion much more so than if he had faced Steve Collins at that stage in his career, but Joe was a world champion boxer and of course, it was a huge vindication for me as a trainer. I thought it made clear to all the naysayers that I was capable of getting Joe to that level at least, even though many at the time thought Joe was so talented, a tub of lard could've stood in his corner and he would still have made it to the top. As it was, in reality it wasn't too long until once again people were suggesting Joe would need to leave his dad who was holding him back, but for that moment and on that night everything seemed simply perfect.

We had a brilliant celebration after the Eubank fight. It was huge for Wales, it was huge for boxing in the UK and you can just imagine the galvanising effect it had on the rest of the boys in the gym to see one of their own walking back into training with a

WBO world title belt.

I was about to unleash two more young, hungry, talented South Wales valley boys on to the boxing world. The dawning of the Team Calzaghe stable was upon us. You'll have heard many things about Gavin Rees and Bradley Pryce and the chances are a lot of it will be less than favourable. But to me, they are two of the best boys around and even though we are no longer together and as much as it hurts me, we barely even speak now, I think of the pair of them as my sons. They were brothers in arms for Joe for well over ten years, day-in and day-out in the boxing gym and Gavin in particular was extraordinarily talented.

Until recently I still worked with Enzo Maccarinelli, I worked for years and years with Nathan Cleverly and I've trained many, many other fighters and seen a whole host of others at close quarters when they've been down for sparring. But without question the second most natural talent I've seen behind Joe would be Gavin Rees. His speed and his power are things that you just can't teach and he has the heart and fortitude of a warrior just like Joe. What he doesn't have, or certainly didn't have under my watch, is Joe's discipline or work rate. Whisper it quietly, but Gavin's natural ability in terms of his picture perfect jab, may even be better than Joe's. That's how good I believe that kid is.

When I first took the shy and cautious Joe to Paul Williams' gym, Gavin, Bradley and Brad's brother Delroy were knocking about there and even as five or six year old kids they stuck out as prospects. But because they were often in trouble, because they had so much lip, I think Paul was thrilled to let me have them! So from day one Bradley and Gavin were my fighters and trying to get them to reach their potential was one of the biggest struggles I faced in my career. I stood in the corner for their first amateur fights and I stood in the corner of their debuts as professional fights. I was also in the law courts when the pair of them did their very best to throw their careers away.

The best way I think I can explain the troubles I had with them is to use the example of Alex Ferguson, a coach I respect greatly, and who is one of the all-time greats. He has always gone that extra mile to protect his players. You might have heard that story about him turning up at a party and dragging out Ryan Giggs when a spy in the camp informed him that Giggs was out drinking with another youngster at the time, Lee Sharpe. Sharpe was sold sometime later just as Paul McGrath was before him because Sir Alex wanted to change the drinking culture at the club. Even though they were excellent players, he let them strut their stuff at Elland Road and Villa Park respectively because of the bigger picture. But he kept Giggs who became a club icon. Well Gavin and Bradley needed that level of controlling. They didn't just need a trainer, they needed a guardian angel to get them eating properly and most crucially not drinking to excess and I wasn't that person. I regret that they aren't richer and better-known after so long in the fight game. Tony Doherty is another one. All three of them could've been remembered as great fighters. I've stated that I saw Gavin and Bradley as being like sons, but when it came down to it I didn't do enough to keep them on the straight and narrow and out of trouble and that's a regret of mine. They've owned up to their own mistakes, but I will always wonder what might have been for both of them if they'd matched Joe's dedication to being the best he could be.

The fact is I couldn't be a full-time voice in their ear telling them not to eat that burger or not to drink those ten pints because I had three kids of my own and a boxing gym to run, gigs to attend and everything else.

Joe absolutely adores Bradley and Gavin and sees them as being his brothers. Gavin and Bradley trained side-by-side with Joe for twenty years and I had no doubt that they would go on to box professionally. Neither of them could wait to turn pro and get their contracts signed so they could start earning some money. Gavin was nineteen when he turned professional in 1998 and Bradley did the same thing a year later at the same age.

I think nineteen is just about the optimum age to turn professional unless the chance to stay amateur and box at the Olympics is there, but you can understand how little faith I had in that route for any of my fighters after the complete and utter shambles in 1992. Gavin in particular I just couldn't hold back, I couldn't stop him from developing so quickly, his speed was electric and my training complemented that well. He had the technique and the speed to throw punches in clusters and so efficiently just like Joe. Punches in bunches came naturally and you could see his amateur opponents utterly bamboozled. Gavin was short but in the ring you could never tell what he was going to do next, he was impossible for his opponents to read. I used to tell him, "Don't wait for the door to shut, hit the targets, if you see an opening, take it and don't ever hold back." Part of my philosophy is like that of a little kid in a sweet shop. What you see, you touch. When you see the other boxer exposed in any way, take advantage of that, take the fight to them. Perhaps Gavin better than anyone else could execute that philosophy. He would overwhelm opponents in every fight and now working with Gary Lockett, he is still doing it.

A few weeks after the Eubank fight, I noticed all the 'Joe is the real deal' talk seemed to change. Instead of praise for the victor, it was more sympathy for the loser, focusing on the fact Eubank had taken the fight at short notice and suggesting otherwise he would have won. I began to wonder what on earth Joe could do to have his talents recognised. It was typical in my mind of the attitude that so many British people had. Joe was a winner and that wasn't as good a story as the valiant loser Eubank, who became more popular with three successive losses at the end of his career than he ever was when he was winning time and time again. Just ask him about it. When Eubank was unbeatable, people though, he was an arrogant prick, but when he started losing, suddenly he became the people's arrogant prick, someone with very British idiosyncrasies. I like Chris, but I didn't understand the shift in opinion.

People didn't seem to acknowledge Joe's phenomenal speed and many critics said he was a slapper half the time which I found amazing considering how many knockouts he had. I think the technique Joe used, the speed all my fighters became renowned for using, set a bit of a benchmark. I watched Matthew Macklin recently and he looks like a classic example of a fighter who has adapted his style to be more like Joe or Gavin Rees. That pleases me. I hope the way we trained will leave an impact. Otherwise, what was the point of giving me all those awards?

But back in the late 1990s when Joe was a fresh-aced twenty four year old world champion, there was no recognition for what we had achieved and in fact the complete opposite was true outside of Wales. Joe had a wonderful homecoming fight in Cardiff against Branko Sobot at what was the Cardiff International Arena (now the Motorpoint Arena) in front of a capacity crowd who completely understood what a massive achievement it was to be a world champion. It was an easy three round fight and I loved how behind Joe the Welsh public was. The rest of Britain couldn't give a shit though, that was how it felt when I read the newspapers.

I could never have even imagined after the Eubank fight that less than two years later I would be 'sacked' as Joe's trainer. Even less real was the prospect that I would have to tell my world champion son that he was a disgrace who I didn't want to be associated with anymore. Yet both those things happened. The Eubank victory was a precursor to our darkest days in boxing and it really is amazing to think how close Joe came to throwing it all away.

Chapter Ten:

Sacked

Imagine finding out you've been sacked via the back page of a national newspaper. Now imagine that the person who has chosen to sack you from the job you love is your own flesh and blood. Been there, done it, got the T-shirt. It hurts like hell and you feel like shit. Trust me.

The weird thing is, while I hold Joe entirely responsible for his dip, his career blip if you like, he was not to blame for the apparent end of our professional relationship. No-one was. Joe was given advice by top people in boxing to move away from me and resurrect his career and it became public knowledge after a series of underwhelming performances. What pissed me off was how it all unfolded.

There was no hiding from the fact it was in the public domain that the split was going to occur and the truth is, I was pretty content and relieved it was happening. Things with Joe had become volatile and rocky and I was no longer enjoying training him. It wasn't that I wasn't enjoying the job anymore, not at all. I loved working with the other guys – like Bradley Pryce, just set for his debut, and Gavin Rees.

I'd feared that my impetuous nature and spontaneity would lead to a moment when I'd wake up and want to take Jackie and the girls on some madcap adventure, but the truth was I had never been happier with my personal life. I loved my wife, the kids, living in Wales and running a boxing gym. I had found contentment I never knew possible. The problem was Joe and I had gone from loving every second of what we were doing to both dreading being in that gym together. Things were good with the other boys, they were really coming along. Gavin Rees had turned professional and won his first five fights looking very accomplished and Bradley made his debut in 1999, also looking a prospect.

So while I was beaming in terms of my day-to-day life, my

satisfaction at being part of a community, Joe was giving me a daily headache. Everything else was perfect. Jackie and I would socialise with local people, my brother Sergio was living in South Wales and I would still see plenty of Uccio when he came up from Milton Keynes. The rugby boys like Byron Hayward had added a gravitas to the gym, a certain prestige that wasn't just about Joe, and things were seemingly rosy. But the Calzaghe father/son professional relationship was falling apart and I felt helpless to stop the rot.

Joe had been experiencing wrist problems throughout 1998, including when he beat Juan Carlos Gimenez in quite underwhelming fashion, and even though people thought he'd do massive things the following year, it couldn't have gone much worse save for him actually being beaten. By the amazing standards I felt he could set, he was slipping beyond all recognition, and having to have an operation certainly didn't help matters. Joe got aggravated with me in early 1999 when he was just on the comeback trail from injury. I thought he'd be all right to start sparring again, but while doing a very light session with his future stablemate Gary Lockett, who had just turned pro, Joe then injured his elbow and faced another few weeks inactive.

Joe was losing momentum. The potentially lucrative earning power that followed his win over Eubank was declining as that performance was reassessed and niggling injuries tarnished his displays. And Joe didn't help. His attitude was poor. He acted as though he didn't care anymore. It was a crisis but I had no idea what to do about it.

Joe had the perfect opportunity to start 1999 right with what I thought was a timely and personal fight against Robin Reid in Newcastle. Joe and Reid had come up at exactly the same time and should have boxed-off to go to the Barcelona Olympics. I knew that there was a chasm between them when it came to talent so this felt like a good opportunity to exorcise some demons. The past wasn't Reid's fault of course, but the fight was nonetheless a great opportunity to dish out some payback on a guy who had run Joe down in the papers. Joe felt Reid did him a disservice too by not fighting him when he was a world champion, only agreeing to the contest after he'd lost his title to Sugarboy Malinga. That was short-sighted as Reid missed a big pay day. There was a lot of needle between the two of them and Joe didn't really like him. He should've been focused on smashing him to pieces. Instead he produced such a bad performance in the eyes of the public that for years afterwards Reid was able to be a braggart about Joe and how he almost won the fight.

Joe hadn't been sparring and was nearly seven pounds too heavy on the day of the weigh-in. He barely made weight by the skin of his teeth using methods I would never normally be comfortable with including running on the spot in a sauna with a sweat suit on. He'd dehydrated so badly he couldn't even eat properly after the weigh-in. He was on soft foods only.

He got even more agitated and pissed off after the weigh-in when he ordered an ice cream that somehow had shredded glass in it. Nothing had gone to plan and the fight was a difficult one, Reid boxing as well as he could and Joe as badly as he could. The judges all scored by a five round margin 116-111, two in favour of Joe and one in favour of Reid. I have no idea how one had Reid winning so convincingly, but there you go. Joe came back to the corner after the third round grimacing and I knew he'd broken his hand yet again and nothing about that fight was enjoyable for either of us. And things were only going to get worse.

I gave Joe plenty of praise for his performance and I meant it. He had to box intelligently and diligently with a busted hand and in my mind had been a clear winner, using his superior skills to get the job done. This wasn't winning a football match 5-0, sometimes you've got to be disciplined and do the basics well and be happy for a 1-0, any manager would tell you that, especially if you've had injury problems.

"Reid, a former 168-pound champ who'd never been knocked down or stopped, was Calzaghe's first tough title defence, and this was the closest anyone has come to beating him. In the split decision, one judge scored it 116-111 for Reid, even with a point deducted from Reid for a low blow. Maybe different judges liked different styles. Calzaghe flung his characteristic barrages, playing bongo on Reid's head, moving his arms as quickly as a clock's second hand. Reid was like a minute hand, periodically

ticking off a right-hand bomb. Calzaghe often ducked to avoid incoming fire and clinched. But the muscular Reid landed the highlight-reel shots, all rights to Calzaghe's face, including one that rocked Calzaghe's head to end Round nine. In Round eleven, they traded blows toe-to-toe, and Calzaghe gave as good as he got. In the end Calzaghe had outlanded Reid considerably, and it was enough for victory." Don Steinberg, ESPN.com

After Joe's hand injury healed, we prepared for a mandatory defence against an Australian named Rick Thornberry who we presumed Joe would steamroller as Henry Wharton had taken him out pretty quick a year or so before. Joe put him down in the first round but it just wasn't the real Joe Calzaghe in that ring. It was a great chance for Joe to cement himself as a superstar in his own country because the fight was in Wales, but he was well below his best and it went the distance. What people didn't know was that because of his injury problems Joe was a one-armed fighter at best. First it was the right wrist and then the elbow and lastly he broke his left hand against Robin Reid. The troubles were relentless. Joe was too nervous about his brittle bones to do any sparring before the fight whatsoever, a situation that was unsustainable. *Sunday Mirror* writer Ken Gorman broke that revelation and compared it to Manchester United warming up for an FA Cup final without kicking a ball in training. When all was said and done it was becoming an extremely unhappy camp whenever Joe and I got together, we were bickering and it needed to come to a head.

As usual after a fight, Joe disappeared for a couple of weeks' holiday to enjoy some downtime. I was also enjoying the break from the pre-fight tensions until I opened the *Sun* and read Colin Hart's story.

"Joe Calzaghe has sacked his father as trainer just as he enters the most important phase of his career. Enzo Calzaghe began coaching his son when Joe was nine and he turned his boy into a star... But Frank Warren, Joe's manager and promoter, has insisted the WBO world super middleweight champion must now make a clean break from his dad after twenty seven unbeaten

fights. Warren said: 'I have been promoting for nearly twenty five years and I've had to make some difficult decisions. But telling Joe and his father the time had come for them to part was perhaps the hardest thing I have had to do. I shall never forget the look of misery on Joe's face when I spelled out what has to happen. Joe and Enzo are extremely close and I felt bad at doing this, but sometimes you have to be cruel to be kind. I happen to feel Enzo has taken Joe as far as he can and someone else should take over. And I didn't pull any punches. I told Joe quite forcibly I think he has become complacent... Enzo agreed Joe has been cutting corners in training and that simply couldn't go on any longer. Fortunately, Enzo is a sensible man and he only wants what is best for Joe. There is no suggestion their relationship won't be the same away from boxing. There is definitely no rift over this. But there's no doubt it will be a terrible wrench for Enzo after nearly twenty years to have nothing more to do with Joe's career." Colin Hart, *Sun*, 4 August 1999

I felt embarrassed, humiliated and victimised and I was incredibly angry. My anger was not directed at Frank Warren. As far as I was concerned it had nothing to do with him and everything to do with Joe. Frank's job was to get Joe the best fights he could and promote his career. When he heard directly from me that Joe had been slacking off in training he had done what he thought best and that was to advise a split. What I was fuming about was that Joe hadn't come to me first, hadn't said a word and now here we were, split without me even knowing! Part of me was relieved to tell you the truth, but pissed off in the manner it had happened.

How could I be sacked? I had never signed any sort of contract to train Joe. That simply had never been on the agenda. As far as I was concerned it was always just a matter of time before we went our separate ways. I was perennially living with doubt that the working relationship would continue. But how fucking dare he let me take the rap for his shit fights? I was furious and the second BBC Wales called me for a response I let them have it with both barrels.

"The camp of world champion boxer Joe Calzaghe has erupted in a row over the dropping of his father Enzo as trainer. Calzaghe senior dismissed comments by manager Frank Warren that he had "gone as far as he can" as his son's trainer and should step aside. The veteran trainer said he was furious at the suggestion he was incapable of doing the job. 'That's a load of rubbish,' he said. 'How much further could I take Joe? He is unbeaten as a professional and is world champion. The bottom line is that he is fighting like a champion and not a challenger. He's not hungry anymore. In that Thornberry fight, he won every round, but I had to take the rap. Why this has happened, I don't know. This stuff about being too close because we are father and son is a joke because father and sons work better than anyone else. I'm a very realistic guy and a positive guy but he (Joe) has hurt me." BBC Wales, August 5, 1999.

That was exactly how I felt. There was talk about Joe going to work with a top trainer named George Francis and I couldn't understand it. To my mind he had endured one stinker of a performance against Rick Thornberry. It was hardly a crisis. But I realised it was Joe who had made me look bad. It was Joe who had created this situation. I stewed on it for days but was determined to keep my cool when he turned up because he was my son. Over everything else, I love him, even though the crap I was getting in the press was tough to take on the chin.

I was sweeping up the gym when I heard the door creak and Joe came in. I could tell he was feeling awkward and I had absolutely no intention whatsoever of making it easier for him. "Hi, Dad," he said. "Listen. Don't worry about all that stuff in the papers. I don't want to leave you as my coach, I just think it's best if I bring in another trainer to work with as well." I simply said to Joe in reply that he was my son, that I loved him and whatever happened professionally that wouldn't change. It was important to me that I make it plain and simple that my father to son relationship with Joe wouldn't be altered because of the work issues. I had always made that promise to him, to myself and to Jackie and I could tell he was relieved. He told me he'd be in for training later in the week and maybe we could have a chat afterwards. Two days later he sauntered in like nothing had happened and it was then that I gave him some home truths about the whole thing. Father first, trainer second... it always had to be that way.

"First off Joe, I need to tell you I am pissed off that you didn't talk to me first about wanting to bring someone else in," I began. "But the problem isn't me, it isn't the training and it isn't about us going stale or me having taken you as far as you can go. The problem is you."

He tried to make a point but I didn't let him get a word in.

"You've become lazy Joe, you've become sloppy and unprofessional and it makes me embarrassed to hear people talking all this shit about me when you are the one who is fucking everything up. The spark in you has gone out. You're training like a champion not a challenger and you've lost the fire in your belly, you've lost your hunger and you're falling flat. I don't want you training like a champion, Mr Billy Big Potatoes. I want you training like a challenger! Forget about being a fucking champion. If you don't sort it out and stop cutting corners you'll lose that title and everyone will forget all about you, whoever your fucking trainer is!"

Joe was stunned. We'd never really had a conversation like that while he'd been professional and it had been many years since I'd told him off. Certainly not since he was a teenager and then it was for getting really drunk and being picked up by a police car. His work rate and his dedication had never been something I'd had to address since he turned professional. We'd only had a problem when he was an amateur but that was just Joe being a typical teenager, which you had to expect.

He was shocked, a bit angry but very quickly accepted what I was saying. The injuries, the pressure of being on top and needing to stay there not just for the prestige and to fulfil childhood dreams but for the more adult, more important reason of having a family to support had changed Joe. I didn't want to shout at him, I didn't want to upset him or stress him out. He had enough on his mind, especially worrying about his hands so often. Maybe he wasn't going to come through this and things weren't going to improve, but I had to try to reach out to him, to snap him back to being the best he could be.

When I reflected on where I'd gone wrong, it hit me hard that for months Joe had been calling the shots in the gym. If I told him to do an exercise he didn't fancy, he'd say, "Fuck that, I'm not doing that. You do it." That wouldn't work and now I was talking as his trainer, not his father, he had to understand that.

I spelt it out to him. "It doesn't matter if I train you, if George Francis trains you or if King Kong trains you. The only person who can change the way you are performing is you."

"Things started to go wrong in my career and the first thing people did was question and blame dad and maybe even I was doing that myself. I'd fucked my hand up and wasn't sparring and I was slacking in the gym. Things were going shit, I was taking a lot of personal criticism from the Press around the Jimenez and Thornberry fights. I went on holiday and though I told Frank I still wanted dad to be involved, there were some names rumbling about to replace him as my main coach. It was just talk, but it got into the papers and I hadn't spoken to him first. Joe dumps his dad was what everyone was saying and it was fucking cruel really for him to find out like that and I was a bit embarrassed. Dad was cool. He was upset but he didn't go overboard. We had a great talk and then I had a long think about it and decided to stick with dad. Frank Warren had told me I needed to train harder and start to cope with my hand problems or give it up and put fear into me. I thought about bringing in a second trainer but realised I was looking for excuses. I lacked focus and a love for boxing at the time and the elbow injury was bothering me too. I was miserable and it meant my performances suffered." Joe Calzaghe.

The next time Joe and I had a conversation that serious and that intense was before he fought Jeff Lacy. But there wasn't a problem between us ever again. His training from then on was back to being spot on and his attitude and desire was never up for question. He admitted to me that a lot of what I said was right and he dropped the idea of bringing in another trainer to work with him even-part time. The whole issue passed and we moved on together ready to turn in a dramatically improved performance in

Joe's next fight against David Starie at the turn of the millennium, January 2000.

Unfortunately, as the cliché says, styles make fights and irrespective of Joe's form, frame of mind or injury problems there was absolutely no way of getting a good fight out of Starie who came to spoil, to ruin the fight and it was a horrible affair again, this time in Manchester with the crowd being made to sit through one of Joe's dullest nights in the sport. One judge only had Joe winning by three rounds, another gave him all twelve but it was far from vintage Calzaghe. Frank Warren made it clear to Joe he wasn't in the least bit impressed and I couldn't blame him. "You boxed shit," he told him in the ring before the verdict even came back. The worst thing of all was it was on television in America on Showtime as part of the Mike Tyson versus Julius Francis bill, so both sides of the Atlantic were bored stiff.

Did we meet Tyson? Yes we did.

"Dad almost got me chinned by Mike Tyson, it was absolutely fucking frightening. We were on the same bill when he came over to fight Julius Francis and I fought David Starie. We were staying in the Grosvenor Hotel and I was there for a week in a training camp. Tyson was staying there too and had booked the entire top floor because he had a huge entourage. Even though I was the one in the world title fight no-one gave a shit about me, it was absolute Tyson mania. I remember seeing Tyson in the hotel and I decided I had to get a picture with him. Tyson looked like he had a hard day but I thought he'd respect me because I was a fighter, so I went over and asked for a picture. He was a bit rude to say the least, uninterested and he just sat there passively but did agree to be in the picture. Dad took it and he fusses around for what felt like forever with the camera and then says, "Mike, are you going to fucking smile or what?" Tyson looked like he was going to rip his head off and dad just repeated the same thing again. "Fucking smile can't you?" Tyson started protesting that he'd had a long day and dad basically told him to man up. I couldn't believe what I was hearing! Tyson shot me a look that was genuinely intimidating. Later on in the week we sat down with him again and he laughed the whole thing off and was more easy-going apart

from when he started talking about boxing promoters. Then he scared the shit out of us! He was a very intense guy." Joe Calzaghe.

The Starie performance had been a disappointment but there wasn't anything to blame this time, other than an opponent who came to survive and yet more injury worries which were beginning to take too great a toll on Joe mentally. He was having more problems, this time with his elbow again and it was now three successive fights without a knockout. Frank was working on bringing over a very dangerous opponent named Omar Sheika and I could tell Joe didn't fancy it one bit. And if I'm honest I could understand why, because at this point it had been maybe thirteen or fourteen months since I had been able to get Joe any sort of sparring. He was defending his world title on pad work and fitness alone and that was a bad situation. Not sparring was unquestionably having a detrimental effect on Joe. He was going backwards alarmingly.

Thankfully Frank Warren laid it all on the line to him and said that other fighters had to cope with injured hands a lot and Joe would too. He couldn't keep trying to find big fights for Joe with the permanent risk of him pulling out injured. They had several heart-to-hearts around this difficult time in Joe's career. He told Joe to go away and think about what he wanted to do. In the meantime we were training daily with Gavin and Bradley and the other boys and then Joe and I would hit the local pitch and putt at Oakdale for what seemed like weeks on end. We were getting quite addicted. I went to Sardinia for a holiday and while I was away Joe stopped going to play golf as he didn't have a partner and reported when I returned that his elbow was giving him less trouble. I never let him swing a club again! We looked at ways to ensure Joe's hands were as well protected as they could be and slowly but surely he seemed to be finding something of his old self in the gym again. He agreed to defend against Sheika and we began preparing for what was inevitably going to be a very tough fight against a man who had just won against Glen Johnson in a performance people raved about.

Joe went to Cheshunt for two weeks of sparring after a request from Frank and after fourteen months without any one-on-one combat in the gym I think Joe felt like a fish out of water and really struggled to regain his rhythm and control. He came back with his pride bruised after being so short of his best – the boys in Cheshunt were taking the piss out of this so-called world champion – and I could instantly tell that fire and hunger was back in Joe. I was incredibly relieved.

Sheika was a Palestinian boy, but he fought out of America and I remember he had a huge entourage for all the press events in London ahead of what was a showdown at Wembley Arena. His camp did every bit of motivating for Joe I could possibly ask of them and then some. I should have paid them commission. It was absurd. Sheika was punching holes in posters, telling Joe he was going to "kill him," and all other kinds of nonsense that was inevitably going to do nothing but make Joe determined to shut them all up. "They are fucking clowns," I remember he said to me at the weigh-in, but I just grinned at them and laughed most of it off. I bit a couple of times and did some trash talking but Joe was cool as a cucumber. I think the previous months had seen him take a good, long hard look at himself and he wasn't up for insults and all of that nonsense. Joe was perfectly content to let his actions speak louder than words after some good sparring and with his confidence high he was like a different person. I was very happy with his preparation and told anyone who would listen that it was going to be the old Joe, the one who had won the world title and proved his talent against Chris Eubank. I thought he'd win inside the distance, I was sure of it.

He badly needed to perform and knew it and as ever when his back was against the wall, Joe fought like a dream and exceeded my expectations. Sheika was a big-hitting tough guy who had lots of hype in the States. But Joe blew him away. It was a great display. He showed strength, character, ability and he was hungry for it from the very first bell. When he stopped Sheika it felt like winning the world title all over again. The critics were silenced and opinions on Joe all changed again after the Sheika fight. It isn't in the Calzaghe nature to turn the other cheek and a lot that had been said and written about us had hurt me and it was fantastic to see Joe back to his best.

"Joe Calzaghe erased three years of frustration on Saturday night at Wembley Conference Centre, retaining the WBO world title for a sixth time with a fifth-round stoppage against challenger Omar Sheika. The Palestinian-American finished with cuts above both eyes, which required 14 stitches. Although Sheika remonstrated with referee Gino Rodriguez when he stepped between the fighters, he later conceded that Calzaghe, now unbeaten in 29 fights, remains the main man in the division. Calzaghe, an intelligent boxer with natural power and an ability to absorb the heaviest of punches, said it was his best performance since beating Chris Eubank to win the title in 1997. Sheika withstood the southpaw champion's clinical assaults in the first four rounds, and was beginning to draw Calzaghe into a tear-up until a clash of heads opened a cut above Sheika's left eye as the bell sounded for the end of the round. Sheika came out for the next round throwing wildly, but was picked off by the champion."

Gareth A.Davies, *Daily Telegraph*, August 14, 2000.

The next fight for Joe was a totally different kind of problem. Boxing is a simple sport really. Two fighters pitched into battle for twelve rounds with only their fists and their wits to determine a winner. It is basic stuff but not so when it's two friends in the ring. That becomes a completely different prospect. I didn't relish the prospect at all when talk began about Joe fighting Richie Woodhall. I was very uncomfortable with it. Initially I told Joe we shouldn't take the fight but after talking with Frank Warren we realised that it was a smart career move. Joe and Richie had been friends for more than a decade, stretching back to their days training side-by-side at Crystal Palace with the GB amateur squad. Richie came back from the 1988 Olympics in Seoul with a silver medal after boxing brilliantly in the final against Roy Jones. Joe spent some time with him in training camps after that and was always really impressed. Like Joe, Richie signed with Mickey Duff when he turned pro and he was always the guy ahead of Joe on our early bills with Mickey. We got to know Richie and his family well and we liked and respected them. Outside the gym, Joe had few close pals in boxing but those two hit it off and would hang about together. It was actually Richie who stopped Joe eating that ice cream with the glass sprinkles. They had a similar class and dignity about the way they went about their careers, inside and outside the ring, and the prospect of them fighting should have been truly thrilling.

I felt uncomfortable for my own reasons as well. Sure, I understood the uniqueness to the bout, what with Richie also being trained by his father. But Len Woodhall was probably the closest friend that I had made in boxing. If it was rare for Joe to pal up with his peers that was even more the case for me. I had nothing but respect for the man, he'd been kind to me when no-one else took me remotely seriously and I didn't like being in competition with him.

There was of course nothing to be done about this. Richie was very keen to take the fight and I sensed the Woodhall camp had fewer reservations about the friendship than the Calzaghe camp. That was a dangerous situation for us and I reacted by keeping things very regimented and serious in the gym, a contrast to our normal preparation.

Joe and Richie met for a head-to-head press conference just a week before the fight and it was incredibly respectful on both sides. The brashness Joe had in his early days, his tendency to talk badly about the other fighter had been disappearing anyway, but the fact it was Richie meant Joe simply didn't have those words in him. And Richie wasn't about to disrespect a great champion either, especially as he knew just how hard Joe had worked to reach the heights he had.

The press conference was in Sheffield, which hosted the fight and as we hit the motorway to head home I was dreading the long drive back. It was an argument Joe and I would have countless times as I drove him home to Wales from gyms, arenas or press conferences across the country. "Let's just stop at the services for a cup of tea and something to eat and then we'll be fresher, Joe," I would say to him.

"Fuck that, Dad, let's get home and then you can have something to eat. The weigh-in is six days away, you know I can't fucking have anything to eat, especially crap from a service station," he replied.

So I sat there quiet for a minute and would then think to myself that he was pissed off now, probably was going to go to sleep all the way home and I needed sustenance if it was a journey in silence. I'd at least stop and buy some sweets. "No, sorry, Joe, I'm the one who is driving and I'm hungry, so we're stopping for some food."

He grunted his disapproval and if things were frosty between us as we walked into the services, they got a whole lot worse.

"Enzo, Enzo, over here, come and join us!" a voice shouted at us. I looked up and there was Len Woodhall with Richie having a cup of tea at the services. "Lovely," I shouted back and over we went. I sat down with them and Joe had no alternative to follow. I would love to think at least one boxing fan saw us in that following hour and couldn't believe their eyes. Less than a week before a huge all-British world title fight, two trainers and two fighters set for battle were sitting in the services off the M6 having a natter about any old nonsense that had nothing to do with boxing. Joe and Richie were like two naughty schoolchildren sitting there with their heads bowed as Len and I put the world to rights over a cup of tea and a couple of jacket spuds with baked beans. Our mortified sons eventually struck up a conversation about their kids and I thought that was a nice note to finish on. South Wales was a bit further away than Telford so we left them there, said our goodbyes and got back into the car. Joe kept his words short but not so sweet. "I am fighting that guy in six days and you've just made me have a tea party with him. You are a fucking dickhead sometimes," he told me before closing his eyes, shaking his head and instigating the predictable return journey in total silence!

It seems an odd thing to do in retrospect, to make the boys feel that uncomfortable, but it was important to Len and me that things remain cordial and it was natural for him to call us over. If the shoe had been on the other foot I would have definitely done the same thing, even though it was incredibly unconventional and something that is highly unlikely to have happened many times before a big fight.

Joe and I talked in the gym about our approach for fight night and his mind was clear, the public wanted to see it and business was business. As much as Joe respected Richie and as much as he liked him, he knew that the entire Woodhall family were dreaming of him returning to Telford as a world champion. There could be no mixed feelings and no hesitations or second-guessing once that bell rang.

I told Joe what I believed to be true, that Richie Woodhall had a lot of silky shots and was a good fighter, but that Joe had far greater speed and far more power and that he had to go out and look for a stoppage win as he would against any other opponent.

It was a very good fight from start to finish and I was proud of both the boys on what turned out to be a tough night for British boxing with another friend of Joe's, Paul Ingle, suffering an horrific injury on the undercard that led to a lengthy battle in the hospital just to carry on living. His boxing career ended that night and it was lucky for everyone that none of us knew ahead of time or I am sure the fight would've been humdrum at best. As it was, it was superb.

Joe caught Richie with a fantastic shot in the first round and didn't capitalise, which troubled me as he was a tremendous finisher of fights. Was he hesitating because it was Richie? Things continued with Joe winning most rounds but Richie showing heart, bravery and no little ability in landing some really good shots of his own.

Richie was the more aggressive fighter as well by the middle sessions and I had to tell Joe, "He's trying to hurt you, stop him," at the end of a couple of difficult rounds. Richie landed some great shots and he absolutely nailed Joe in the seventh and the crowd were on their feet. But Joe didn't flinch, didn't wince, didn't crumble whatsoever and I think that broke Richie's spirit. He'd thrown his best shot and Joe didn't take a backward step. At the end of the eighth Joe was on top and I told him to get Richie out of there quickly. "He's finished, it's done," I told him.

Within two minutes of the ninth Richie had been down and hurt and the referee stepped in at the right time when Joe had him pinned to the ropes and no shots were coming back. I launched myself into the ring as I always do at the final bell, but I went straight over to see Richie and Len before I went to Joe. Len and I embraced; in fact the commentary team referenced it on Sky that

I appeared to snub my own son! I was worried about Richie's health. But thankfully he was fine and it wasn't until we returned to the back of the arena and heard the news about Paul Ingle that my great mood vanished away. Thankfully Paul won his fight for life and Joe received decent plaudits for winning what had been a hard fight.

"Joe Calzaghe's power proved decisive as he defended his WBO super-middleweight title against good friend Richie Woodhall. Referee Roy Francis halted an excellent battle at Sheffield Arena after 28 seconds of the 10th round, with Woodhall confessing afterwards: "No complaints". Woodhall, the former WBC champion, gave it everything, but it was a night when Calzaghe's combinations were in good working order." www.bbc.co.uk December 16, 2000

It was a great time for Joe who was about to receive real recognition for his achievements in the boxing world... In the UK anyway. And things changed for me. From being viewed sceptically at best as Joe's coach, I was suddenly gaining a reputation and respect. I had helped Joe to victory in a battle of the fathers in the eyes of the press and with Gavin Rees and Bradley Pryce winning every fight they were in, the praise kept on coming. I even heard rumblings from the *South Wales Argus* boxing correspondent Paul Tully that the paper had been enquiring as to whether Joe might be lined-up to be in the Queen's New Years Honours list.

But I knew that any such praise coming my way could easily be temporary. Joe was being mentioned in terms of fighting in America against some huge names and I knew that sooner or later, he was going to be forced to show in a fight that he was only human after all. His reign had been so supreme, his whole professional career, that he'd never been knocked down, never hit the floor even once. In my heart of hearts I knew that time was going to come. What would it be like if Joe finds himself tested, knocked down, in the doldrums? I had started to think about it, to concern myself with that thought. It was because I was reading more and more that his chin had never been tested. I thought that was absolute bollocks, but it sets your mind racing.

Against Robin Reid and Richie Woodhall, Joe's chin had been tested. Hell, even in some sparring sessions, you find a boxer might take an unexpected shot that can be a test of your chin. I was as confident as I could be. I eventually decided that when it did happen Joe would be just fine. But that nagging doubt, that little voice in my head just wouldn't go away. I was always fearful of that moment arriving.

I was also pre-occupied with thoughts of Joe reaching that next level and getting that super fight he craved. It seems shallow to look back now, to be so obsessed and feel you are entitled to something. But at that time a big fight in America, thoughts about Joe being knocked down and all those little details I wanted to work on following the Woodhall fight were matters of huge importance. I live in my own little bubble sometimes and I felt those things worthy of obsessing over.

Maybe what was driving me was the fact I was coping, for the very first time, with a loss that changes any person forever. The loss of a parent is a difficult rite of passage and my mother Victoria passed away in 1999 after illness aged sixty-nine. Mum dying hit me very hard because I felt as if I was just positioning myself in life as she had always dreamed. I was becoming a top professional and a good family man and a devoted follower of the rules and values she tried to instil in her kids. Finally I was the man she hoped I would be and then, just like that, she was gone.

Everything my mother ever did she did for her children who she adored. She was blissfully happy in marriage and worked exceedingly hard to ensure her children would have opportunities in life. I know that at times, more than a few times, I made her feel sad and angry. I desperately hope I also made her proud and I believe that to be true, but only after years of deciding I was the black sheep of my family and acting out accordingly. I wrote at the start of this book that my father is my hero. Thinking back on everything makes me realise that is just my tradition and heritage speaking. Both my parents are inspirational figures and I wish I had caused my mother less stress. I love her more than I could ever put into words. If Dad is my hero, Mum is my heroine.

What I was about to learn as I obsessed over little details of our professional life is that life deals you all sorts of cards and you can only play the hand you get, not the one you think you've got. My little issues seemed very unimportant considering how the next couple of years unfolded as there were far more important matters to be dealt with.

More matters of life and death.

Chapter Eleven:

Knocked Down... But We Get Up Again

Joe would without question reflect on the years immediately leading up to the Jeff Lacy fight in 2006 as the most difficult in his great career. We dealt with a situation that caused us all considerable heartache – a matter of life and death.

The first half of the decade was a far cry from the glory era where we became the most lauded boxing gym in the world. I seemed to be permanently fretting over some looming disaster. When I look back and reflect there was a lot of misery on my part and none of it warranted. I stressed myself out far too often without just cause. I regret it now.

After beating Richie Woodhall, Joe had become the top British fighter on the radar in terms of landing a big-name American, but each and every time Frank Warren tried to get that done there would be circumstances beyond his control that changed things. Joe could've fought Roy Jones, Bernard Hopkins, Antonio Tarver and Glen Johnson, but something always scuppered it. Normally it was because, despite talking about wanting the fight, they'd ask for the earth when negotiations started because Joe wasn't known in America and was too dangerous. The politics were exceptionally prohibitive. Or there would be an injury issue, another common hurdle we failed to clear. Joe would hurt his hand or one of the American guys would bust something in sparring and we'd go back to square one. The worst was when deals were agreed in principle but it was dependent on the outcome of another fight with boxer X facing Joe after retaining a title. That situation was set a couple of times and on both occasions the wrong fighter ended up winning from our perspective and then the rematch would be in the way of Joe's opportunity. It was maddening and scuppered deals with both Tarver and Hopkins.

It makes me laugh that people are already pointing their fingers at Nathan Cleverly for not taking a unification fight as if it is that easy. Boxing just doesn't work like that, or not in my experience. The big, name American fighters will have zero interest in splitting the purse fairly with Nathan at this stage in his career, in his mid-twenties with no huge scalps on his record. It's nobody's fault, that's just the way boxing is.

The worst culprit of all for not wanting anything to do with Joe was a guy I grew to despise, Sven Ottke, the IBF and WBA super middleweight champion who retired unbeaten in thirty-four fights in 2004. He never fought away from Germany and that protected his status as a champion.

Having slept through some of his fight footage I was in no doubt that Joe would wipe the floor with him, but Joe and Frank Warren both agreed that it was wrong that Ottke never left Germany to fight. He had controversial points victories against Charles Brewer and Byron Mitchell and in his penultimate fight, a lot of people think he was very lucky to get a points verdict over Robin Reid. Joe wanted to face Ottke for a long period, but the guy was never willing to discuss fighting in a neutral country and generally didn't fancy the prospect of ever fighting my son. It was like he saw the super middleweight division as being split down the middle and was happy with that. He'd do his thing in Germany and Joe could do his in Wales. Why spoil the party?

It bothered Joe that people tagged him with the 'Stay at home Joe' tag, because he was as keen as anyone to face the best calibre of fighter. One simple thing his critics don't understand about him is the fact that Joe was always more worried about being accused of ducking fights than he was of being beaten in the ring.

I had another concern too, a big one. At the back end of 2000, I began to hear whispers about the authorities taking an interest in the state of disrepute our gym was in. That was a key worry. I dread to think how many sleepless nights I endured. How could I train without a gym? Things were great in terms of the quality we were producing. I was no longer working with Paul Samuels who had licensing issues and left me when he was unbeaten in eight, along with another boy called Mark Hughes who was unbeaten in five fights before he stopped fighting. But Joe, Gavin Rees and Bradley Pryce were all undefeated. If the gym was going to be closed, or need renovating, where would we go and what would we do for training? That had me panicked.

On the plus side, Joe had rediscovered an ability to find that key shot that ends a fight early and he made very short work of Mario Veit in Cardiff even though the German got a big build up. It was an easy fight to sell – he had won thirty fights without defeat, exactly the same as Joe – but when it came to fighting away from home, on the big stage, Veit froze like Bambi staring into headlights. It was a lopsided and embarrassing affair. Veit couldn't protect his chin so his height and reach advantage meant nothing and Joe had him down twice before the referee waved it off with Veit being pummelled on the ropes. Bradley Pryce also fought on that bill and won an Inter-Continental title, which we viewed as a good stepping stone for him. At that point he was catching the eye more than Gavin.

Even though it was a lightly-regarded title, I was immensely proud of Bradley earning his own gold. Bradley, and I don't think he'd mind me saying this, wasn't only less talented than Joe and Gavin but he was even the least talented boxer in his own family! Bradley's eldest brother Byron was very tidy and another brother, Delroy Pryce, could've been a stunningly good fighter. He had the most picture-perfect jab and it was unfortunate that matters outside of the ring stopped them turning professional. They both loved the sport whereas I think Bradley had really wanted to do judo or karate when he was a kid and turned to boxing because that was what his father wished.

But Bradley reached a very good level because he was such a proud fighter, a true warrior in the ring. I knew how passionate he was about proving his worth, showing that he could come from nothing to be a success. He has the sweetest nature of anyone I've met in the sport and I always really enjoyed being in his company. Bradley and Gavin won nine fights between them in 2001 and people were noticing them as they had an exciting style.

"Joe Calzaghe demolished Mario Veit in just 112 seconds in Cardiff last night to enhance his credentials as the best super-middleweight boxer in the world. The Welshman hammered Veit to the canvas in the opening minute with a left hook and followed

up with a merciless assault which sent his opponent crashing down for the second time. The German, like Calzaghe entering the bout with an unbeaten record from his 30 fights, clambered to his feet but Calzaghe continued to connect with big shots and referee Mark Nelson had no option but to wave the contest off. Few could have predicted the sensational nature of his win which, following so soon after the demise of both Lennox Lewis and Naseem Hamed, has now established him as the leading British boxer of the moment. The emphatic manner of the Newbridge fighter's victory will surely impress even the most cynical observers across the Atlantic, who will watch the fight via tape delay on the Showtime television network... Promoter Frank Warren confirmed that the way forward now was for Calzaghe to fight in America and refused to give up on the possibility of securing a fight with American light-heavyweight Roy Jones."
Daily Telegraph, 29 April 2001

As ever though, when it came to it, Roy Jones had other options that took priority.

Joe didn't fight again until October and it was another chance to impress in the States as he was on the undercard of another Mike Tyson bill, this time in Copenhagen as we left Britain for the first time in Joe's career. He fought an American called Will McIntyre, who was in essence a blown-up middleweight and it was an easy night, Joe getting the stoppage in the fourth round. Again Joe told everyone who would listen he was off to the States.

Joe was named British boxer of the year after beating McIntyre, more an indication of the lack of sparkle at world level from the UK than him having a particularly stellar year by his standards. To crack America, Joe needed a top American fighter and Charles Brewer represented a good challenge at that time. The idea was that the fight would be in America hosted by US network Showtime who had a deal with Frank Warren, but that was scuppered by of all things, the Winter Olympics. Showtime's coverage of those games, staged in Salt Lake City, Utah, meant they didn't have the filming equipment they needed to host the fight so it was moved to Cardiff. It was the least happy we could be about having home advantage.

However, for what was unquestionably a tough fight against a guy many people thought had been robbed against Sven Ottke, Joe's preparation couldn't possibly have been more difficult. We were used to battling the aches and pains that are part and parcel of a boxer's life, but nothing prepared us for the call we got two weeks before the fight.

"I called Enzo on the phone, on his mobile and it was actually Joe who answered. I asked Joe where they were and he said training and I said they'd better sit down. I explained that Uccio had been in an accident and it was very, very bad indeed. I was at the hospital and they had already told me to expect the worst. I told them to get down here quick because he probably only had a few hours." Rhona Calzaghe, Uccio Calzaghe's wife.

I felt like I was going to be sick, pass out or maybe both. I was shaking as Joe relayed what Rhona was telling him. Uccio was Joe's godfather and with those two it had never been a name, only title. They adore one another and this news hit both of us for a loop. We drove straight to Coventry where he was in a critical condition in intensive care, hooked up to many machines.

Uccio had lost control of his car at high speed, skidding across both sides of a dual carriageway before smashing into a grass verge as the car flipped over. Groggy and barely conscious, my brother attempted to crawl away from the wreckage through the smashed driver's window. But as he tried to wedge himself out, the worst happened. Uccio was crushed as the car fell on top of him. My brother had suffered a broken back, severe head injuries, a collapsed lung, two broken legs and a broken arm and also had internal bleeding. He was in a coma when we got there and covered from head to toe in casts, bandages, tubes, bruises and cuts. It was like observing someone in a horror film, only this was real and one of my worst fears was coming true before my eyes.

Amazingly Uccio survived the first forty-eight hours which are critical and slowly, slowly, his condition improved. The doctors were astonished. He was hospitalised for five months, spending weeks in intensive care, and by the time Joe and Brewer stepped into the ring, he was still hooked up to ventilators. He had multiple surgeries and several of them were classed as high risk. Yet every time, my brother rallied and refused to give up the fight for life.

Joe coped admirably as I was barely there to train him, I was either at the hospital or phoning the family and my head was a mess. Luckily Joe managed better than I did to cope with the unique and stressful situation even though his heart was breaking about his uncle.

"The first major upheaval for Uccio in getting better was the prospect of not being there to watch Joe face Brewer, because he'd never missed a fight, not since Joe was an amateur. Uccio wasn't out of the deep water on the night of the fight, but he had already asked Joe when he came to visit him to arrange a helicopter because they couldn't get Sky TV at the hospital. He was deadly serious! He wanted a helicopter to pick him up, take him to the fight and then fly him back to the hospital. I had to do a running commentary on the phone to his mobile which he hid under the pillow during the fight. Halfway through the ninth round the nurse was doing her rounds and rumbled Uccio and she took the phone off him. When the judges' decision came in I phoned the hospital and said you've got to go and tell my husband the result of the fight. I was worried that if they didn't he'd do something totally stupid to try and find out. I really didn't fancy him jumping out of the window." Rhona Calzaghe.

"I would have done that too, I had to know the result!" Uccio Calzaghe

Most fighters only get out of bed a few minutes before the press conference on the day after a championship fight – if they get up at all – but Joe was in his car first thing, heading to Coventry so he could talk Uccio through the fight that had turned out to be an absolute humdinger.

Born and raised in Philadelphia and nicknamed 'The Hatchet' Brewer was as tough as old boots and the bullet mark in his chest was testament to that fact. He punched hard, really hard and had been a world champion when Joe beat Eubank. He was a fighter of real pedigree. They traded almost from the off in a very aggressive fight and with what was going on around us, I overstepped the mark in my criticisms of Joe after he got drilled by Brewer with a huge right hand in the seventh round. I screamed and shouted at him and that wasn't something I generally ever had to do with Joe and some of my other fighters like Gary Lockett and Enzo Maccarinelli. They don't respond to me being hysterical, simple as that. Joe got the message though, stepped it up to end the fight looking a million dollars and proved his point to a few people in the US with a great performance.

"Joe Calzaghe braved an awesome hail of leather thrown at him by Philadelphia hard-man Charles Brewer to maintain his iron grip on the World Boxing Organisation super-middleweight title at Cardiff International Arena last night. Following a savage duel of the type that had been fought on the mean streets of Brewer's native city, Calzaghe, 30, was given a unanimous points decision by margins of 117-112, 118-111 and 111-109.... As the bell went to signal the end of one of the most keenly contested world title fights of recent times, both men embraced in the centre of the ring. It may not have been very pretty, but the fight had been a classic."
Mike Lewis, *Telegraph*, 20 April 2002

Beating Brewer was supposed to be a defining moment in terms of moving on to the next level and into boxing's top tier. I believed that Joe had finally cracked it, the Americans were finally interested. Frank Warren was excited that he'd made great progress towards getting a stadium bout against Bernard Hopkins agreed but once again it didn't happen.

"A teleconference was set up in my office in New York for July 30th, 2002, and on the call was myself, Don King who was in the room, Frank Warren and Bernard Hopkins' lawyer, Arnold Joseph. Along with Arnold was a woman named Linda Carter, who was there on behalf of Bernard. We asked Arnold if Bernard wanted to fight Joe Calzaghe and we asked him how much money would he want if he did. The response we got was $3million and the fight would have to take place in the United States. After a little scratching of the head, we said 'Okay, done.' Frank Warren agreed

on the spot, Don King agreed and we agreed so, as far as we were concerned, all parties were singing off the one hymn sheet. Arnold excused himself with Linda and I can only assume it was to call Bernard. Either that day or the next day, they came with a new demand: $6million, double the sum that had been agreed, the deal blew up.....he had then no desire to fight Joe Calzaghe, that much is pretty clear. Joe got criticised sometimes for not having fought the big-name Americans, but in this case the fault never rested with him." Jay Larkin, then Showtime's Senior Vice-President of Sports and Event Programming.

That was that. We still couldn't entice the biggest fighters to face Joe because in my opinion they were scared of him. Two more victories, against Miguel Jimenez and stand-in Tocker Pudwill, were nothing more than pay-days fought in special surroundings. The Jimenez fight was in the open air at Cardiff Castle and was a really lovely evening and the Pudwill defence was in Newcastle on a bill Joe shared with Ricky Hatton. From then on I would say Joe and Ricky became good friends. They were thrust together because of who promoted them but they went on to be the two marquee fighters of an era in British boxing. Joe always respected Ricky and vice versa, but it became a genuine friendship.

Joe crushed Pudwill in two rounds and two years previously Pudwill had taken Sven Ottke the distance but of course this time Pudwill was dismissed as a bum because that's the British way. Even thinking about Ottke angers me to this day. That was a fight that needed to happen. It damages boxing when two men the public wants to see fight – like Manny Pacquiao and Floyd Mayweather – let politics stand in the way.

There were two downsides to an otherwise spotless 2002 and one was a first career defeat for Bradley Pryce when Ted Bami upset the bookies and our camp with a KO win. It came late in the final round of a fight Bradley had been controlling. There were only a few seconds left on the clock but it was a symptom of the fact I was losing the battle to keep Bradley focused on boxing and completely dedicated to his training. By his own admission he was drinking too much.

In the early days with Frank Warren. He's showing me how a running order works here. I didn't have that same closeness with Mickey Duff.

Here we are in the ring with Richie and Len Woodhall after the boys' great fight. They were and are true friends of the Calzaghes.

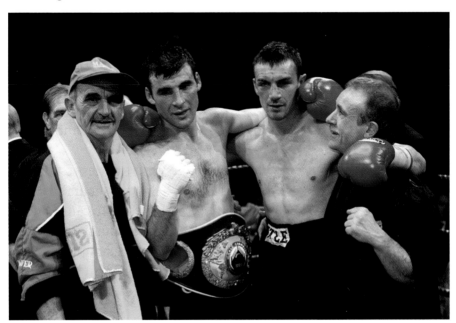

In the gym with the team that we had in our prime. From left to right, Nathan Cleverly, Kerry Hope, Vince Cleverly, yours truly, Sergio, Gavin Rees and Bradley Pryce. PIC: Chris Tinsley

In the ring with Gavin Rees after another easy win for him. I always loved Gavin and he was the easiest of all my fighters to put on my shoulders!
PIC: Mike Lewis

With Sugar Ray Leonard, an absolute legend in our sport. Ray was in Cardiff to promote Joe's fight with Peter Manfredo. He came to my gym and my home. I was humbled. PIC: Mike Lewis

Calzaghe Promotions. This was supposed to be our dream team. Back row, Gavin Rees, Paul Stretford, Joe, Tony Doherty, Bradley Pryce and Hari Miles. Front row, Mo Nasir, me and Serge. PIC: Malcolm Morgan

This was the day I called the local paper out of the blue to tell Michael Pearlman that I'd started demolishing my own gym to rebuild it. I think he thought I was joking.

And here is the result. I built one of the rooms into a kind of wall of fame. I love it.
PICS: Mike Lewis

With Nathan Cleverly
back in his early days.
I generally always
took a softly, softly
approach with him.
PIC: Nick Morrish

And still! Enjoying another
successful world title defence.
These were always the greatest
moments. PIC: Nick Morrish

With Enzo Maccarinelli. He's the heaviest hitter I've trained and I feel like I'm the only trainer who could get the best out of him.

And with Gavin Rees, my second most talented fighter, pound-for-pound.

Rocking in the gym with Sergio while fighters trained. This was for a charity song we did, but is my idea of heaven! PIC: Mark Lewis

Self portrait. I drew this looking into the mirror when I was feeling a bit down. I've always loved art and it's a flair my daughter, Sonia, inherited.

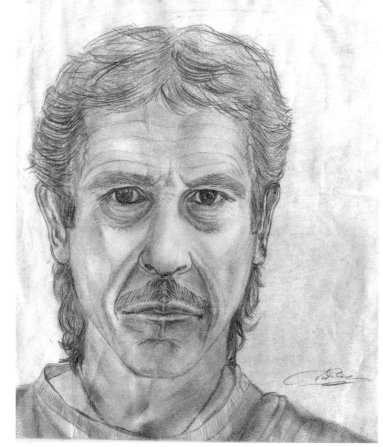

Playing ref at a local tournament in Trinant, something I do annually.

Joe and Robin Reid. They used to be huge rivals but Joe has let go of all those feelings now he's retired. It's a similar story between him and Carl Froch.

Joe and I with Roberto Duran in Cardiff at the WBC world convention.

Best Pals.

Me, Rocky, Uccio and Sergio at Planet Hollywood. Meeting him was like a dream, such was his influence on Joe as a child. I must've said "Hey Adrian," 20 times, I was so nervous!

Joe and I with Barry Jones and his father. Barry was always very helpful to Joe in terms of offering advice.

Sergio, JC Lewis, me and Uccio jam in the gym, something I'll often be found doing to this very day. My guitar is never far from my side.

Wise guys! Left to right: My uncle Gavino, uncle Rino and Dad in Sardinia. As far as I am concerned this picture could be a DVD cover for the Sopranos!

Sergio and I with Roy Jones Jr, who is a total gentleman.

Vanity – not bad for 63!

Joe's MBE, what a proud day.

Me with my MBE, an even prouder day!

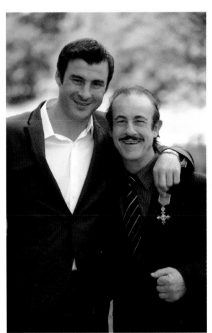

Celebrating my MBE with Joe. PICS: Malcolm Morgan

Joe and I in Little Italy enjoying life after Joe's destruction of Roy Jones.

Unveiling the bridge named in our honour. What a privilege. PICS: Malcolm Morgan

Training my friend Kerry Katona in the gym.
PICS: Malcolm Morgan

Chatting with our great mate James Dean
Bradfield of the Manic Street Preachers.
James came to interview me for BBC Radio
Wales. He's a family friend and we've
known him since he was a little boy.
Musically he's an inspiration and he is also
a huge fight fan. PICS: Mark Lewis

Meeting HRH Prince Charles at Cardiff Castle as he presented a Lonsdale Belt to Joe for services to boxing as he celebrated 10 years as a world champion. It was a great honour and I did my best to crack some jokes! PICS: Mark Lewis

Soon afterwards Bradley was arrested and convicted of assaulting his girlfriend and had his licence revoked for a year. But by then he had been beaten again and during his hiatus I heard he was drinking a lot. I talked to him and we agreed that I wasn't getting him focused and it would be best if he went and trained elsewhere. I couldn't put up with watching Bradley piss his career away and he went to train with Tony Borg in Newport. He didn't return to train with me until a heart-to-heart in 2005. I really didn't want him to leave because I cared for him. Don't let his arrest paint your view of Bradley as a person, because I believe passionately that he's a wonderful boy with a great heart. Alcohol can have a horrible impact on people, something I remember only too well from my nomadic rebellion across Europe.

A year after Bradley's troubles I went through the exact same thing with Gavin Rees. He got drunk and had a fight at, of all places, a funeral, and he too lost his licence for a year. Gavin kept training, avoided prison as Bradley did and stayed in the gym. But it felt like a complete waste of an amazing talent. I feared I couldn't ever bring them to their full potential the way things had gone. Perhaps in retrospect I needed to play 'mother' more. Maybe I should have been physically dragging them out of the pub like Sir Alex Ferguson would've done, but they were grown men and that's how I treated them. As far as I was concerned the day they had both turned professional I had to stop thinking of them as little kids, the same as with Joe.

Not only did I lose Bradley but the place I'd come to love was finally demolished. For everyone else it was a blessed relief, but for me it was an abomination, a travesty that the Newbridge Boxing Club was torn from the rafters on orders of the council on the grounds that it was unsafe and unfit for purpose in every single regard. I say torn from the rafters, the truth is the floor fell through with four people jumping on it and a gust of wind could've knocked the rest of the place down after that. Never have the council workers who demolished our gym had an easier day than they did then. Much like my first sexual experience, it was all over in minutes!

Community is everything. That was the message I was putting out in my battle to save the old place, but while it was a fruitless battle the good PR helped us immensely. The council were the driving force behind the demolition, but they never cut us adrift and promised to do all they could in relocating us. Simply put, they didn't want Joe Calzaghe training in Cardiff or Bristol. I have nothing but gratitude to everyone at the time who helped us and that was a long list. Other local boxing coaches including my good friend Gary Butcher from Cwmcarn ABC and another pal Keith Jefferies contacted me and said that they thought they might have found somewhere that would be a perfect home for a world champion. There was a building for sale set back on an industrial estate, right on the doorstep of where we had been, a few miles away on the Newbridge border. I went to have a look and it was perfect, absolutely sensational, I had goose bumps on first sight.

There have been many scratched bonnets and damaged tyres from cars that have taken the narrow, windy off-road lane that leads to a rugby playing field, totally protected from the thriving hub of business just a few feet away. The small disused rugby clubhouse is the first thing you see and to me it was perfection, hidden away like a jewel. And when I did that journey for the first time and parked up my car to inspect our potential new home my heart was beating hard. I went to the doors and pushed, but not until the third time of trying could I get them open. Large, corrugated metal barriers protect our new home better than the old one ever did, both from the elements and unwanted visitors. I saw two large, dank and dark corridors leading into one large room that was perfect for setting up exercise equipment, weights and whatever else. I continued up another dark passageway and passed a little kitchen area with a sink and a desk and then came to the main area that was wonderfully sized with space for a boxing ring (a proper one) and several punch bags. It's no exaggeration to say it was four times the size of where we'd been and it even has a toilet, though showers remained a luxury too far.

The clincher for me though was the land and especially the steep steps leading up to the industrial park. They have become the most trodden steps in Wales with so many boxers sprinting up and down them, day after day. Not only did we have everything a trainer could ask for inside the gym but outside too – steps for sprinting up and down, roads and mountains for pounding out the miles and rugby posts to hang from and do pull-ups on. The complete set! I love when we take training outdoors. That building has been my true home since 2003. It is infinitely better than our older premises in every regard and feels like a palace. It's perhaps not to all tastes though...

"The sign outside, "Newbridge Boxing Club," is beige, hand-painted, black trim. Little piles of trash dot the weedy yard. At one point, Enzo wrestles with the mulish front door to yank it open. Indoors, Joe intermittently spits on the floor during a congenial interview in the room next to the boxing gym. In places, it's just a few notches north of squalid. The walls do boast posters of the champ, and one of Stallone's "Rocky," but an Observer reporter spotted a dead mouse floating in a sink, and it's cold and dank in there." Chuck Culpepper, *LA Times*, April 18, 2008

Maybe it's not quite a palace then. But to me it's everything. If that is squalor I can't begin to imagine what they would have thought of the old place! In 2010 I changed the gym beyond recognition, but throughout the glory era the second incarnation of the Newbridge Boxing Club never altered and for Joe, Bradley and Gavin, it was a temple in comparison to a shack.

Thankfully, my brother Uccio made a full recovery from his accident after two tough years. It was touch-and-go and a bloody long road of rehabilitation, but he faced up to adversity and defied it. That was also the case for Joe in his only fight of an injury-hit 2003. Byron Mitchell had been a world champion but lost ludicrously to Sven Ottke by split decision in Germany. It was clear that Rocky Balboa wouldn't have beaten Ottke in Germany and everyone in British boxing knew Joe faced a major test when it was announced he'd be facing the 'Slama from 'Bama' as Mitchell was known. He had eighteen knockouts to his name and after the fight was delayed twice, first because of venue conflicts and the second because of TV scheduling, both guys were desperate to impress.

They faced off in Cardiff in June and I was keen Joe box, not fight or brawl on the inside and stand toe-to-toe, but the crowd got into him and the tactics went out of the window. Joe overwhelmed

Mitchell in the first round which was stunning, a blur of combinations and smart footwork and I was dead calm as they stepped out and the bell rang for the second round. It wasn't the fight I had planned, but Joe was revved up and that relaxed me.

They went back at it, toe-to-toe. Then, after only eighty-one seconds, the unthinkable happened. Joe was on the floor. At first I thought it was a slip but then I could see from Joe's legs that he'd been put down by a punch. The Cardiff crowd hushed. I was staggered. The father felt fear, shock. The trainer also felt shock as my brain scrambled to react. Joe looked at me as if to say, 'What the fuck is going on?' All he got back was, 'I haven't a clue.'

I had worried about this moment for years. Now it was reality and I didn't have a fucking clue what to do.

I snapped out of that quickly. There was no element of panic in me whatsoever after a matter of seconds. I needn't have worried so often and so long about this moment. As he was picking himself up I was thinking the same thought, over and over. 'Get up, get up.' My head had cleared. When he did get up I shouted at him to wait, to take the full count and give himself time. Then I started shouting instructions because I had no idea what he had left after being decked.

"Three Bs," I shouted at him as Joe threw three successive shots to the body. "Four Cs," I said and realised he'd come through absolutely fine as he snapped off a combination of straight jabs that forced Mitchell to crouch and lose his posture. How was this possible? "Four As." Bang! Bang! Bang! Bang! Joe fired in four great cross-shots as he stepped forward and shifted the momentum. I'd always believed Joe had a great chin and tremendous resilience and I believed he would survive his first knockdown. But this was more than surviving. "Stay clever," I yelled at him.

I realise now that the fact Joe threw the numbers of punches I shouted was possibly coincidental. Or a reflex action based on years and years of doing padwork together. All he was seeing was red mist. Being put down had stunned him more than me or the crowd and what followed was one of the most sensational sequences you'll see in any fight.

Within forty-five seconds of taking the first count of his career,

Joe stopped Mitchell with what I can only describe as a brutal succession of punishing and varied shots, many to the head. It was crisp, sharp, phenomenal boxing. To my mind it was the sport at its most exciting and just as Mitchell was dreaming of a world title, Joe roared back and put him down with a fantastic left hand. He followed that up with a blistering onslaught after the count and the referee was forced to step in. It had been incredible.

"WOW! Sensational is an over-used word in sport, but it summed up the way Joe Calzaghe defended his WBO super-middleweight title for the 13th time last night. Bring on that career-defining fight against Bernard Hopkins, Roy Jones, whoever. Because the Welshman proved categorically by stopping American Byron Mitchell in the second round at the Cardiff International Arena, that he is the best 168-pounder on the planet. It was just under six minutes of the most heart-stopping drama. The first round was a thrilling brawl that saw Calzaghe stun the challenger to the core. The second? We never got to the end of it, but what we did see was Calzaghe knocked to the canvas for the first time in his career only to pull off boxing's equivalent of The Great Escape... *In round two, Vesuvius erupted. It all started with the shock to end all shocks - Calzaghe was floored. He uncharacteristically walked into a brutal right-hand from Mitchell and, make no mistake, he was in trouble. But somehow, and heaven only knows how, he managed to turn the fight on its head within the space of no more than a minute. Instead of trying to grab hold of Mitchell, who was sensing a sensational smash-and-grab raid, Calzaghe decided the best form of defence was attack. Himself dazed, he pulled out some blitzing shots that hammered into Mitchell's head and suddenly things had gone full circle. Calzaghe knew he was on the verge of something dramatic and produced wave after wave of punches. Mitchell crashed into the ropes at first, but there was no way back for him. His eyes glazed over as he tried desperately to avoid the annihilation. But his senses had been stinted to the point of no return. And as Calzaghe threatened to do him serious damage the referee jumped in to stop it and that was that. Unbelievable!"*
Delme Parfitt, *Wales on Sunday*, 29 June, 2003

This felt like Joe's eureka moment, where everything would fall into place. In terms of excitement and sheer entertainment value for all lovers of boxing and sport in general this was going to take some beating, I reckoned. The pantheon of the greats beckoned and everyone in the United Kingdom was wising up to that fact. Joe was given an MBE a year after we'd first heard rumblings and Showtime TV Network promised us they were determined to get Joe fighting in America against a top name. Frank Warren had been doing all he could and would continue to do so. We were finally there.

But incredibly and ridiculously, it took another three years to really have Joe arrive as a superstar. And when the chance finally came, Joe and I came within a whisker of blowing the whole thing.

Chapter Twelve:

Career Defining to Re-defining

Joe was well placed to move on to the next level as we headed into 2004, but circumstances went against him and he started slacking off a little bit, thankfully snapping out of it before any great damage was done. The year was one of transition in the Calzaghe gym and if I am brutally honest the same was true of 2005.

For Joe the year saw boxing overshadowed by his divorce. It's not a subject he felt it appropriate to discuss in his book for the sake of his children and it's certainly not my place to discuss it here. It wouldn't be fair to Joe or to Mandy. However, many people reading this book will have gone through the same thing and will know what an impact the end of a marriage can have on every aspect of your life and certainly your professional career.

Joe won a routine mandatory challenge against Mger Mkrtchyan, a tougher test than he made it look and yet another fight that we hoped would be the one to elevate him. However, when Joe pulled out of fighting Glen Johnson at light heavyweight because he threw out his back, the whispering started again that he was cherry-picking opponents. It was before Johnson beat Roy Jones and Antonio Tarver, but it would still have enhanced his reputation. Between missing that fight and the divorce, Joe was pretty low and the camaraderie had completely gone in the gym at that time. Gavin Rees was banned from boxing while Bradley Pryce had hit a losing streak, beaten three times in five fights, and after our heart-to-heart had left our gym too. Things weren't working with us at all well and I think Joe felt lonely and isolated. When that happens I tend to overcompensate in giving him attention and end up annoying the life out of him.

The one absolute beacon of light during that time was our newest recruit to the stable. He was a modest, polite, extraordinarily talented travelling boy named Tony Doherty who dropped in from time to time as his family were living in

Pontypool. Doherty trained in Manchester with Gary Lockett at Brian Hughes' gym but he wanted to be closer to home and came and trained with me instead. What a talent. He's extraordinary. Just like Gavin Rees he has sensational flair in the ring, not just speed or deceptive power but intelligence, a grace that you simply can't teach. Watching Tony Doherty boxing at his best is like watching David Gower bat at cricket or Lionel Messi dribbling a football, pure poetry to the trained eye.

The problem with Tony was always an issue with weight. He didn't have that magnetic attraction towards a pub door like Gavin and Bradley, but Tony struggled to be disciplined with his diet in between fights and unfortunately he remains a largely unfulfilled talent after a blistering amateur career. As a person though Tony is absolutely first rate and his massive family always made welcome additions at ringside on the bills we had leading up to Joe's retirement.

Aside from Tony's visits things were flat for us in the gym as Joe struggled with the nastiness of divorce and a quite serious back injury causing him pain, worse than he usually experienced with his various hand injuries. He was lined up to fight Kabary Salem, an Egyptian who fought out of New York. Salem might as well have been a native New Yorker because he did all the trash talking you associate with some American boxers. It was unbelievable. At least when Bernard Hopkins talks, bored as you become, you know you're listening to someone worth hearing from. Salem talked like he was the baddest man on the planet, but as far as I was concerned he hadn't earned the right. Things got really heated at the head-to-head press conference. Even though Joe tended to play down the pre-fight hype these days, I was sure he would eventually bite when he heard Salem, but instead it was me who snapped at the rubbish being spewed out by Salem's trainer, Nasser Nettles, who we had come across previously when he was in Omar Sheika's corner.

"If tomorrow's Edinburgh showdown between WBO super-middleweight champion Joe Calzaghe and Egyptian challenger Kabary Salem contains as much action as yesterday's press conference the fans should be in for a treat. And if the Newbridge

southpaw and his New York-based foe do not provide enough entertainment, there is always the possibility of a supporting bout involving the two trainers, Enzo Calzaghe and Nettles Nasser. The meeting, at a city centre hotel, started peaceably enough, with each side showing due respect to the other. But when Joe told Salem that if he wanted to go home with a belt he should go to a superstore and buy one for his jeans, things began to get a little out of hand. Nasser, who was in the corner of Arab-American Omar Sheika when Calzaghe halted him four years ago, told the Welshman he was in for a bloody and tough evening. 'I feel this is going to be Calzaghe's last fight,' he insisted. 'Come Friday, he's going to be history.' The champion's father decided to put in his two-penn'orth.' Salem has a better chance of running across the Sahara barefoot than he has of beating Joe Calzaghe,' said Enzo. 'I'm fed up with all your yapping. Take a tablet and shut up.'And for a moment, it all turned a bit nasty. Happily, everyone calmed down before coming to blows. But it certainly adds a little spice to tomorrow's event at the Royal Highland Showground." Gareth Jones, South Wales Echo, 21 October 2004

I badly wanted Joe to beat seven shades of shit out of Salem to shut up his trainer once and for all, but I wasn't helping matters and I actually pissed off Joe far more than usual in the hours before that fight. It seems funny now but, trust me, at the time Joe wasn't laughing. It started when we were heading down to the weigh-in in the hotel when the lift made a series of funny noises which I pointed out to Joe. I don't know what possessed me, but I jumped up and down to 'test' the lift. Guess what? It failed my test. The thing broke down in between floors and after an hour of being trapped with a son who was hungry, dehydrated, anxious and increasingly likely to murder me, we crawled on our hands and knees out to safety thanks to the engineers. Joe was beyond angry at me. And when I then spilt his bottle of energy drink that he'd been longing for, for six hours, all over a WBO official wearing a tuxedo a few minutes before he stepped onto the scales, he snapped.

"I remember that day. Perhaps the closest I ever came to actually

punching dad in the face. I was so dehydrated when he spilt that drink I could have cried. He was trying to help but I wanted to kill him. I told him to get the fuck away from me and he skulked off. Then I felt bad." Joe Calzaghe.

When the opponent's camp subsequently accused Joe of cheating after weighing in at exactly twelve stone and wanted him to tread the scales again it set the stage for an enormously bad tempered fight and a very forgettable night for us.

By this stage Sergio, my younger brother, had been learning the ropes and training alongside me in the Calzaghe gym for around three years. I had also started working again with a kid who'd first come to the gym when he was nine years old. Nathan Cleverly idolised Joe and dreamed of being a boxer and his dad Vince dreamed of taking him there. Vince was also now assisting me so we had a good team in place.

But while Sergio was a very good trainer in his own right, he point blank refused to work Joe's corner and he never did. Sergio just couldn't stand the anxiety of watching Joe fight from such close quarters. He'd instead sit with Joe's two boys, and later his girlfriend, at ringside and scream his head off. However, for this particular fight he was needed to carry Joe's belt into the ring and when he got there he marched right over to Salem's corner to make a point to their noisy trainers. It was an act of defiance. Nettles reacted badly and things turned ugly. Nettles made some wise crack about being able to take the belt and made a grab for it. Serge saw red mist and the pair of them went nose-to-nose. It almost got out of hand, but thankfully the fight got off on schedule even though Joe's performance might as well have been phoned in.

I blame a lack of motivation after a tough year but Joe was awful that night. He got dropped in the fourth round, though this time there was no panic on my part as I saw he wasn't hurt. Only his pride had been damaged with just the second knock-down of his career. He did enough to win clearly on points but he's never watched the fight back and I didn't until writing this book. It does not make pleasant viewing and I can promise you I won't be watching that rubbish again.

Both fighters were dirty on the night, Joe let Salem set the tone in that regard and the crowd grew frustrated and I couldn't blame them. There was a clash of heads and I could see the frustration in Joe, he was pissed off. He felt he was treading water at all times, fighting this guy and that guy in defence of his title but never really making a significant step forward in terms of enhancing his reputation. We felt his critics had decided Joe had gone as far as he ever would and he was unable to prove them wrong.

The press didn't slam Joe but everyone knew that without a defining fight his star which only shone brightly in the UK anyway was going to fizzle out. It was a shitty time and things seemed to only get worse for him. The WBO refused to sanction a fight with Brian Magee in Belfast at the last minute because Mario Veit had become mandatory contender again. Veit's promoter won the purse bid and it was set for Veit's backyard of Germany, so the Magee fight was called off at the last minute on their instructions and both Joe and Brian missed a pay day. Joe was annoyed about that but was far less bothered than you'd expect about going to face Veit in Germany. The fact it was away from the UK was the most exciting aspect for us.

At a time when it was necessary from a PR standpoint, 'Stay at home Joe' was going to someone else's backyard and you have to think that Veit really fancied his chances after Joe's stinker in his previous fight. We were out of our comfort zone and everyone was warning that in the hands of the judges over there justice might not be served. German judges were notorious for hometown decisions and having taken an interest in the career of Sven Ottke I could well believe that to be true. With Joe's morale down, it was potentially a dangerous night ahead, but luckily Joe found a way of getting out of his depressed mood.

He was totally convinced after a chat with Frank Warren that he could get a fight with another newly-crowned super middleweight world champion, Jeff Lacy, and that had snapped his focus right back. He assured me not to worry about the judges in Germany and promised to knock out Veit and then take care of Lacy. He was focused and hungry again and of course was true to his word with a great display over Veit that silenced the crowd.

"Joe Calzaghe never wanted a rematch with Mario Veit and he never wanted to fight in Germany, but on Saturday night he fought intelligently to stop Veit in six rounds. Calzaghe, 33, retained his World Boxing Organisation super-middleweight title for the 16th time and is now, so he claims, looking for another title or two. In Brunswick on Saturday night he looked as composed and aggressive as he had in any other fight, which is surprising considering his on-going divorce problems and an unintentional break of six months. In 2001, Veit was knocked out in just 112 seconds and Calzaghe had claimed that he would do the same in their totally unnecessary rematch. By round five Veit was ready to go and was knocked down for the first time, but somehow survived until the bell. He had no chance in round six when he was again sent sprawling. Calzaghe insists that he wants to meet the winner of the August International Boxing Federation super-middleweight fight between American Jeff Lacy and Robin Reid."
Steve Bunce, *Independent*, 9 May 2005

Joe was super-excited about tackling Lacy after he bumped into him and his trainer at a Ricky Hatton press conference. They told Joe to his face they'd come to England for a unification fight and Frank Warren was getting closer and closer to getting a deal agreed. The dream was on from that moment for Joe. The deal was done for November 2005 and we couldn't wait, even insisting on a warm-up fight first to get prepared. That was Joe's idea and I was both surprised and impressed. His brittle hands could've stopped him, but he decided he needed to be as sharp as possible. Frank lined up Evans Ashira and to our complete and utter incredulity and terrible frustration Joe did injure his bastard hand in that fight.

Joe stopped Ashira in five rounds in Cardiff but the cost was massive. The plan had been to eat Ashira for starters and then devour the main course of Lacy, but after sailing through with one hand, in the dressing room Joe was disconsolate. Frank Warren sent a photographer in to prove Joe's hand was really broken in case the Lacy camp cried foul, but it was clear the fight was going to be postponed at best. There was no way Joe would heal in a month and we had no way of knowing how Lacy would take the news. He had a warm-up fight too, with Robin Reid, so I didn't expect a problem but I was wrong again. Lacy's promoter Gary Shaw tore into Joe through the media and said he didn't want to do business anymore.

"X-rays have revealed Joe Calzaghe has broken the metacarpal bone in his left hand in the course of his one-sided points win over Kenyan, Evans Ashira. The 33-year-old Welshman, who was forced to jab his way to a 17th successful defence of his WBO title, will now be in plaster for a month and out of the ring until next year, with no guarantee of a rescheduled date with Jeff Lacy. Lacy's promoter Gary Shaw who had previously criticised Calzaghe for taking the fight against Ashira in the first place, said, 'Tell Frank Warren that he and Joe Calzaghe don't rule the 12-stone division any more.' If he (Warren) is actually serious about February then he should bring Calzaghe to the United States because that is the only way he will ever see Jeff Lacy again. I have absolutely no interest in wasting my time with Joe Calzaghe anymore,' Shaw said. Shaw's deteriorating relationship with Warren puts even a New Year meeting in major doubt, irrespective of the negative X-ray results which Calzaghe was given during a trip to hospital in Cardiff." Mark Staniforth, Press Association, 12 September 2005

It felt devastating to have come so close and seemingly have injury completely end Joe's dream of a fight he craved with every fibre of his being. Lacy had, as I expected, steamrolled through Robin Reid, putting him down four times in a fight that the American public seemed to think signified Lacy was the real deal. I had my thoughts on Lacy, but until the fight was made official there was no point in me sharing them with Joe or anyone else.

We all endured a miserable run-up to Christmas as the whole family felt the anxiety that Joe was feeling. He couldn't continue at the same level he'd been at. There was no point. His injuries were becoming more and more of an issue and had left him at a crossroads. If he went the way of more (in the eyes of the public) mundane defences, there would be no turning back. He'd been a world champion eight years without losing a fight and yet in 2004

Ring Magazine named Joe as only the twenty-seventh top boxer in the world. To my mind he was a guaranteed top-five fighter, but the world needed convincing and we were running out of time.

But then we all got what we wished for that Christmas. While Joe and I were feeling sorry for ourselves, Frank Warren had persevered and eventually got the deal done with Gary Shaw when it seemed to us to be dead in the water. I was ecstatic. Joe against Lacy was rubber-stamped and set for March 2006. Frank saw the opportunity to fill out the Millennium Stadium, but unfortunately Six Nations rugby commitments scuppered that plan. It meant the fight had to be in an arena and it was eventually booked for Manchester at the M.E.N which is far bigger than the arena in Cardiff. Frankly, by that time we'd have happily taken the fight in a barn in Jeff Lacy's Florida backyard. This was everything Joe had been working for and the opportunity was ginormous with US television companies immediately stating a desire to screen it live.

Preparation began just after Christmas and Joe virtually ignored the celebrations as 2006 got under way. He was training like he was demented, his focus, desire and attitude all unfathomably brilliant. He forgot all about his injured hand and was transfixed by the fight. Nothing else mattered to him. I was just happy his hands were holding up.

Then, of course, came the troubles and that visit to Harley Street. It truly was a horrific feeling waiting for the diagnosis when Joe headed down to London and as I've detailed, I was forced into some serious soul-searching. There was a great deal at stake and ultimately, I felt like I was doing the right thing for everybody when I talked him into taking the fight.

Better things were coming to all of us aside from just Joe's super fight with Lacy. We were a team again in the truest sense of the word. For the first time in a couple of years we were a gang who would spend hours and hours a day together. Joe's isolation and dissatisfaction was a bad memory. Nathan Cleverly was showing great promise and talking about going professional and Gavin Rees and Bradley Pryce were back. They were both on the winning trail and boxing well and were moving onwards and upwards as was Tony Doherty. If Joe beat Lacy there were some big pay days ahead and the boys wanted a slice of the action on the undercards. Both of their attitudes seemed better following all the trouble with the police. Bradley had been alarmed by how badly he was regressing in the ring since leaving our place and looked at our stable and thought he should be part of it again. He asked me like a man to take him back and when he promised me he was fully focused, I was only too happy to do so. He quickly proved himself to me too. That, by the way, is no slight on Tony Borg. Tony has done absolutely amazing things at St Joes with the likes of Gary Buckland, Lee Selby, Fred Evans and Sean McGoldrick. The next generation of Welsh stars have been coming from his gym.

It was nice having Vince Cleverly, Nathan's father, around the place. It was a lot like all those years earlier when I studied Paul Williams intently and tried to learn all I could. Vince had that same desire. The similarities didn't end there. Vince was a musician before he was a trainer – I've gigged with him many times - and of course he would go on to take his son to a world title. Hell, he was even married to a woman named Jackie!

Nathan, Gavin, Bradley and Tony Doherty fought fifteen times between them in 2006 and won every contest. Another kid came to our gym looking for somewhere to train when he turned professional and I took him on as well. He was a Merthyr boy named Kerry Hope. Kerry might be the most quiet, softly spoken boy I've ever trained but he was a pleasure to have around the place. Both Gavin and Bradley used to wind Kerry up incessantly though, and I'm not sure he enjoyed the camaraderie aspect of the Newbridge Boxing Club as much as Nathan did. But Kerry has his part in the Calzaghe story without a doubt. And with his three victories in his debut year of 2006 we were set for an unbeaten year with over twenty fights. But of course the main attention was all on Joe's clash with Jeff Lacy.

The nice thing was it wasn't just Joe fighting in Manchester on that night. Kerry and Nathan were on the undercard and so I prepared all three of them together. Nathan and Kerry could spar, Joe couldn't. But the fitness drills, the stuff we did outside of the gym, we did as a team. That's how it always had to be. If Joe would have done his steps circuits and road running solo it would have conveyed the message to the boys that Joe thought he was superior and above them and he didn't want that. He loved the companionship and it was only going to get better, though little did we know it then. Even for the biggest fight of his career Joe happily shared the spotlight with two rookies because they were his stablemates. It's ridiculous to suggest Nathan and Kerry didn't benefit immensely from that experience.

The true struggle once we got past the wrist issue was totally changing our normal training regime. Joe was fighting at 2am for US television and the whole bill was starting late as a result. It meant evening and night training sessions, so I barely slept. Enzo Calzaghe does not lie-in, not ever! Being lazy and lying in bed all day is a reminder of when my life had no direction and I hurt people. I don't like to think about that anymore. Besides, it's a waste of a day full of opportunities to just sleep and be idle. That's how I look at it.

Come fight night it was a lot of waiting around, because there was a huge hiatus between watching Kerry and Nathan enjoy routine wins and then the main event. I remember I kept mentioning to Joe that the day before at the weigh-in Lacy wouldn't look Joe in the eyes. "I know Dad, I know what it means too, I get it," he kept saying over and over, but never coming out and stating that he believed as I did that Lacy was scared. But Joe knew he was in Lacy's head.

Finally the hour was upon us as a security guard knocked on the door and said, "It's time," and it was an explosion of noise as Joe hit the ring. During the introductions Lacy was still avoiding eye contact. The enormity of the situation he was in had finally dawned on old 'Left Hook Lacy' and he didn't like it one little bit. The bookies rated him as the clear favourite, but Joe was at his stunning best as the gamble to fight with one good hand paid off spectacularly. I was responsible for convincing Joe to fight, but that display was all him. It was Joe as his genius best in every regard.

In the very first round Lacy hit Joe precisely in the temple with his best shot. That big right hand that had Robin Reid reeling and everyone else convinced Lacy was the real deal, the super middleweight Mike Tyson, Iron Jeff. He snapped it and Joe never even winced. He could deal just fine with Lacy's power, now it was time to see how Lacy would do up against Joe's phenomenal skills and ability to dominate with his relentless style and speed. Within three rounds he'd 'slapped' Lacy so badly he was a swollen mess. The American looked completely startled and he had no answer at all. Joe was electric as I knew he would be in a fight that just meant so much to him. At the end of the first round a barrage of punches had connected with Lacy and Joe had his hands raised. It continued in that vein and at the end of the third round I told Joe to take a breather, have a round off. "I don't need it," he said. "I'm flying and he's nothing," he told me. "He can't punch for shit."

It was pure theatre, Joe was delivering like a dream and Lacy was being blown away. Shot after shot, combination after combination, it was a complete massacre, total and utter destruction, and Joe said afterwards he felt like Superman. Lacy's eyes were cut, he was swinging wildly and Joe was picking him off time after time, throwing flurries of so many shots I couldn't count. This wasn't punches in bunches, it was destruction by the dozen. I felt bad for Lacy. He expected to come over and beat up a washed up old man and instead he was dissected by one of the best in the business at his absolute peak.

There was no let off and the Manchester crowd were electric. When you know, you know and those fight fans were witnessing an historic performance and realised it early in the fight. I didn't think Joe lost a single round. He collapsed at the final bell and I lifted him up and told him he'd done it, that it had been a masterclass. And when we got out of the ring, I made sure he heard me. "You were fucking brilliant," I told him.

The plaudits came and from that point on, they never stopped coming. The judges confirmed what I thought. It had been a shut-out victory. Lacy didn't win one round. Joe's career had transformed in the space of thirty-six phenomenal minutes and I got to stand there and watch my son's dreams come true. The world was watching and Joe had delivered the performance of the year. It remains one of the proudest moments I have experienced, one of total and utter contentment and happiness.

"Joe Calzaghe defied injury to produce one of the greatest

performances of all time by a British boxer and unify the world super-middleweight titles in Manchester. Calzaghe crushed Jeff Lacy, America's IBF champion and supposed next big thing, flooring him for the first time and claiming every round on all three judges' scorecards. Calzaghe's mesmerising display was put into context by Lacy's venerable trainer Dan Birmingham, who said: "I have never seen a better performance by any fighter, anywhere in the world." And it was all the more remarkable, given a serious left wrist problem which Calzaghe revealed had almost forced him to pull out of the fight three weeks ago." Mark Staniforth, Press Association, ringside reporter

No-one could have ever predicted just how one sided the fight would prove to be and Joe had reached a new level in terms of recognition. People tried to claim Lacy was overhyped until the people claiming that realised they were the ones who had overhyped him! There could be no doubt whatsoever that Joe was the real deal and the best thing of all was that now the United States fight fans knew it. Even though Manchester staged the massacre, Joe was happy to start in the middle of the night to ensure US fight fans saw their new Tyson fighting live against this washed up has-been. So Joe's performance reverberated on both sides of the pond as Lacy had had a good following and viewing figures were decent.

I would like to express my gratitude to Jeff Lacy. All credit to him for coming to the UK and taking a fight many other American boxers had claimed to want but never delivered on. I hoped he would come back strong, but feared the manner of defeat meant he wouldn't. Joe put him down in the final round for the first time in his career and almost won by stoppage and Lacy appeared completely broken long before the final bell. Sometimes you see that happen in boxing, which can be a cruel sport, when a single defeat or the manner of it removes your aura and you're never the same again. Lacy has lost three of his last four fights at the time of writing this and definitely was never the same again. That is a shame.

"The Jeff Lacy fight was of course the biggest night of my career

and the catalyst for me reaching new heights. And Dad is right in saying that I wouldn't have been prepared to take the fight if it wasn't for him talking me off the ledge. When you are a professional sportsman who is always expected to be at their best it can take a toll on you. At times I have felt overwhelmed by that and when I got on the train to London with shooting pains in my wrist I just wanted to disappear and forget all about the fight. The doctor told me it was at least a week of no action and as far as I was concerned, with where my head was, that was that and there could be no fight. I fully expected Dad to back me up. When he didn't I was taken aback but his passion and conviction that he was right and I was wrong was convincing. I trust my dad more than anyone and I was willing to put my faith in his words. I talked to Frank Warren and he was telling me exactly the same thing. All I could do was get as fit as a fiddle. I couldn't spar and there was no getting around that, but I did everything else with the most intensity I physically could. It was clear Lacy wasn't comfortable in the press conference and at the weigh-in and I felt that outside of the ring he was beating himself. I just stared him in the eyes and talked about how great I was and could see he believed it all and that fired me up even more. On the night the crowd were amazing and I couldn't have fought better. I was nowhere near rested enough as I was struggling with sleep and my hand hurt like hell but it was like a dream, I felt untouchable. Dad had been right all along about me taking the fight and it was the key moment for us as a partnership, I guess. I put all my faith in his decision and I am very thankful for that." Joe Calzaghe.

It dawned on me the next day as the pride set in that it had also been a huge night for me, a huge event in my training career. Suddenly I was legitimised; people decided that I really was the real deal as a coach and it wasn't just Joe's talents. I stood in the corner for twenty fights in 2006 and they all ended in victory for a fighter from my stable. I could do no wrong all of a sudden and I absolutely loved the feeling of recognition. It's vain I know, but to pretend otherwise would be untrue. It had aggravated me that people didn't know how good Joe was and didn't appreciate my part in that. What more could I do? All my boys were winning.

Like I said earlier, if you tell someone something for long enough they start to believe it. For years I had heard anyone could train Joe. Now all I was hearing was that I was the best trainer in Britain. How can I pretend I didn't love that?

The fact I had a stable had almost been by accident. Bradley, Gavin and Nathan all came to the gym from a very young age and made it whereas dozens of other boys never got that far. Tony Doherty had been a familiar face over many years and only Kerry Hope was 'sent' to me because of his location and mutual promoter. We were a decent unit but other than Joe it was very low profile.

Shortly after Joe beat Lacy, Frank Warren called me to say that his cruiserweight Enzo Maccarinelli, a giant puncher from Swansea, would need a new trainer because Charlie Pearson had decided to retire. Enzo fought on the undercard in Manchester on the Lacy bill and as a Welshman with an Italian father I had always taken an interest in his career. It sounded potentially like a good fit to me but I asked Frank to get Enzo Macc to give me a call. I thought it was important we were on the same wavelength before I agreed to anything for both our sakes.

Enzo went one better and came to Newbridge to visit the gym. Joe liked him a lot and after five minutes in his company I was only too happy to take him on. A few months later he was training with us full-time and doing some light sparring with Joe, who I could tell relished the competition. Enzo in my mind was a world champion in waiting and he'd been delivered to me because I was trusted and respected. That was all I had ever wanted. As I watched Joe and Enzo laughing and joking, it dawned on me what we had built.

I continued to scan the room as Gavin and Bradley worked on the pads and Kerry Hope and Nathan Cleverly did likewise. I was working some drills with Tony Doherty, and Vince Cleverly and Sergio were both in attendance, watching and advising. It was all focus until Joe turned and told his uncle Sergio in fairly robust language that it was time for him to get the kettle on! It sounds silly, but it was a moment I felt really captured what we were all about. Joe had become a superstar and as far as I was concerned that meant only positive things for everybody else. Opportunities were going to come our way. It was the most exciting period of my life. Pure exhilaration in knowing you were on the verge of creating something special.

We called ourselves Team Calzaghe and suddenly, instead of being known as Joe's trainer, I was known for my stable of fighters. I thought I had six potential world champions in the gym but we were just a small coaching team in a fairly poor area of Gwent in South Wales. It was unheard of for such accolades to come from such humble surroundings. I also felt I had at least three fighters who were capable of being champions immediately in Bradley Pryce, Gavin Rees and Enzo Maccarinelli. Nathan Cleverly wasn't there yet, but the rest were destined to wear gold as soon as their chance came I felt.

Incredibly I was right. One of the greatest success stories in the history of British boxing was already underway.

Chapter Thirteen:

Winning

Once Joe was finally given due recognition across the world, things changed for everyone in the gym.

I'm not giving away insider secrets by explaining how this works. Boxing is like any other sport, which in essence, is like any other business. If you have a small gym in South Wales with several fighters on small cards and small purses, it is hard to get them more lucrative opportunities. If you have a world champion, obviously it becomes somewhat easier for his stablemates to be on larger, televised cards. If your main man is the best in Britain, that lucrative window opens even wider. If he's propelled overnight to being one of the hottest commodities in world boxing, the slipstream of opportunity for everyone else becomes a tidal wave. I was determined to take advantage.

It took a bit of time, but after the Lacy victory the momentum changed for all of us and there was a buzz about Welsh sport that I'd not known for a long time and wouldn't again until the rugby side reached the World Cup semi-final and the soccer side flourished under the tragic Gary Speed in 2011.

Joe was signed to fight IBF light-heavyweight title holder Glen Johnson at the Millennium Stadium in July 2006 in a bid to become a two-weight world champion after missing his first chance to face Johnson with a back problem. It was billed as a homecoming show and was a massive card for British boxing with Danny Williams against Matt Skelton as a heavyweight clash and other up and comers from Frank Warren's stable including Kevin Mitchell, Matthew Hall and Stephen Foster all getting an outing.

The rest of the bill was all Team Calzaghe. That afternoon and evening I made my way to the ring on six separate occasions as Bradley Pryce, Enzo Maccarinelli, Tony Doherty, Gavin Rees, Kerry Hope and Nathan Cleverly were all victorious. It should've been a glorious debut at the Millennium Stadium, but we were a man down.

Sadly Joe pulled out with injury. His hand wasn't in the best of shape and he felt he wouldn't do himself justice. He'd come pretty close to changing his mind and I recall it was on a Thursday that he was waiting to chat to the doctor before telling Frank Warren what he'd decided. Joe had a column in the *South Wales Argus* for many years and when their boxing writer, Michael Pearlman, called Joe, they did the column on the presumption the home-coming fight was a go. Joe never mentioned the injury and I remember feeling quite pleased to hear him saying all the right things, totally relaxed. But it was all a front. About six hours later Michael was frantically shouting down my phone that Joe hadn't let on at all that the fight would be off and now he wasn't answering any calls. Michael informed me he'd just had a call from Richard Maynard, Frank Warren's media man, to say Joe had pulled out. I didn't even know myself at the time for certain. I had to speak on Joe's behalf so they could change the column and when I saw Joe later I could tell he was upset. He was so gutted that he had to pull out of the fight he turned off his phone and locked himself away in the house. People never saw that side of Joe, but he was low and worried what people would say about him.

It would have been a tremendous opportunity to cash in on the Lacy victory and move into the realms of the two-weight world champion greats. Joe vowed that once his hand healed he was ready for any big challenge and for the first time I could remember, he faded into the background for a couple of months and his stablemates overshadowed him.

Joe went on holiday with his girlfriend and the gym was absolutely buzzing about the big night at that wonderful stadium in Cardiff. In Joe's absence there was a huge window of opportunity for the other boys in the camp. I think they relished the chance to step out of his shadow.

It would be unfair to take any credit for where Enzo Maccarinelli was in his career when he joined us. The guy was already fighting at a world level and his challenger for the Millennium Stadium bill was an absolute colossus from Argentina called Marcelo Fabian Dominguez in a battle for the interim WBO cruiserweight title. Essentially my very first outing with Enzo was when he became a world champion. But I would like to think the manner of victory had my stamp on it. Enzo fought with crispness and a level of intensity that I don't think we'd seen before and he dealt out severe punishment to a legitimate heavyweight. He stopped the guy with an onslaught in the ninth round and for me it was a show-stealing performance and a magnificent feeling.

For Enzo to realise his dream in the Millennium Stadium was a true triumph. The credit though, in honesty, goes to Charlie Pearson, his previous trainer. My glory with Enzo was in the way he followed up the victory. It was a shame Enzo never got to win the title in the manner it was expected he would. He was supposed to fight Johnny Nelson but that bout never happened in circumstances similar to when Joe had been set to meet Steve Collins, Nelson retiring on medical grounds just weeks before he was facing Enzo.

Kerry Hope and Nathan enjoyed points victories in the afternoon and Tony Doherty didn't keep me hanging around with a first round KO win. Gavin Rees won on points over six and if I am honest looked a little uninterested and that left Bradley Pryce who, as it transpired, was set for the biggest night of his career.

Bradley returned to our gym that year with a completely new attitude and application. The competitive nature of the stable by then, the breadth of talent all around pushed him on like never before. He had a terrific comeback fight with me against Michael Jennings up in Preston after being inactive for nearly a whole year. He lost on points but was unbowed by a guy being tipped for world titles and never wilted under strong, sustained periods of punishment. The warhorse was absolutely back and on a decent local show in Newport in March, headlined by Gary Lockett, Bradley upset the odds to take Ossie Duran's Commonwealth light-middleweight title. He made his first defence against Hassan Matumla at the Millennium Stadium and never looked classier, winning with a stoppage. For those few months, Bradley was as good as anyone else in that gym. He belonged at the top table too and that first defence in the Millennium Stadium was an awesome moment for him.

Probably the best fight of the night was Gary Lockett's successful WBU title defence against his friend from the amateurs

Ryan Rhodes. It was a terrific battle between two fighters with excellent technical proficiency and in Gary's case underrated power. I had never been more impressed with Gary than I was that night, and I had followed his career closely. How lucky for me that some months later he too joined our stable. Gary trained up in Manchester for many years and that suited him, but once his first child was born he wanted to stay settled in South Wales.

We ended 2006 with a big night back at the MEN Arena in Manchester. Joe faced a tough, tough guy named Sakio Bika on an evening where other Team Calzaghe fighters came of age. Bika had a head made of granite, wasn't afraid to use it and has rightly been described by my son as fighting like a bad guy out of the WWE. That is totally accurate. I think the fight remains one of the few times Joe's machismo meant he fought the wrong way, letting his heart rule his head as he got into a toe-to-toe or more accurately head-to-head kind of contest against an awkward street fighter. It was like the Byron Mitchell fight only without the stunning finish. He so wanted to impress for the TV cameras, more in the States than the UK I suppose, and to put on a show for the Manchester crowd. It was as if in 2006 Joe hailed from Stretford or Moss Side. The backing the local boxing fans gave him in those two fights at the MEN was phenomenal. He was on the verge of being a stadium fighter and the MEN became a temporary home from home and Manchester a key city in the Calzaghe story.

The fans might have loved it but I was fuming after he got caught with a massive headbutt that split him wide open above his eye. I couldn't get him to execute the game plan. "Just fucking box him, Joe. What the fuck have you been doing? Box away, jab him and you'll dominate. You don't even need to take one punch let alone a fucking head butt," I yelled at the end of the round.

He didn't listen, or couldn't help himself. There was never a fear of Joe losing that fight but even he admitted he'd been wrong to box as he did and he was very disappointed afterwards.

"Joe Calzaghe last night wrapped up a 19th super-middleweight title defence - but he was made to fight all the way by brawling rival Sakio Bika. Bika was docked a point for butting Calzaghe,

but the Newbridge southpaw won comfortably on points and may now turn his attention to Antonio Tarver or Clinton Woods – if he opts to step up a weight. But despite a wide margin of victory, Bika's rough-house tactics upset Calzaghe who will have hardly impressed a watching US TV audience. 'I'm disappointed with my performance, I wanted it to be a spectacle but I just couldn't get off, I wasn't 100 per cent and it showed,' said Calzaghe. 'I'm disappointed I couldn't finish it off. It was a great fight last time but not this time. He came in with his head, he was strong and my lack of ringside sharpness showed but a win's a win. I didn't get my tactics right'. " Peter Shuttleworth, Wales on Sunday, 15 October 2006

But while Joe was licking his wounds backstage after a come-back-down-to-earth sort of an evening, I was unable to stay with him and worry about where it all went wrong. Even though about ninety-nine percent of the crowd had left the arena, our night wasn't over with a huge examination for Nathan Cleverly. Nathan fought another unbeaten prospect called Tony Quigley who started a massive favourite and had a win more than Nathan on his also unblemished record. He was tipped to fight at British title level straight after he beat Nathan and it was supposed to be open and shut. As it transpired Nathan looked like a potential world beater, albeit at joke o'clock in the morning in front of no more than a handful of hardcore fans and two journalists. Quigley had a terrific first round but Nathan took everything he had, smiled and worked behind his jab. As the rounds went on he became more and more dominant and ended it with a stoppage in the fifth round after systematically breaking down Quigley. It was the first time Nathan exhibited the wow factor that makes everyone take notice of a prospect.

Enzo Maccarinelli capped off a successful night for us collectively with a destructive win. He'd been in a barnstormer with Mark Hobson over twelve rounds when Joe defeated Lacy, but the rematch was more comprehensive, a concussive blow to the head ending the fight in the first round. I was pleased with that. I felt Enzo was progressing well and we headed into 2007 full of optimism for some great nights and big pay days for everyone.

Boxing is a sport where money and glory tend to go hand-in-hand and luckily for the rest of our stable Joe's final two years in the sport included three of the biggest fights in his career.

It seemed unlikely politics would allow for a unification match with fellow super middleweight world champion, Mikkel Kessler, who also had an undefeated record and Joe was itching to move up to light-heavyweight anyway. Into his mid-thirties, Joe found it harder and harder to make twelve stone and it was painful being around him in the week leading up to any weigh-in. He was surviving on thimbles of water and a lettuce leaf or two and that's no exaggeration. But it seemed a real shame not to commemorate what would be Joe's twentieth defence of his WBO world title and he agreed to celebrate the landmark if the venue and opponent were right.

Frank Warren needed to bring over a fighter who could carry interest in the US, because it was blatantly obvious from the July show at the Millennium Stadium that fans wanted desperately to see Joe have at least one last fight in Wales. After he pulled out against Johnson the ticket sales dropped off markedly. The Millennium Stadium was available and in Peter Manfredo, Frank Warren had found a fighter that carried at least some fascination for the US fight fans. Manfredo had made his name not in the professional ranks but in something far more significant sadly, in the current day and age, as he was a big time reality TV star. Manfredo had been on *The Contender*, a show devised by Sylvester Stallone and featuring Joe's all-time hero Sugar Ray Leonard as one of the judges.

It was perfect really, a chance to say goodbye to the UK fans as Joe was adamant he was going to close out his career over in America. Joe was comfortable financially and was consumed with his legacy, so it had to be the States, a chance to banish the 'Stay at home Joe' tag once and for all. He'd won forty-two professional fights on the trot and yet still he felt he had something to prove to the public. I found that extraordinary. The downside of his quest to step up in class though meant relinquishing his IBF super middleweight title that he won from Lacy. He had to make a mandatory defence for them and wasn't willing to do so. I thought it was a short-sighted stance by the IBF, but that was how it had to be.

Perhaps Joe's desire for recognition was heightened by a knock at the end of 2006. The world and his wife began tipping Joe to be Sports Personality of the Year at the famous BBC awards. Even Darren Clarke, the red-hot favourite with the bookies, commented that Joe should win. The buzz built and built and I had a good feeling. As it was, neither Joe nor Darren won. Zara Phillips did. Joe was a statesman and so was Darren and they praised Zara and her achievement. I thought it was a fucking outrage. Basically Joe unified his division, proved himself the best of the best and lost to a horse. Did Zara Phillips jump over fences herself? No. I vowed never to think about that shitty award ever again. How I would change my tune. My ranting about it at the time in the papers makes me look silly now. We live and learn.

The April show was going to be fantastic and got even better when Enzo signed a deal to fight David Haye in a massive unification battle. Arguably, that would've contended as the true main event notwithstanding Joe's historic twentieth defence. However, it was all off twenty-four hours later with a contract dispute and Enzo's best chance to beat Haye maybe passed with it.

The main event was a big challenge for me personally because Manfredo was trained by Freddie Roach, generally considered to be the best in the world. As it was, he was busy with Oscar De La Hoya on the night so Sugar Ray Leonard stepped in and was in Manfredo's corner. That was ultra bizarre. Leonard is an absolute god in the Calzaghe household, Joe thought he could walk on water and he made for a nice subplot. He was so unbelievably nice too; it was hard to imagine he'd been in some of the fiercest battles in the history of the sport as he is such a gentle soul. We got to know him well during the fight hype, he even visited our gym and my house and that was wonderful for Joe. Never meet your heroes? What a load of bollocks.

Come fight night though there was no fairytale story for Manfredo in front of thirty thousand fans and nor did I ever fear there would be. Ordinary fighters look ahead to their next opponent when they are overly confident. Normal champions can also get caught out when the pressure is on to deliver, but Joe doesn't fall into either category. Within three rounds Joe had Manfredo out of there, some felt prematurely as the referee Terry O'Connor arguably stepped in sooner than he needed to, but everyone agreed they were poles apart in terms of class. What will stay with me more is the atmosphere, the electricity inside that brilliant venue. I had three big fight nights at the Millennium Stadium and they were as exhilarating as it got and certainly the most draining evenings I've had in boxing. I needed a rest after those evenings, the mental energy expended and time spent running around trying not to miss anything was daunting.

On the undercard, Bradley Pryce had a twelve round title defence and Nathan Cleverly went eight rounds for the first time. Gary Lockett dispatched Lee Blundell in three rounds in his first fight with me and Tony Doherty stopped Taz Jones in the seventh in a rematch following a controversial encounter earlier that year. Kerry Hope and Gavin Rees both went the six round distance and Enzo Maccarinelli was even faster than Joe, blasting away bare-knuckle champion Bobby Gunn in just a couple of minutes to win his second world title defence. Total that all up and I was in the corner for almost three hours and forty rounds on the day, with every fighter victorious. Intense doesn't begin to cover it, but I had to be there for my fighters.

I'd come back to our dressing room and pause for breath and then before I knew it another one would be up. I don't think any coach could ask for anything more than what I got from the boys either. Halfway through Kerry Hope's victory though, I called out: "Don't let him get too comfortable, Tony." My mind was so fried I momentarily forgot who was fighting. Only the adrenaline carried me through. Even though I am a very fit man for my age, the mental toll was considerable, but it was impossible not to get caught up in the atmosphere and gee yourself up for the next fight. Ridiculously, despite all that, I couldn't sleep when I got home and I drove Jackie mad, waking her up to tell her all about it all at 4am.

I wouldn't trade those bumper nights though and magnificently, that was just the warmup ahead of the most intense night in boxing I ever experienced.

A significant development for Joe was that Kery Davis, the Senior VP of HBO boxing sat at ringside in Cardiff as Joe dispatched *The Contender*. He confirmed afterwards that HBO were essentially interested in Joe fighting any of the big-name Americans, or indeed, Mikkel Kessler, the WBA and WBC champion if that fight could be made. After so many years HBO were very keen on Joe, and Frank Warren explained to us that it would be a big fight with a huge interest. Frank Warren and Kessler's then promoter Mogens Palle were in negotiations for months and months, but the success of Joe's defence against Manfredo swayed the deal, I believe. If Joe could sell 30,000 tickets to fight a largely unknown name (in the UK anyway) like Manfredo then a huge unification fight was likely to attract a phenomenal live gate.

Another key to the fight getting made was Kessler having an absolutely brilliant attitude towards the whole thing. As far as he was concerned, it was yesterday's man versus today's star and the venue was irrelevant. He saw beating Joe on television in front of live audiences across Europe and America as the chance to write his own ticket and as a trainer of a champion I can only admire that bravado.

The fight was signed in the summer and it astounded me the bookmakers made Kessler the favourite even though there was little in it in truth. Kessler was undefeated and he'd seemed invincible up to that point, but quite honestly when were people going to wise up? I told everyone in the lead up to the fight that Joe would beat Kessler, I guaranteed it and I'd been studying the guy for the best part of two years by then. I respected Kessler enormously but I didn't fancy his chances against the Bernard Hopkins or Winky Wrights of this world and thought Joe would beat both of those guys. Kessler was at the time just too orthodox. He boxed in straight lines and though he hit hard, no more so than other fighters Joe had faced. As I saw it, he wasn't dynamic enough to beat Joe and had a significant disadvantage as pertained to fighting in the biggest fights on the grandest stages.

I thought, however, that Kessler was a far superior fighter to Clinton Woods or Carl Froch, two guys with big mouths who banged on about fighting Joe for years and years. They weren't in his class and in my view, not much of a step up from someone like Robin Reid (though I now rate Froch higher than I did, he's proved his calibre). Kessler on the other hand had a great deal to admire about him and was a dangerous opponent.

The reason I think the Calzaghe versus Kessler fight will stand the test of time is that there was a great simplicity to it. By way of example, Joe's next fight would be notorious before it began because of the build up. There was something very artificial about the way that fight came to be with Bernard Hopkins making what could be taken as a racist comment. But there was none of that boxing hoopla and brash behaviour with Kessler. This was about two undefeated fighters going head-to-head for three shared titles. A great venue and a great prospect when you factor in the classic ingredient of one being the next big thing, an up-and-comer looking to be at the top of the food chain, against the cool cat that is king of the jungle and has been for a decade. As a fan, that would've sold me. I didn't need theatrics and we didn't see them.

Joe told me as soon as the fight was signed that he thought he would beat Kessler, but it'd be his hardest night ever. I told him I agreed wholeheartedly and I am not sure that is what he wanted to hear. Joe trained with tremendous energy all summer and was probably never better physically prepared for a battle. Brilliantly, the public responded and estimates are that there were just over fifty thousand fans in attendance that night, though it felt to me like about two hundred and fifty thousand.

While Joe put in the hours – largely under Sergio's supervision – in the gym and flew across the globe to promote the Kessler fight, we had a big old night to prepare for at the Cardiff International Arena that was coming up fast.

And in a lot of ways, I think that night was probably the pinnacle of my career.

Chapter Fourteen:

Defining Nights

Even though the Kessler fight was looming large, in the spring and summer of 2007 Joe was at the back of the line in terms of my attention. My hands were full with fighters set for action in weeks not months and they needed me to prioritise them. That was how it had to be. I can't stress that enough. I would never have taken on any other fighter, let alone another eight or nine, if I felt I couldn't give them the same level of care as Joe. Many times I would spend an entire session working with four boxers as a group, but when we were done I would only talk to them about battle plans one-on-one. My ethos was that they were all individuals and if they wanted to talk, it should be just the two of us so they put their own ideas across and know they had my attention. Each fighter worked on strategy with me individually and that was always my approach. Joe never had a problem with this system and I think he loved just being one of the boys.

Enzo Maccarinelli was the headline act for that upcoming show at the arena in Cardiff and he faced by far and away the toughest challenge of his career against Wayne 'Big Truck' Braithwaite, an American powerhouse who had been a world champion and defeated only twice, his résumé was stellar. Everyone had question marks over Enzo because he'd been decked by a journeyman called Lee Swaby earlier in his career and this was a considerable jump in class. Nathan Cleverly, Kerry Hope and Tony Doherty were also in action that night and incredibly another fight was mooted that had my heart pounding.

Frank Warren had a Frenchman named Souleymane M'baye signed to a deal. He had won the vacant WBA light-welterweight title in Bolton against Raul Horacio Balbi. It wasn't a great fight and I wasn't so impressed by M'baye who looked lucky to me to be given a draw in his first defence against Andriy Kotelnik. I fancied Gavin could step up a weight and do a number on him and become a world champion, but I didn't know if that was even a possibility.

We had a meeting with Frank in London to discuss something to do with Enzo or Joe and I remember bringing up Gavin Rees and saying he could step up in weight and beat M'baye. I think initially Frank thought I was crazy. Gavin was 26-0 at that stage and had never really had anything resembling a defining fight. Because of his troubles, it had taken Gavin nine years to accomplish very little, even though he'd proved unbeatable on a domestic level.

Brilliantly all the stars aligned and it worked out. Frank made the fight. It was a wonderful prospect to me because it was so unexpected. No-one was talking about Gavin Rees as a world champion. With Bradley Pryce as Commonwealth champion, Nathan Cleverly beating Tony Quigley and Joe and Enzo leading the way as world champions, Gavin had if anything got lost in the pack. Now he was facing the chance of a lifetime.

To my mind he was still my second best boxer. For pure talent, he was Joe's only challenger. If any fighter could step up in weight and be trained to shock a champion who had yet to be tested it was Gavin. If it wasn't against the rules I would have bet a very large sum of money on that fight. When the bell rang Gavin was a 7-1 outsider with the bookies to win. I completely understand why given how underwhelming his professional career had been, but we all knew how good the kid was. The whole of Newbridge was planning on visiting the bookies with their hangovers because they all had bets on Gavin to win.

It was another glory night for us and in many ways I feel it's the night in boxing I hope people most remember me for. This wasn't a night where a superhuman boxer produced his scintillating best. This was about hard working, exciting but often underappreciated top talents from Wales shining on a world stage and I felt like everything I had worked for had come to fruition.

I had come a long way from the dingy bars and nightclubs singing with my brothers, the days of walking by the river high as a kite in Amsterdam and balmy or plain barmy nights in Sardinia, and I had dedicated my life to a career as a boxing trainer. That had been my passion for over twenty years and now, suddenly, a kid with me for that entire period has a chance to be a world champion. The little sod whose father Mike and I would scream at until we were blue in the face when he was a cheeky little bastard at only ten years old had a chance to join the greats. It made me so proud to have reached that level with Gavin.

Enzo absolutely dominated Braithwaite, forcing him around the ring and threatening to win it inside the distance. Braithwaite had brilliant power and did catch Enzo once or twice, but he couldn't land anything like the sense-numbing left hook which Enzo put him down with in the fifth, one of the best punches I've ever seen. Braithwaite just managed to take it the distance but Enzo won by a massive margin on the scorecards and the crowd stood to show their appreciation of a stunning display. From being rated as a standard fighter who was maybe lucky to be a world champion, all the talk was suddenly of a unification fight for Enzo, but I hadn't been surprised by the quality of his performance. I had total faith in him beating Braithwaite. Because of the huge size differential, Gavin's fight gave me more concern.

We had worked on a simple plan to beat M'baye. Gavin is relentless and very quick so it was obvious that he'd box on the inside and work the body, throwing in clusters so that a feigned shot to the head would open M'baye up. He is a rigid fighter and I studied him and imagined seeing him bamboozled by Gavin who had the speed to keep going back to that tactic and then hitting the road and backing up out of range. I thought Gavin could do that for long enough to rack up round after round and didn't think M'baye would know how to respond.

Our approach worked beautifully. Tactically I don't think there can be any doubt at all that it was my personal highlight as a trainer in my entire career. Gavin and I came up with a plan we were both very comfortable with and he executed it to perfection. Gavin has done practically an entire life of sparring with Bradley Pryce who is bigger than him and furiously trying to smash Bradley's head off several times over twenty years of friendship was the perfect preparation for M'baye.

Gavin to my mind won each of the first seven or eight rounds as M'baye looked like a robot that was malfunctioning. He hadn't bargained for the speed and fluency Gavin had and he looked desperately out of his depth. Gavin's fitness at the time was no problem but the step up in weight brings with it an obvious pitfall in terms of the damage inflicted when you take a punch. Gavin has a chin to be proud of, but in the final half of the fight he was struggling to stay out of reach and his own punches lacked that zip they had earlier as body shots began to take their toll. M'baye was limited, but still the heaviest hitter Gavin faced. Gav hadn't been twelve rounds in six years and a world title fight is a hell of a time to return to that level of intensity.

In round eleven, Gavin suffered swelling around his left eye and M'baye landed some stiff, punishing shots from thereon in and the ones coming from the left were hard for Gavin to pick as his vision was impaired. It was getting pretty hairy as to whether Gavin could hold on and survive. I feared I'd have to throw in the towel even though he was within sight of the finishing line.

It was Mickey and Rocky stuff in the corner after the eleventh round. "How much do you want it? Three minutes! You are three fucking minutes away from living your dream. How much do you want it," I screamed at Gavin, slapping his face – on the good side – to make sure I had his attention. I had faith that he would see it through but the question was did he still believe he could shrug off the exhaustion he felt for just one more round?

As he rose from the corner I made him jog on the spot to show M'baye he had all the energy left in the world. A massive part of my training technique is based on psychology, of building up my fighters and making them feel invincible, like they are superheroes. That's what I was doing in making Gavin jog on the spot. Push yourself beyond your limits Gavin, I know you can.

One the bell sounded for round twelve it was a tough three minutes which felt a lot longer. M'baye went for broke and Gavin stood firm, stalling and holding and scratching and clawing his way to the final bell. Whenever M'baye pinned Gavin to the ropes he would slip his head inside, tag M'baye and retreat to the middle of the ring, winding down the seconds until finally that bell came. I felt as sure as you ever can that he had won it. Colin Hart and Ron Lewis and all the other journalists at ringside all had Gavin as the winner with a margin of between two and six or seven rounds. I know this because I shouted to them. Frank Warren thought he had done more than enough to win too. But would the judges see it that way?

There is probably no tenser moment in boxing than waiting for the verdict in the ring, both fighters usually full of bravado and a belief that they have won, many times without any idea how it's going to go. "I have done it, haven't I?" Gavin asked me over and over. "We think so," I said as we waited and the Cardiff International Arena prepared to riot if the wrong verdict came in. Remember that it might have been in Wales but M'baye was the house fighter, Gavin was the one in the away corner but naturally had the crowd fully behind him.

Then came the verdict, a unanimous decision and yet still your heart beats like a drum. Not until you hear that one tiny little word that your brain is searching for can you truly celebrate.

"Your winner, and NEW..."

And then mass celebration. I hugged Gavin and as I did, as the CIA erupted, I felt exhilaration and vindication.

Let them try and tell the world anyone could have trained Gavin Rees to a world title, I thought. Let them try and question a guy with three world champions and a WBU champion and a Commonwealth champion all fighting out of one gym. Still don't believe I belong in boxing? Still whispering about me being lucky and becoming a world champion trainer because of my sperm not my talent? Go fuck yourself!

I was proud that I had finally succeeded in demonstrating how talented my stable was and how unique I was as a trainer. It doesn't bother me to admit that, even if it sounds vain and arrogant.

My conscience is clear because as happy as I was for myself it paled into insignificance compared to how thrilled I was for Gavin. This was different to when Enzo won earlier in the night. It was the same feeling I got when Joe won, like my son and friend was living his dream. I felt pride as a coach and satisfaction for a kid I think of as one of my own.

"The Welsh have never had a Cinderella man, but they've got one now and his name is Gavin Rees." Colin Hart, ringside commentator.

It was an extraordinary time. We now had three fully fledged world champions in our gym and a reputation growing by the fight. I say we had three world champions, but I never particularly understood why people didn't consider Gary Lockett a world champion. He held the WBU belt and to me that was significant. It was the same title that Ricky Hatton held until he beat Kostya Tszyu and also became IBF champion. Are you trying to tell me Ricky Hatton wasn't considered a world champion before that fight? Bullshit. He was a bigger name in British boxing than Joe for a long time.

So to my mind we had four world champions even though Gary Lockett would tell you he'd have preferred to be a British champion than hold the WBU title. He certainly never considered himself a world-title-level fighter until he was one in 2008 in Atlantic City. And I felt Bradley Pryce was right there on the bubble at that time too. I had three world champions but dreamed it could be five. And then in a couple of years Nathan Cleverly could round out the half dozen.

Bradley went to London the week before Gavin's triumph and beat the unbeaten next big thing Anthony Small in a fight few expected him to win. Bradley was supposed to be a rung on the ladder for Small but Bradley battered him up pretty badly in the seventh to end it prematurely in what was a real tear up. A month before the Millennium Stadium bill, Bradley went and did it again, this time knocking out Martin Concepcion in the third round as his stock rose and rose. Unfortunately, after one more defence against Marcus Portman that also ended in a stoppage, the wheels fell off in terms of Bradley going to that next level.

But his hunger was typical of the gym at that time. He wanted a world title like Gavin had and Gary Lockett also desired the biggest fights and pay days going. Nathan Cleverly, Tony Doherty and Kerry Hope wanted to challenge for British or Commonwealth titles and everyone was striving and most importantly believing in their dreams. Anything seemed possible the more we all kept winning. The gym had an aura about it.

As soon as the show in Cardiff ended we moved into promotion mode for the Kessler fight and it was different to normal. To my surprise Joe was nothing at all like his usual self. Whereas my other fighters and I used to get more and more on the same wavelength the closer we came to a fight, Joe and I usually went in the opposite direction and argued incessantly. It became an outlet for his tension I suppose. Despite this being the largest fight of Joe's career he was never more relaxed than he was for Kessler and he wasn't snapping at me and calling me a fucking idiot two weeks before, which made for a lovely change.

The fight had captured the imagination of the public and within the sport it was all anybody was talking about. Everyone had a different theory on who was going to be victorious and it was a pleasure to be part of the promotion as two gentlemen prepared to go to war.

Kessler, throughout, was a picture of respect and restraint. There was absolutely no trash talking from him at all but I got the same impression as before the Jeff Lacy fight, that everything wasn't totally rosy in the Kessler camp. He limited his media commitments far more than was usual – a work-out and Q&A with journalists on one morning and that was it. I was hearing on the grapevine that Kessler turned down loads of press interviews and it seemed that while his spokesman Michael Marley – a colourful character who used to work for Don King – wouldn't shut up, Kessler was very withdrawn. I liked that for Joe. Not until the head-to-head press conference the day before the weigh-in did we hear a peep from Kessler. He was the young pretender here to vanquish the old champion, but he never truly seemed to me to fully believe he could win the fight.

I really did like Kessler though, I respect him hugely. He had great composure and class and it wasn't his fault that I got very heated at the weigh-in. Kessler had to take to the scales twice, the second time in his birthday suit. The two fighters then went nose-to-nose for a photo opportunity and Michael Marley started doing throat-slashing gestures in Joe's face. I wasn't having that. "You get the fuck out of here doing that bollocks or I will give you a slap," I told him. It's all part of the pantomime and those moments are always highly charged but I found myself close to snapping in that moment.

In private Joe expected Kessler to be a tougher test than Lacy, but I wasn't overly concerned. Even if Kessler coped with the atmosphere and environment, I didn't believe he could sustain any sort of dominance over Joe. I felt he was durable and technically sound but a little bit unremarkable. Kessler has the class to beat most contenders comfortably, but he boxes in straight lines and can be predictable and that suits Joe very well indeed.

The fight night was incredibly my third time in just over a year at the Millennium Stadium and as the previous two shows flashed away in a blur, I vowed to myself to try and take time to smell the roses, as they say. This time I wouldn't rush about like a blue-arse fly and would attempt to savour it all.

By the time that November date came around I'd taken on another boxer too. I didn't like to do things the easy way. Hari Miles joined us just in time to get a bit of a pasting from Enzo Maccarinelli in sparring but I think he was grateful for the experience. Hari was a talented kid too, not always totally focused but rarely a problem and a humble enough boy from Newport who came to us after working full-time as a dustman. He wasn't afraid of hard work or long hours and I liked that.

Hari was on the bill at the Millennium Stadium along with Nathan Cleverly and Kerry Hope, but with just five fights in total it was a somewhat calmer evening for yours truly. All the boys were victorious as was a very comfortable Enzo Maccarinelli who was far too good for stand-in opponent Mohamed Azzaoui, a blown-up light heavyweight who did well to last four rounds.

I had some time to relax before Joe was due to make his ring walk and as he got in the zone I happily left him to it. I had a little stroll around that big old stadium. I started to feel utterly euphoric. I had that feeling in the pit of my stomach that this night was going to take some topping. There is always noise when you step out of that curtain, but a national treasure – and by then Joe was a national treasure – coming out at the national stadium takes some beating. The flashes from the thousands of camera phones twinkled in the night sky and Joe's music, some thumping hip hop, boomed and the bass reverberated. The people were absolutely enthralled by the spectacle. While big days at that stadium are nothing new, this wasn't rugby or football. The backing for Joe, one of Wales' own, was visceral and as he made his way to the ring the place got louder and louder. I had goose bumps.

It's strange, but as fifty thousand people greeted Joe and me with a crescendo of noise that I can vividly hear in my head to this day, I was repeating the same thought over and over and I couldn't believe it hadn't occurred to me earlier. That afternoon Joe and I walked to the stadium after a meal at a Cardiff hotel and I guess that set my mind racing. Because as Joe made his slow walk down to the ring the same few words kept repeating over and over in my mind. "I used to sleep right outside this stadium in a phone box."

Over thirty years before that defining night in my son's life, I had shivered and suffered for too many nights in a phone box on Queen's Street in the centre of Cardiff, right around the time I met Joe's mum. I could've seen the stadium from where I slept had it been built back then. I had gone from that low, being desolate and desperate, to this feeling of utter elation as over fifty thousand people screamed and shouted at the top of their lungs. If a moment like that can't bring out the emotion in you, what would even be the point in living, let alone working?

I was practically in tears by the time the ring introductions occurred and I was just in awe of how calm, composed and most of all happy Joe looked. He knew what was at stake, he'd waited for such a long time to be in this position and there was absolutely no way in hell he was going to lose that fight, I knew it without consideration for anything anyone else said or feared. I can't explain or justify with logic why I felt so confident. It was blind faith I suppose, but you can't get your brain to convince you to be scared, wary or apprehensive if you don't feel it in your soul. Before a punch had been thrown I felt deliriously proud, happy, excited and wistful for the adventure we had been on. I was in danger of being overcome by elation, the response from the crowd was simply the greatest I'd ever known or imagined. To me it felt like Beatlemania, only with an audience that had drunk a lot more beer.

I'd been adamant with Joe that the game plan had to be a softly-softly approach with a bit of spoiling for at least three rounds, as Kessler would then struggle to get his jab going which was essentially his plan A, B and C. Joe could fight in so many different styles and I knew that rounds that were tentative and close, he would edge because he had better ring awareness and would throw more punches. That was how it was in the early sessions and I was content. Joe had given himself a platform to produce a great performance. He essentially reverted to a Kessler style initially and punched very accurately, very sharply and very straight, packing everything down the middle and imposing himself with double jabs and combinations. It was close and cagey but you felt both men were ready to explode into action with the crowd way ahead of them on that score.

In the third, Joe was looser and cleverer than Kessler and hurt him a few times. From then on the fight completely lived up to the billing as the action became more and more spectacular. "The super fight is becoming a super super fight," the HBO commentator said in round four, a round that Kessler enjoyed, one uppercut especially really stunning everyone.

"Start shining, start sparkling, show everyone all that you can do," I said before the fifth and from then on Joe did just that. It was beautiful. "More, more, more, I want more like that," was the only message I had to deliver for the remainder of the fight. I don't think I'd underestimated Kessler's skills, everything I felt before the fight was coming true. But Kessler's courage, his heart and his durability were superb. If his power had been overestimated by others, his conditioning was certainly better than I expected it to be. Kessler had never been in this situation before and Joe was landing more shots, more varied punches and it was difficult to see how on earth the judges weren't going to be giving him round after round.

Somewhere in the back half of that fight Joe broke Kessler's spirit. Kessler's punches didn't lack sizzle, his defence was still admirable but you could see in his face he'd been bamboozled by Joe, he didn't know what to do next. The kid was totally out of ideas and looked shell-shocked. He did everything right, but Joe made it look wrong. Despite a brilliant effort in the last round, Kessler didn't even raise his hands and pretend he'd won the fight at the final bell. Everyone knew and Michael Buffer's announcement contained no apprehension for me, just pure happiness as I tried as hard as I could to soak up every second and somehow trap the moment in my memory banks.

"Two champions collided late in the night, each of them proud and unbeaten – but Joe Calzaghe, at 35 and 10 years a champion through 20 defences, added a 21st to his log to send back the spirited challenge of Mikkel Kessler. It was one of the Welshman's very finest performances. The Italian Dragon, son of Newbridge and hero of Wales, keeps his WBO super-middleweight title and adds those of the Dane's belts, sponsored by the WBA and the WBC. It will, more than likely, be Calzaghe's last fight at 12 stone; he can't take the suffering to shrink his frame to the weight anymore and he will probably go looking now for the American light-heavyweight Bernard Hopkins. That is a mouthwatering prospect, as well. The margin at the end of 12 tough, absorbing rounds was 117-111, 116-112, and 116-112 for Calzaghe. And that was about right, although Kessler did himself proud... The crowd were in no doubt who was bringing home the titles as Calzaghe waded into Kessler in the 12th, a confident and inspired champion at the top of his form against a fine adversary." Kevin Mitchell, *Guardian*, 4 November 2007

Joe's crowning glory made him the hottest commodity in boxing behind Manny Pacquiao and Floyd Mayweather. Having won the three world titles against the best opponent in the world at twelve stone and the *Ring Magazine* title, known in the sport as the true indicator of who the best in the division is, I knew without a shadow of a doubt that would be Joe's last fight at the weight he'd killed himself to make time and time again. After a decade of super middleweight dominance it was time to move up.

"That night at the Millennium Stadium was exactly the stage I had dreamed of my entire career. I fought so many times against guys I knew who didn't belong in the ring with me and it was very difficult at times to keep up with the standards I had set for myself and dad expected me to maintain. But Kessler was a fighter I truly respected and admired and I knew it would be incredibly tough to beat him. But I was so prepared for the fight it was impossible for Mikkel. He had probably been thinking about fighting me for a couple of years. I had been planning to unify the division since my debut as a professional. It was a truly great evening and the

noise from the crowd was something else. Probably only one boxer in ten thousand will get to experience fighting in front of 50,000 people and it was a phenomenal feeling. I also knew I had a reputation to maintain. My stablemates were shining and winning titles all over the place and I couldn't be the one to let the side down. I felt it was one of my very best performances and certainly it was the biggest fight I was involved in, including the two in America. It was the perfect way to bow out of the super-middleweight division and fighting in Wales or the United Kingdom and was a special, special night in my life, not just my career. I knew I didn't have long left in boxing and to enjoy something like that was perfect." Joe Calzaghe.

Joe was privately already plotting a final route to retirement having vowed to his mother that he wouldn't be still boxing as an old man and risk getting badly hurt. He was thought determined to follow in the footsteps of some of his heroes and become a two-weight world champion first and talk had been intensifying about a clash with Bernard Hopkins or someone of that calibre.

But as thrilled as I was that Joe had made it to the very top of boxing, I simply had no concept of how big an impact his victory had made on the British public, nor how dramatic his final year as a fighter would be for all of us.

Chapter Fifteen:

Recognition

Never again did we collectively hit the heights of 2007 and in truth I would be stunned if such a run of success was replicated again by any gym in British boxing. Nevertheless, there were to be some absolutely massive occasions in our final run at the top with Team Calzaghe in 2008 and it was also a time when I was given recognition beyond my wildest dreams.

I am not going to bullshit you that awards don't matter and that it didn't mean as much to me as the victories in the ring. I have never attempted to hide how insecure I have felt at times and this, to me, was validation. If that makes me sound pathetic then so be it, at least it is honest. It felt wonderful to return home to Jackie with awards and accolades. She had to sacrifice a lot of time without me because of my boxing commitments and I felt happy to make her proud of me, or at least show her that the sacrifice had meant something.

At the end of the year, Joe, Enzo Maccarinelli and some other pals went on a boys' holiday to Las Vegas to watch Ricky Hatton fight against Floyd Mayweather. Joe's plan was to cut loose and hopefully bump into Bernard Hopkins while he was over there and maybe get some business done too. It did, however, mean missing BBC Sports Personality of the Year.

With Joe in Vegas I was glued to *Sky Sports News* to see if he was on and my mind wasn't really on Sports Personality that Sunday. I had never won anything significant and the coach of the year award always went to a team boss, normally in football or rugby, so I didn't have my hopes up whatsoever.

A day or so before the Hatton fight I remember getting a call from Joe in Vegas and he was unbelievably excited. "Turn on the TV Dad, you won't believe it," he said. "I've just bumped into Hopkins and we ended up being pulled away from one another. You won't believe what he said. Can you see it on the television Dad? He just told me in front of loads of press that he'd never be beaten by a white guy."

Did I just hear that right? I couldn't believe it, Hopkins had made a ridiculous statement solely to garner attention and I finally believed for the first time he did want to fight my son. As soon as I saw that ticker bar flash up at the bottom of Sky Sports News I knew the fight was a done deal. Until Joe beat Jeff Lacy and Mikkel Kessler nobody wanted to know him but now he was getting the attention he deserved, even Hopkins wanted a piece of the action. And the best part was that it had all been captured by reporters in a Las Vegas casino.

It got even better. Ricky's lawyer Gareth Williams got Joe accredited for the weigh-in between Mayweather and Hatton. It was a big event hosted by Michael Buffer with several thousand Ricky Hatton fans in attendance. Joe wanted to go on the stage because Bernard Hopkins was on there but security wouldn't let him through. Luckily Michael Buffer called Joe's name while he and his pals argued with the bouncers and Joe raced past security with Enzo Maccarinelli in tow onto the stage. The crowd started to do that "super, super Joe, super Joe Calzaghe," chant and when Hopkins was introduced they chanted, "Bernard Hopkins, what a wanker, what a wanker!" As you'd imagine, he wasn't best pleased and he and Joe went nose-to-nose. Yet more pictures to go with the white boy headline. This was all going to be global in no time at all.

"The idea was largely to party in Vegas but one of the girls from HBO called me as soon as we arrived and said they'd love to sort us out with some tickets for the Hatton fight and everything else and would I maybe come to the hotel and do a bit of a meet and greet. I said ok, no problem. They were quite specific on the time and I just hoped Hopkins would be there, I figured that was the plan. I was doing my rounds and I clocked Hopkins from a distance and thought it was going to kick off the way he snapped his head back when he saw me. It was like he was suddenly all about business when he'd been laughing and joking two seconds before that. It wasn't planned per se, but as soon as he made that white boy comment I was buzzing, because I thought that means the fight is done. The racism, all the controversy, it was brilliant,

I couldn't have asked for him to do anything differently. He knew exactly what he was doing and I remember Frank Warren on the other end of the phone straight away saying he'd call Golden Boy Promotions who represented Hopkins. It was the best holiday I ever had!" Joe Calzaghe

Unfortunately, Ricky lost to Mayweather who frankly along with Manny Pacquiao was the only boxer in the world I felt was on the same level as Joe. I headed to London for the Sports Personality show and there was a growing clamour for Joe to win which I was excited about. All the press guys were talking up Joe and while I was cynical because of our experience the previous year, it is an event we always watched when Joe was a kid. It was important to me, more than it should've been. He had already won the Welsh version about eight hundred times but to win across the United Kingdom would be much bigger. When we arrived everyone was talking about Joe and I got so excited I was hardly concentrating when they announced that I had won the Coach of the Year award.

It was a brilliant moment for me. I was the first Welsh/Italian/English hybrid nationality winner and the thing everyone said was significant was the fact I was the first person to win it for coaching an individual. I told everyone I thought that was bollocks. To me, trite as it sounds, we genuinely were a team at the gym. There was never a time when it was just about an individual, but there you go. I was also the first boxing trainer ever to win it.

And of course, Joe won that night in a big upset. When Lewis Hamilton was announced as a runner-up my heart was in my mouth and when they cut to Joe and Ricky Hatton in Las Vegas and Ricky presented Joe with the trophy my heart swelled with pride. People were congratulating me and I felt overwhelmed, like I could've burst into tears at any time. The entire family was watching back in Wales and it was a wonderful night for the Calzaghe clan.

Sports Personality continues to be one of my favourite social events. There is something special, humbling even, about being surrounded by the best of the best sporting talent in the UK and

I've generally always found it a brilliant experience to meet new people from other sports. There is only one exception to that, an encounter with one of the rudest people I've encountered. And this one broke my heart! It was Fabio Capello. When I saw the England coach at the 2009 event I was really excited because of course he was a huge presence in Italian football. I introduced myself in Italian and thought he might like that, but the response I got roughly translated to: "Leave me alone, can't you see I am busy?" I was absolutely gutted. I felt absolutely affronted that an Italian hero of mine was so bloody rude, but what can you do? And Fabio, if you're reading, when you're standing on your own vacantly staring into space, no, I can't see that you're busy!

I won seventeen awards in total in about fourteen months. The *Ring Magazine* trainer of the year award, never achieved before by a British trainer was a huge honour and it was the same with the Boxing Writers' Association of America Award for Trainer of the Year which I went to collect in the States. I won the British Boxing Writers' Association award, the British Boxing Board of Control one and the only exception was the Welsh version of Sports Personality of the Year because they refused to include Team Calzaghe in the Team of the Year category which pissed me off and they don't have a Coach of the Year category. It was an historic list of accolades and it makes me Britain's most decorated boxing trainer. That is a fact and one I will hopefully be remembered for.

I could easily have got a big head with so many people suddenly telling me I was a success, but fortunately we simply didn't have time for soaking up any platitudes because there were some major nights on the horizon. Besides, I already had a huge ego and big sense of self-importance, so it didn't change me. I was still my own biggest fan, as I had been before.

Joe was inching towards a deal with Hopkins, and it was a lot easier thanks to the "I will never lose to a white guy" comments, and Joe reacting by calling Hopkins sad, old and racist. The needle was there, the public wanted to see the fight and there could be no backing down from Hopkins this time. Finally the deal was done in February. We were all set for April at The Thomas and Mack Center with the Planet Hollywood Casino the major host and sponsor, and Joe embarked on the most tiresome press promotion tour you can imagine.

But ahead of that fight were two huge nights in March with Enzo Maccarinelli first up. A deal had finally been struck for a cruiserweight unification clash with David Haye and everyone was saying it was the most exciting al-British fight since the days of Nigel Benn and Chris Eubank. I was extremely confident based on the way Enzo had steadily improved since joining our gym that he would beat David Haye. I think my style of training was well suited to a guy with natural punching power like Enzo and his attitude was always impeccable and still is to this day. I felt Haye was incredibly talented, but I saw it as a 50/50 fight and felt Enzo could definitely win.

There was certainly a charm offensive in place from Haye who had never been adored by the British public but he seized upon the fact this fight was in 'his manor' at the magnificent O2 Arena in London. Haye predicted he would win in under a minute but our game plan was to survive any early onslaught if Haye came out flying as we expected he would. David was preoccupied with being heavyweight world champion and I saw it as extremely unnatural for him to fight at cruiserweight. I felt Enzo had no disadvantage when it came to power, certainly not when you factor in them both being knocked down before and a significant advantage in conditioning. I thought Haye would wilt like Wayne Braithwaite did after doing too much to make the weight. I'd seen Haye blow himself out against Carl Thompson and believed he could be made to make the same mistakes again.

In my heart of hearts I just couldn't see Enzo losing. His preparation was amazing, Joe was able to spar with him and his punching power was spot on. I had faith that David Haye could not cope if he was taken to the trenches to steal Chris Eubank's phrase and that was our game plan, we were taking Haye to war.

For me it went one of two ways. If they traded bombs Enzo would show he had a better chin and he'd stop Haye within three rounds but the strategy was risky as Haye is a puncher. If it went long Enzo would outwork Haye and win it on points decisively. Enzo and I watched Haye together on DVD but you can't train a fighter's brain. A week before the fight Enzo got a cold and I think

Haye got into his head along with the sniffles. At the pre-fight press conference Haye turned up two hours late and conducted his own media event with Enzo, myself and Frank Warren long gone. Haye oozed confidence and at the weigh-in Enzo saw that. It got to him.

The fight was at midnight broadcast on Setanta in the UK and Showtime in the USA and it was going to mean massive things for the winner. Haye came out looking like the coolest cat on the planet and Enzo, who was greeted with a chorus of boos, looked agitated. He walked so fast to the ring I could barely keep up with him and I wondered what the fuck had got into him, because he was usually very calm and collected. Nothing in the dressing room had indicated to me any panic in Enzo, but his charge to the ring as *I won't back down* by Tom Petty blared over the speakers, had me concerned.

The first round was a tickling contest, but it was clear the packed arena was completely behind Haye and Enzo was losing the plot. He was not relaxed and it cost him big time. I felt like my words simply weren't resonating at the end of the first round. Enzo was just totally out of his stride. In the second round he got caught because he failed to protect himself and went down. It unravelled from there, the fight over and Haye a clear and decisive winner and now undisputed cruiserweight champion. It was hugely upsetting, not least because Enzo had to face up to the fact that on the night, he simply didn't do himself justice. That expression about don't die wondering? He'll always wonder what would have happened had he been at his best. That's the harsh reality of boxing. In June 2008 Enzo got back into the ring and knocked out a heavyweight named Matthew Ellis, but the Haye defeat had harmed him a lot and he would have a very mixed couple of years ahead. It's sad to say, but Enzo's chin wasn't as good as I'd believed and the Haye defeat was one he never fully recovered from.

I was really upset for Enzo but that's the way boxing can be. Whatever the reason, he didn't perform anywhere near to his best on the night and he was no longer a world champion. He'd trained as hard as he possibly could and had lost to the best guy in the division, who as it transpires was better than I imagined he would be. Haye was a credit to Britain in becoming a world champion at heavyweight and I have nothing but respect for him despite the subsequent antics with Dereck Chisora. It was a massive fight night in my career and I am proud that we were part of it even though it ranks high on my list of most disappointing nights in boxing.

We had been extremely proud to have three world champions and suddenly we were in danger of having none. Joe, after eleven years as WBO king vacated all his belts to challenge Hopkins at light heavyweight and Gavin Rees had an extremely difficult defence in Cardiff against Andriy Kotelnik whose size advantage was significant.

If Enzo had lost on the big stage, Gavin went out with a whimper two weeks later in anything but a grand manner on my worst night in boxing. For whatever reason Gavin can't sell tickets like some of the other boys in the gym and it was a world title bill at the Cardiff CIA with less than three thousand fans in attendance. Frank Warren was obviously far from pleased with the box office returns. My concern was Gavin's attitude. He was never the most disciplined, but he was off the chart in the build up to this fight. Being a world champion went to his head and he was behaving recklessly.

Don't believe me? Take the fucking joke of a diet he revealed to the world through the local papers – while training twice a day, he was starving himself for 24 hours then eating a McDonald's burger!

I had no idea how bad things had gotten until the week of the fight and if that suggests I was losing my touch then I can't argue. I always treated my fighters like adults and expected them to do the right thing. Gavin actually weighed-in over the limit and that was at light-welterweight where he looked tiny in comparison to some fighters. It was ludicrous that he made two trips to the scales. I felt embarrassed.

On fight night he got found out. Gavin started like a train as he had done to win the title against the odds but his dominance was short-lived. His stamina wasn't there because he'd been cheating in training and Kotelnik was certainly ahead on the cards when he stopped Gavin at the death, Gavin having suffered a perforated ear-drum. Within an hour of losing even though he was hurt, Gavin was making plans to go for a drink and I was crushed that he'd thrown it all away and seemed so calm about it.

To make matters worse Kerry Hope also lost that night in a brutal fight where Matthew Hall punished him and even the bright spot of the evening was a disappointment to a degree. Tony Doherty beat Rhonda fighter Barrie Jones, who is as lovely a lad as you could meet, but it was a horrible atmosphere because some of the Jones fans abused Tony and his family because of their travelling background. As the crowd was so sparse, it was really noticeable and tainted what was a very good fight.

Tony was another fighter who was struggling outside of the ring. His brother died in 2006 and that hurt him badly. Subsequently he lost focus and his weight was ballooning between fights. I am sad to say he's only fought once in the four years since that Jones fight and if he doesn't have a second coming in him it's a waste of a huge talent.

So it was over to Joe, once more our sole world title fighter. We'd had a fortnight from hell and Joe wasn't faring much better as he spent day after day listening to Hopkins go on and on and on and on, be it in London, Vegas or New York at the press events. HBO were filming both fighters for a special documentary and the press commitments seemed endless. We were looking forward to finally getting to America where we'd spend a fortnight acclimatising before the big night and the plans were meticulous, thanks in part to a good friend.

Ricky Hatton had fought in Vegas numerous times and he was full of advice to Joe on what to do. Apparently the first rule of Vegas is never under any circumstances stay on the strip and that kind of thinking appealed to Joe because he loved quiet and privacy. We arranged a lovely villa to stay in away from the bright lights with a pool table and hot tub and the plan was that it would be Sergio and I, Joe, plus Nathan Cleverly and Bradley Pryce who would fight on the undercard and provide Joe with sparring options. A small team, but giving us everything we needed.

Unfortunately, we couldn't get a visa for Bradley because of his past indiscretions and had to fly out without him. Despite regular contact with the American Embassy in London we couldn't get them to change the decision. So Nathan was on his own in terms of sparring options and we were a very small group compared to Hopkins who seemed to have the biggest entourage in boxing.

We had a nice week of training and adjusting our sleep patterns with plenty of games of pool and some crazy golf and then the madness began as we headed into the big fight week in Vegas. The whole thing was like a crazy dream. Joe had got used to Hopkins' histrionics, but he wound me up no end. That led to my biggest ever meltdown at a press event when Hopkins and I went nose-to-nose at the final press conference. The whole thing is on YouTube and I meant every word I said to that big headed idiot. Emotion poured out of me as Hopkins picked at my insecurities so soon after Gavin and Enzo's disappointing defeats.

Hopkins had said that I would be the reason Joe lost, that my pride would lead to Joe's downfall because I wouldn't know when to pull him out and I snapped big time at essentially being called the weak spot in the Joe Calzaghe armoury. "You'd better get your whole camp to realise how quick Joe Calzaghe is. I know how to beat you. I've watched you, only once, only on one video. That is all I needed to watch to realise how to beat you. You are a 43-year-old man and if you beat Joe I will pack it in myself, let me tell you this now; I know how to beat you easy, easy, easy. You've never met someone like Joe before and he will beat you easy. Forget shit, you've got nothing," I screamed at him, jabbing him with my finger as Joe and Frank Warren stood by our side. There were hundreds of press there but I didn't care. When I finished ranting – and yes, I realised what I said doesn't really make sense – Hopkins turned to the press and said with a big grin, "I am more scared of him, I'm more afraid of Enzo than Joe!" It was great humour and it calmed me down but, believe me, I meant what I said, I thought it would be easy for Joe to beat Hopkins.

I thought he was past it, not as fit as he thought and was someone who had lost four times and had become a guy renowned for sneaking fights. I watched the Jermain Taylor fight, saw what hard work he made of it and thought, 'he's never met a Joe Calzaghe; he won't be able to handle it.'

People made a lot of Hopkins 'dream team' as he had four

world-renowned coaches including Freddie Roach in his corner. But I had the same arrogance and faith in my ability as a trainer as I did as a musician. So what if the Beatles are on first, was my thinking... it doesn't mean we can't blow the audience away.

The whole build-up felt surreal. One minute we were chilling in the villa, the next we headed to a film premier at the hotel and met Al Pacino who is an absolute hero to Joe for his role in *Scarface*. I think he's one of the greatest actors of all time and it felt a million miles away from our gym in Newbridge when we posed with him on the red carpet for his movie, *88 Minutes*. We didn't stay for the film and with a rating of 5% on Rotten Tomatoes that was perhaps a wise choice. Interestingly, Al Pacino didn't stay for it either. He obviously knew...

When we went down to the press events at Planet Hollywood, we got a clearer picture of what a huge deal this fight was. There were thousands of British fans in the hotel and all along the Strip, and there were massive billboards advertising the fight. It was easy to get swept away with it all and lose a bit of focus. One day in the limo after Joe's public workout, my phone rang. I hate answering my phone abroad because it costs a fortune, but it was Michael Pearlman from the local paper and I thought it might be something important.

"Where are you Enzo?" he asked and he sounded agitated. "We've left the hotel now, Michael. Did you not speak to Joe or something? You had your chance with the rest of the press, we'll be seeing you again in the morning anyway," I told him. "No you've left something here Enzo. You need to come back to the hotel straight away. You've left without Nathan!"

I looked around and he was right! Everything was so hectic that we left Nathan Cleverly stranded in the hotel and buggered off without him. Luckily Michael was with him because Nathan didn't have a phone and we were already heading away from the Strip in heavy traffic. As you can imagine he wasn't best pleased when we arrived back an hour later to pick him up, but I'm sure the overall experience of being involved in the build-up to a massive fight will have been invaluable to him. Presumably Nathan will have his own mega fights in the US and his experiences with Joe will be vital.

It was Nathan, not Joe, who became the first Welshman in twenty-five years to fight on the other side of the Atlantic and both Joe and Enzo Maccarinelli were at ringside supporting him. That was amazing to me on both counts. Joe was only two hours away from a huge fight and Enzo Maccarinelli drank so much beer that week it was incredible either of them took their seats, but that was how much they thought of Nathan. Nathan looked a million dollars and easily beat Antonio Baker. I loved working with the kid and I would never have believed it if someone told me that night it'd be the last time he fought with me in his corner.

Joe was cool and calm and it was a phenomenal atmosphere by the time the main event came around. Michael Buffer introduced a string of celebrities and it was clear that Joe had a very positive and receptive crowd. You'd imagine fighting an American that wouldn't be the case, but the majority of the fans were in Joe's corner and nearly all of them had flown over from the UK. It was remarkable. Tom Jones sang the national anthem and the stage was well and truly set. I was totally confident but that faith evaporated a little when Hopkins floored Joe in the very first round. It never looked likely to end the fight, but it was still the exact opposite to the way I envisaged things working out. Hopkins caught Joe almost with his forearm across the nose and it was a terrifying moment. Joe recovered, but barely and things didn't improve.

Hopkins took the second session on points as well and I was a bit dumbstruck as to how this was possibly happening. Joe wasn't in the fight at all and he was three points behind on the cards after two rounds. We had some harsh words in the corner. "Are you listening to me, Joe?" was always my first question. If he wasn't, why waste my breath? I told him to start throwing combinations, to get the jab going. Joe looked shell-shocked and he needed to start fighting his fight. I was really concerned. I had underestimated Hopkins and I wouldn't be the last by any means.

Joe definitely started looking more like himself around the fourth round and I kept pressing home the importance of using his speed and combinations to trouble Hopkins. "Do you want him to stop you or do you want to stop him? That's the way it is going to go," I said at the end of the sixth, actually one of the best rounds Joe had in the fight.

"Where are the fucking four As Joe? Where are the fucking four Cs gone?" I was desperate for him to land more clean shots because I was concerned close rounds would go to Hopkins in the USA. Joe was throwing more single shots rather than combinations than I had ever seen before, yet the HBO commentary team still seemed to think he was winning. I wasn't sure. We were planning on working the Hopkins body but his defence was so canny Joe was simply landing where and when he could.

In rounds eight and nine Joe was definitely the aggressor and then in round ten Hopkins went down for a low blow that never was and bought himself a five minute rest. It was laughable and I couldn't believe Joe Cortez the referee was swallowing it. It was pathetic gamesmanship when Joe was gaining more and more momentum and Joe cleverly amped up the crowd while Hopkins delivered his Oscar worthy performance. The fight was slipping away from Hopkins and he knew it. It was the first time I relaxed a little. By the eleventh round, more punches had been landed on him than ever before according to the stats. Whenever Hopkins decided he wanted to trade shots, Joe landed more.

"I can't pretend otherwise, Hopkins was a much better fighter on the night than I had expected him to be. Physically it was about what I expected. The guy had superb conditioning but so did I and even at thirty six I had seven years on him and he slowed, he weakened and he pretended to be hurt when he wasn't to waste time. But he's hands down the cleverest fighter I've come up against, his ring knowledge was amazing. He anticipated certain things I did better than anyone else had been able to. It was such a hard fight. I knew I was upsetting his plans and winning rounds but I still knew it was close at the final bell. I hadn't been at my best, but I thought I had done enough to win the fight." Joe Calzaghe

At the end of the eleventh, Joe told me: "He's cheating, he keeps cheating, dad." I was worried. "Fuck his cheating up my arse," were the words I used in response. We were both feeling the tension. I was exasperated and gratuitous swearing is normally the route I take in such a situation. "This fucking water bottle is empty, get Joe some fucking water. Now, you, Joe, how much do you want this? Don't you get it? If you don't win this round it's over. You've got to stop him, beat him up Joe." That was how I set him out for the final round which I suspected he needed to win handsomely. Joe fought great in the final round, but it was just a case of waiting to see what the judges thought and by the time Michael Buffer came to make his announcement I was bouncing around, a bundle of nervous energy. It was a split decision and heart in mouth time. Never before had I not had an instinct for who was going to get the decision. It was a completely alien feeling. Over to you Michael Buffer.

"Ladies and gentlemen, we go to the scorecards. Adalaide Byrd scores it 114 to 113 for Bernard Hopkins."

Shit.

The crowd booed.

"Ted Gimza scores it 115 to 112 for Joe Calzaghe."

Cheers from the crowd. I was unable to control my movements, my head swinging and hands wringing as I tried desperately to catch my breath. What if he loses?

"Chuck Giampa scores it 116-111 to your winner by split decision...."

Please. At that moment you're all father. Every ounce of your heart and soul is desperate that your little man isn't crushed with disappointment. Just please let it be my boy who has won.

"From Newbridge Wales...."

I know he went on but the second I heard Newbridge I lost myself completely in the moment and lifted Joe high into the air. I felt as strong as ten men. Joe landed 232 punches, more than any other fighter had against Hopkins and his percentage of landed shots rose throughout the fight.

To go to America and beat an icon of the sport and become a two-weight world champion was everything Joe had dreamed of. In the post match interview it was mentioned that Kelly Pavlik could be next or perhaps Roy Jones Jr, who ringside interviewer Max Kellerman said had been "campaigning" to fight Joe. That was absolutely true. To my amazement, I found out later that Roy

Jones, a four-weight world champion and absolute bona fide legend of boxing, who had ducked Joe for years, spent the fight doing commentary for BBC Radio Wales. It was an absolutely incredible coup for their producer Graham Davies who couldn't believe his luck. But there was Roy Jones, sitting next to commentator Steffan Garrero broadcasting exclusively to Joe's Welsh public. That was how much Jones wanted to fight Joe. It's astonishing really.

"Joe Calzaghe drew on reserves of sheer bloody-mindedness after an atrociously slow start to steal the decision from the aged phenomenon that is Bernard Hopkins. The 36-year-old Welshman, decked inside two minutes, got up to carry a winning argument to a 43-year-old opponent who already considers himself a legend - thanks to Ted Gimza who saw it 115-112 for Calzaghe, supported by Chuck Giampa who gave it to him 116-111, against the lone verdict for Hopkins, 114-113, delivered by fellow Philadelphian Adalaide Byrd. However close it was, this morning Joe stands at the top of the mountain, The Ring's acknowledged light-heavyweight champion, owner of a log that reads 45 fights 45 wins, undefeated in 18 years.... Proceedings took a nasty turn at the press conference; however, when Hopkins refused to give Calzaghe due acknowledgment for what the winner admitted was a close win. "I got beat tonight," Hopkins said, "but not by Joe Calzaghe. The people know I won that fight." Struggling to keep the lid on his sometimes volatile temper, Hopkins hinted strongly that was it for him in the ring, and repeated that he had secured his legacy by his performance. He looked agitated when asked more than once if he'd give Calzaghe any praise at all. Calzaghe had already said there was no animosity between them, despite pre-fight exchanges. But, when Hopkins declined to pay tribute or even shake his opponent's hand, an obviously peeved Calzaghe, feeling perhaps that his night of triumph was being hijacked by a sore loser, called after him: "I whipped your ass. You got your ass kicked by the white boy." Kevin Mitchell, *Guardian*, 20 April 2008.

I personally thought Hopkins humiliated himself at that press conference, but notwithstanding his hissy fits everything about that trip was like something out of a dream for Joe and me, even if the fight was less than it could have been in terms of style. Hopkins spoiled it in my opinion. But the experience was sensational. We flew with British Airways, in business class and it was the first time I'd ever experienced such luxury on a plane. After most fights in Cardiff we'd celebrate afterwards with a session at one of the local pubs around Newbridge or Blackwood, but post fight parties in Sin City are a little bit more exciting than that.

We went back to the Planet Hollywood Hotel and we had a suite there for the night and Joe had flown out several of the family. Uccio and his boys were there and Joe's sister Sonia as well, of course, as Sergio. Jackie was back in Wales. She didn't want to come out and was more than happy to stay in with Sonia's kids and wait for our phone call. Joe's name was up in lights in Vegas and we were ready to celebrate. Some security guards came to collect Sonia and me from the room and we were escorted into this nightclub where there was a party for Joe. As we passed through they announced my name as we walked the casino floor. It was like my own Beatles moment. People stopped playing the slots and the tables and they clapped me and cheered my name. It was mainly fight fans but there were celebrities around too. Bruce Willis I remember was there and also Simon Cowell. I strolled right past Bruce Willis and heard a Welsh fan start drunkenly singing "Under the Boardwalk" at him which I found hysterical. Sonia grabbed my arm in a protective manner as people came up to shake my hand and it felt wonderful her being by my side as the public showed me great affection.

In the next few hours we met hundreds of people, from fans to celebrities and it was amazing. The names are impossible to reel off without sounding like a dick but you'll have to indulge me. These people came to meet us, not the other way around and it was surreal and wonderful. We spent a good hour or so with Rocky Balboa himself, Sylvester Stallone, who was a lovely guy. He was a huge boxing fan, obviously, and he really was a wonderful character, full of interest about our story and Joe's achievements. To get that approval from the star of our favourite movie was surreal. I even told Stallone that Joe used to copy *Rocky* and watch the films over and over and I think he liked that. Tom Jones came in too and had loved the fight and being a part of it. If there was a big Welsh party, it was only fitting Tom Jones be there.

We stayed in that nightclub for a while until it became very busy and Joe decided to move our little private party on to another room. It was just family and close friends and as we made our way through the hotel we saw Michael Douglas and Catherine Zeta Jones. That was very exciting to me as Catherine is such a beautiful and talented girl, an Oscar winner and someone for Wales to be very proud of. She had a nice chat with Joe and then came and surprised me by patting me on the shoulder and I was so gobsmacked that she was interested in chatting about Joe that I remember I spilt a bottle of Budweiser beer all over her shoes! I was mortified. Luckily she saw the funny side of that. She talked about the influence her mother had on her and I think she related to our relationship and respected our bond. It was quite a night and by the time I crashed out at about 6am I had nothing left to give after one of the longest and most momentous days of Joe's life.

Once we got back to the UK it was holiday time for Joe but not for me even, though I barely had a reason to unpack my suitcase. Within a month I had another absolutely monumental fight to prepare for because Gary Lockett was facing a guy who I thought was America's new Jeff Lacy in being dramatically overhyped. His name was Kelly Pavlik and the fight was set for Atlantic City. America was calling my name once more.

Chapter Sixteen:

American Dreams

Gary Lockett had been waiting a whole career for an opportunity like this and I think the high profile we'd established for the gym helped his case. Like I mentioned before, Joe being Joe gave opportunities to everyone in the gym. People totally dismissed Gary's chances, but I didn't rate Pavlik whatsoever. If the truth be told, I couldn't fathom what all the fuss was about. The guy was the most awkwardly upright, punch-in-straight lines fighter I think I'd seen at the top level and it was clear to me he just needed to be properly tested. I figured Gary Lockett was the man to do it and felt confident that if he executed the game plan, Gary could pull off an upset that exceeded even what Gavin Rees had managed to achieve.

The problem was convincing Gary of that. In a gym full of jokers and dreamers, he was the most serious and straight-laced guy around. That isn't a compliment nor is it an insult, merely an observation, but Gary would be the first to tell you his attitude in the gym was different to some of the others. For example, before they had kids, Bradley and Gavin lived to box and the same is true of Joe. For Gary, boxing has always been work, a job rather than a passion, he boxed to live and his pragmatic nature meant it was tough convincing him that Pavlik was beatable.

I think that stemmed from getting an opportunity he simply never expected. Gary had been waiting for a chance to fight Arthur Abraham for the IBF title but when John Ruddy was injured, Pavlik needed a new opponent and chose Gary, the number one contender with the WBO, from a list of potential replacement opponents. Why? I think that's simple, it was because he saw Gary as a way of getting to Joe. Even though Pavlik was a middleweight and Joe was now the light heavyweight champion of the world, many commentators seemed convinced that was the fight that needed to happen.

Part of my training philosophy is the need to make my fighters believe they are indestructible, to give them a total conviction that they would triumph when they stepped into the ring. That approach didn't work with Gary. He's his own man and however many times I dismissed Pavlik, I had no idea if the message was getting through.

We went to Atlantic City, a kind of 1980s Vegas or the Blackpool version of Vegas, and I was becoming increasingly pissed off with the repeated low blows from Pavlik's big-mouth trainer Jack Loew. He had been slaughtering us in the press for a long time.

Kelly Pavlik's trainer, Jack Loew, has aimed a broadside at the Enzo Calzaghe camp in the run-up to his man's WBC/WBO middleweight defence against Gary Lockett in Atlantic City on June 7. "I see Lockett has been inspired by Joe Calzaghe's victory over Bernard Hopkins and is predicting the same result against Kelly," said Loew. "Maybe Enzo can teach Lockett to slap like a girl - just like Joe. You can get away with that style of fighting against a 43-year-old geezer, but don't try that against Kelly. That's how rockets crash and burn," he said. "We didn't work this hard to win the title just to have Lockett and his troubadour trainer take it away from us."

I've taken that from the *South Wales Argus,* but that big-mouth was spouting the same old crap to anyone who would listen. Pavlik was like Clinton Woods or Carl Froch, trying to raise his profile by trash-talking about Joe. The same old shit, just a different name.

Preparation went fantastically well for Gary and I felt proud of him as he did the head-to-head press conference and everything else. It was totally new for him to be fighting at that level, but he coped admirably with seeing his name up in lights as the saying goes. There were thirty-foot-high billboards with Gary's face on all over Atlantic City and I think it dawned on him quickly just what a momentous fight this was. It was truly a once in a lifetime opportunity but he was the ultimate professional throughout, as if that was ever in doubt.

Unfortunately, on the night, Gary couldn't get it done. He had acknowledged before the fight that he was a level below the likes of Pavlik or Winky Wright – even though I felt he had enough talent to win the fight – but he knew about his own strengths too, most notably his world class power. Gary had a puncher's chance if he boxed smartly and kept Pavlik at range in the opening rounds, but he couldn't do that and he got put down twice and had to take a knee on another occasion. Just like with Enzo Maccarinelli and David Haye, I felt Gary was beating himself, not coping with the occasion and not showing his best. Gary thought the gulf in class between him and Pavlik was bigger than it is in reality, but that was an insurmountable hurdle for him to overcome.

In the third round I had seen just about enough and felt Gary was absolutely toiling. Pavlik is relentless when he gets on a roll and it troubled me that the referee still hadn't waved the fight off. So I took the decision out of his hands and threw in the towel to end the fight and I would do it again in a heartbeat. Gary was very understanding and his father thanked me for taking the action I did and while it was a shame that it had been a disappointing night for us, it wasn't the end of the world. Gary was such a realist it was depressing at times for a dreamer like me and I believe in his heart he thought he'd reached a peak and wasn't capable of going to that next level.

But as well as being too pragmatic for my idealistic ways, Gary is also an incredibly responsible and dedicated family man who never wasted a penny of his earnings as a fighter. He invested wisely and was making plans for retirement years before it would occur to most boxers. In short, he's a smart cookie and not long after losing to Pavlik and getting his day in the sun, Gary retired to become a boxing manager, physical trainer and property developer. As it transpired, our paths would cross again soon after.

That night in Atlantic City completed what had been a miserable six months for the Team Calzaghe stable, Joe aside. Little did I know but things were only going to get worse.

Less than a fortnight later I was in Birmingham for an Amir Khan bill as Bradley Pryce was successfully defending his Commonwealth title against Marcus Portman. It was a great night, though Joe who had said he'd be there to support Bradley, never showed up. He was keeping a low profile and about to make public via the *South Wales Argus* on the Monday his intention to promote his remaining fights himself and split with Frank Warren. It ended in dispute and in court and was an extremely difficult and upsetting time for everyone involved. What I can say is that I regret it happened and wish it never did. As a promoter I have the upmost respect for Frank Warren and as a person I like him a lot.

There were obvious consequences to the split and regrettably, the first major change came when Nathan Cleverly told me he was going to leave to train with his father Vince. Vince had been training amateur fighters in a couple of small rooms above Bargoed Social Club and felt ready to start with Nathan alongside his co-trainer Alan Davies. What could I say? I didn't want to lose someone who I thought was legitimately moving towards a world class level, but by the same token, if people can't see the similarities between Nathan and Vince and Joe and myself they are mad. Can I really be angry at them and the success they've enjoyed together? Of course I can't. Nathan didn't leave me to go elsewhere, he simply left to go home.

Nathan cited 'boxing politics' for his leaving and despite some negative press releases in the first few months after our split, he has never said a bad word about his time in our gym to my knowledge. 'The Clever Boy' is well known for having a maths degree but I would argue it wasn't just at Cardiff University where he got a first class education. The chance to spend so many hours with Joe and our other top calibre fighters was ideal preparation for the next chapter in his career. Since he left our gym Nathan has become the Commonwealth, European, British and finally WBC world champion at light heavyweight and I love the fact he acknowledges the part we had to play in that. Nathan boxes like an Enzo Calzaghe fighter and that is because Vince Cleverly trains with a style he learned in our gym. Good for them. They are both people I still count as friends and Joe and Nathan remain very close.

Joe was targeting at least one more big fight in America and didn't see Kelly Pavlik as a viable option. Pavlik was a middleweight and it was impossible to pair them up, or so we thought. To our astonishment Pavlik signed up to fight Bernard Hopkins, who even at forty-three appeared determined to fight on despite losing to Joe. For me the Pavlik camp had got greedy and maybe because they started to believe their own hype about Joe's shortcomings, they thought Hopkins possessed no threat. I thought at light heavyweight it was a total and utter mismatch. Hopkins was way better than Joe and I had expected and I certainly wasn't surprised when Hopkins completely and utterly destroyed Pavlik. Kelly might have gone in undefeated, but he copped an absolute hiding on the night as Hopkins tore him to pieces like a hungry lion with a startled gazelle. He was so clever and so dominant. It was an aggressive display and people were shocked. Hopkins went on to reclaim his *Ring Magazine* title as the top light heavyweight in the world after Joe retired and is still going strong. People who think he was washed-up when he fought Joe need their heads examining.

Having beaten Hopkins too, Roy Jones really represented the only viable option left for us. He had looked a million bucks in his previous fight against Felix Trinidad, had a huge profile and was desperate for the fight. HBO had stated they were perfectly happy to cover the contest live from the UK, but Joe was seduced by the idea of Madison Square Garden in New York. It was a romanticised venue, arguably boxing's Mecca where all the greats had fought and I certainly wasn't going to argue. They split the purse and Setanta were on board again and the fight was made for November. In the end it was very easy, which is funny since we'd been trying to do a deal with Jones for ten years or more.

I don't know if it was things happening outside of the gym or if it was because Joe was underestimating Jones, but our preparation was awful. Twice in one week, Joe came in for training and I knew he'd been drinking the night before. He had a degree of comfort with his weight because it was light-heavy not super-middle and I didn't like his attitude. I lashed out at him and he got a double shock in one afternoon and that snapped him right back to his best.

"Sometimes Dad could read me better than I could myself. I thought everything was fine and I was looking forward to the fight with Roy Jones. Four weeks before we were going to America I turned up at Mum and Dad's house to go for a run and Dad told

me to "fuck off," and asked me what I was doing. What are you talking about I thought? He said I was in the pub too much and not working hard enough. "It's probably your last fight, you've come to the end and you're fucking it up and cutting corners," he argued and I knew instantly he was right. It was exactly the kick up the arse that I needed, a proper wake-up call. I went running on my own and when I got back my younger son Connor was upset. He had been watching Roy Jones clips on YouTube with a pal and was more than a bit impressed. "Please don't fight him Dad, he's absolutely amazing, he's the best fighter in the world. Please, please don't fight him," he pleaded and I was taken aback. From then on I knew I had to step it up. I assured Connor that Jones wasn't that good anymore but I knew I had to be at my best and wasn't working hard enough. Two wake-up calls in about an hour and a half were all I needed." Joe Calzaghe

From then on we saw the real Joe again and I was relieved, but nevertheless thinking that probably this should be Joe's last fight. He loved boxing and that hadn't changed, but I think the training and restrictions on his lifestyle in terms of what he could eat and how much he could socialise were starting to seem like sacrifices not worth making. Joe was thirty-six years old and financially set for life. What more challenges were there for him? He'd gone undefeated in fifteen years as a professional, eleven as a champion and was now the best in the world at light heavyweight as well. Realistically, what was left? I kept my thoughts to myself and looked forward to the opportunity of seeing a city that apparently never sleeps.

New York is a wonderful place and I thank my lucky stars that the Calzaghe boys were afforded the opportunity to be involved in such a massive night of boxing. When I made that phone call to Uccio all those years before to tell him I was quitting Foreign Legion and wouldn't go to tour in America, Madison Square Garden was exactly the kind of venue we had dreamed of playing. We booked an amazing apartment right by Central Park for a month and Sergio, Uccio and I all stayed with Joe and Kerry Hope who came over for sparring and to feature on the undercard.

We had also planned to take Bradley Pryce with us after his

well-documented problems trying to get a visa for Las Vegas but sadly it was the same old story. This time he even got to travel on the plane to the States. Unfortunately he was detained at passport control and never made it out of JFK Airport. He was incarcerated for an hour or two and then escorted onto the first plane back to London! I guess it's funny to think of now but at the time we were cross and Joe especially wasn't pleased because Bradley was always a terrific sparring partner.

Vegas had been the most surreal experience with the people we met, the neon lights and the glitz and glamour, but to me New York felt like the most amazing boys' holiday. We had a great time in the apartment cooking meals and playing music and it was a magnificent autumn in NYC with bright sunshine and proper short-sleeves weather. We arrived before the New York marathon which finishes in Central Park and Joe's daily run would be along the final stretch of the marathon route. It was so picture-perfect it was like being at home with the beautiful scenery and crisp fresh air we'd always had on our doorstep. Everything about New York appealed to my sense of romance and adventure. I felt the kind of feelings I encountered on my travels and I was starry-eyed.

We ate some fantastic meals in little Italy and Chinatown and went up the Empire State Building and really behaved like tourists. Joe was being filmed by a crew from HBO for their 24/7 documentary series and because of that I even got to do some busking with a homeless guy which I think shocked the cameraman but was probably not a surprise to anyone who knows me. That was one of the highlights of the trip for me and I think it goes without saying, I always show homeless people respect wherever I am. I will always be a poor man in my heart.

We were calm and collected heading into the big fight. Unfortunately, Kerry Hope's opponent failed to make the weight and Kerry missed out on his dream of boxing in the Garden. It capped off a memorable trip for Kerry for all the wrong reasons. He had to try and keep up with Joe in tip-top condition and it was a struggle. When we found out Kerry wasn't going to get to box we consoled him with a slap-up meal in Little Italy and now his weight wasn't a factor he wolfed down a spaghetti carbonara. Unfortunately two hours later Joe wanted to do a work-out and the short version is that Kerry's lunch ended up all over my shoes!

Joe was fantastic though, the most serene I had ever seen him. He loved the lifestyle in New York and we got in some great sparring partners. Despite all his previous problems, his hands were fantastic and the only drama was created by yours truly. I almost caused a riot at the final head-to-head press conference.

I should explain that the backdrop to the fight was the US Presidential election which was happening in the days leading up to the fight. Barack Obama or John McCain were about to become the new President and there was a real buzz in the air, with the word "change," being bandied about a lot. The day before the head-to-head, Obama officially won the election. Jones was very proud of America after Obama's historic victory as the first African-American President and played into the whole "change," "Yes we can," slogan in saying he was going to beat Joe. I went into rant mode in front of a room full of Jones' friends and fans. "Change mate, what change? There ain't going to be a fucking change," I told everyone in America.

Here are some of my quotes from the press conference.

"The road has been very long. Twenty-five years of being a pain in the ass to Joe. I remember the first fight and now we are going to Madison Square Garden. As many of you know I never boxed in my life. It has been exciting. One thing I would like to make clear is that Joe was the first to say to me, 'Dad I want to box Roy Jones. Dad, I want to box in America. Dad I want to box at Madison Square Garden.' Of course I was thinking we could box in Wales. And he said no, Dad I want to go to America and I want to fight at Madison Square Garden."

"Joe is going to kick Roy Jones' ass. What do you think of that? We have just come across the shore to kick ass. We don't need cheerleaders. On fight night, Joe possesses what no other fighter does; and it's called a heart. When Joe's been down in the fight, he always finds a way to win. The harder the fight, the harder he works to win."

(To Jones) "Roy you are a good friend, but make no mistake,

Joe Calzaghe is coming to kick ass. On Saturday night, he is going to become 46 and 0. You are going to see a fantastic display from Joe Calzaghe. Roy is going to fight his heart out, but it won't be enough to beat Joe. Change? There ain't going to be no fucking change! We didn't come here to fight to lose. We are going to be at Madison Square Garden with all the Americans pulling for Jones. We picked this place. We picked this place to kick ass."

Some people reacted furiously, but I didn't give a fuck. It was pure passion and some people told me afterwards they enjoyed my, shall we say, *eccentric* performance.

The only change on fight night was that we didn't have Dean Powell with us who used to work Joe's corner, as he is Frank Warren's matchmaker. Dean is fantastic at what he does and I shared many a beer and good evening in his company. But I still had the services of Frank Black and Brian Coleman and we were a formidable team.

Frank Black and Ernie Fossey before him were two guys Frank Warren had paired up with us. They became true friends and both merit their own credit in Joe's success. Ernie worked with us until his death in 2003 and he was an honest and reliable presence in the corner, meticulous in his preparation. I really respected him and both Joe and I paid our respects at his funeral. A former fairground booth fighter, Ernie's canny matchmaking had played a big part in helping Frank Warren overtake Mickey Duff as the top promoter in town. He had a wicked sense of humour and was a man of real integrity. He used to get really annoyed when British crowds abused foreign fighters and for a man of his generation I think that speaks volumes about his amazing character.

Frank Black was a much quieter sort of a guy but he also had a wonderful understanding of boxing and was in Joe's corner for his last nine fights. Frank died peacefully in his sleep just a month after our New York adventure. He's greatly missed too.

Everything was familiar and as it should be and Joe didn't even have the needle and conflict to worry about that came with doing promotion with Bernard Hopkins. Roy Jones was a class act from start to finish and not a word of trash talk was spoken by either fighter. Joe and I felt that Jones was dangerous, but had less left to give than Hopkins, even if he was the younger man. Your actual age and your boxing age often don't correlate. Joe was thirty six but boxed like he was twenty-six and we were confident that would be the story of the fight unless Jones landed a bomb.

Two minutes into the first round, Jones landed a bomb.

More accurately, Joe walked right on to a bomb, coming out of a clinch and walking with his hands down into a combination that left him crumbled on the canvas. The alarm bells went for me big time. I've seen fighters hurt and knocked down and I'd seen Joe knocked down three times. I'd never seen him this hurt. His legs were a mess, wobbling all over the shop when he made the count and he still had forty seconds until the end of the round. 'He's gone,' I thought. When he recovered within ten seconds I felt guilty for my moment of doubt. But if it had been Roy Jones at his peak maybe the fight would've been over. We will never know and the only person to blame for that is Roy Jones. He could've fought Joe long before.

It was Joe's intention to make this a much more entertaining fight for the American public than his dirty clash with Hopkins. This was also a different situation. Before he beat Pavlik, America had fallen out of love with Hopkins and he had little or no support in Vegas, it was a Calzaghe crowd on the night. But the USA loved their Olympic gold medal-winning, four-weight world champion and icon Roy Jones and at the end of the first round the crowd were raucous. Joe was losing badly and had been beaten up by the all American hero. He was in the Lion's Den now and the sense of occasion in Madison Square Garden was everything we dreamed it would be. It was just the dream was turning into a nightmare.

That has always been the situation where Joe thrives and while there were no fireworks in the second round, all three judges scored it in Joe's favour. The next ten were clear cut. From round three Joe looked invincible. He began dropping his head and his hands and showboating like he was a teenager in the exhibition halls and he dazzled Jones with his speed and the sheer velocity of his punches. He was throwing ninety punches a round as a minimum and by the eighth session Jones suffered a horrendous cut above his eye. He was partially blind for the remainder of the fight and there was simply no way back for him.

I really must take issue with some ringside commentators saying Joe disrespected Jones in the final rounds by showboating and geeing up the crowd. I think that's a disgusting accusation. Before that fight Joe had thirty-two stoppage wins from forty five fights and once Jones got that cut, as they'd say in New York, "forget about it." Jones was a goner and if Joe had desired I know in my heart he could've stopped him and hurt him. Joe didn't go hell for leather to take out Jones because he respected him and he respected the fact that most of the public were there because they loved Roy Jones. Joe had put on a boxing masterclass, an absolute clinic in Madison Square Garden and that was enough for him. But to suggest he tried to embarrass Jones is absolute bollocks, the total opposite is true. He allowed Jones to be on his feet at the final bell.

It was a glorious win for Joe and the praise was positively gushing.

"THIS was the night when Super Joe became Superman with an out-of-this-world performance. The night when Super Joe Calzaghe turned himself into a real-life hero amid the skyscrapers of New York. As Roy Jones Jr left the Madison Square Garden ring with a badly cut left eye, a bruised face and battered ego, Calzaghe waved to his fans and screamed: "I am Superman". Not many on the wet streets of Manhattan would have disagreed as the Welshman dismantled Jones over 12 gripping rounds with the same kind of powers The Man of Steel used against villains. Superman's famous arsenal of power, speed, stamina and vision were the elements Calzaghe used to put Jones in his place in front of 14,512 people inside an arena that rocked from the ring to the rafters. Calzaghe showed character when Jones delivered a first-round insult by catching him on the side of the chin with a flashing right cross — although it appeared the American's forearm did more damage than his fist. The Welsh dragon was up off the canvas after referee Hubert Earle reached four — he was floored in the same round by his last opponent Bernard Hopkins in April. Speedy Calzaghe went on to unleash so many turbo-charged punches that ringside officials were left dizzy trying to keep count.

For the record, to retain his Ring Magazine *light-heavyweight belt, Calzaghe threw 985 punches compared to the American's tally of 475. The Pride of Wales landed 344, the most ever by a Jones opponent. His vision was underlined by the uncanny way Calzaghe slipped Jones' counter-punches. Slip here, duck there as Jones landed just 12 jabs — that is ONE a round... Calzaghe's critics will write off Jones as an old man at 39 who was shot after too many tough ring battles. But all a fighter can do is beat the opponent in front of him. And Calzaghe did more than that, producing arguably the best performance of his career to underline claims as the best pound-for-pound puncher around. Calzaghe wanted to step outside the comfort zone of fighting in Europe. He has done that twice now and seen off Hopkins and Jones in the States to take his 100 per cent record to 46-0."* Pat Sheehan, *Sun,* 10 November 2008.

Jones was sadly beaten up badly and couldn't even attend the post fight press conference as he needed to visit the local hospital. Yet again Joe had beaten a legend of America. We had a wonderful evening of celebration. Setanta put on a party in a downtown Manhattan bar and we drank the night away with friends, family and well-wishers. Everyone was talking excitedly about what was next for Joe, but I had a feeling I knew. I couldn't bring myself to say the words though and it wasn't the right time.

"Everyone had warned me not to make a rash decision about retirement. You are a long time retired and I didn't want to say I was retiring only to come back. That's tacky to me when fighters do that. I knew it was going to be pretty amazing to fight at Madison Square Garden and the way I fought made it a proud day because I was pretty close to my absolute best. I had my kids there with me, most of my family in fact and I was very content with the experience. A load of people were calling me, out including Chad Dawson, Bernard Hopkins and Mikkel Kessler, who did so within half an hour of the fight, but I didn't see the point in staying around for any of them. What was left for me to prove? I had already beaten Hopkins and Kessler and was anyone really convinced by Dawson? We had a great party after I beat Jones

and everyone was asking me what is next, what would I do, who would I fight? I was non-committal but told five or six people there who I trusted that I was pretty certain I was going to call it a day. I figured it was just about the perfect way to bow out. Plus I was getting earache from my kids to retire and I had promised Mum years before that I would quit by the time I was thirty-five. I'd already gone back on that one, so I figured I owed it to her to (nearly) keep my word. I promised to wait until the New Year but in my mind I knew I was done from that night onwards. Anything I said otherwise was just bravado." Joe Calzaghe

I knew the time would come that we would have to have a heart-to-heart and a few weeks later I made it clear to Joe I thought his instinct was right when he told me the news I had expected and dreaded in equal measure. "If your heart is telling you to retire, that is what you must do," I told him.

I was happy for Joe even though I had no idea what that meant for our future. Joe was thinking about life outside of boxing and I just had to deal with it.

As we headed into 2009 I knew he was done and it was only a matter of time until that became official. I still had my other fighters but none of them had been enjoying recent success apart from Bradley Pryce. It was going to be a period of readjustment and I joked to Joe that I didn't know what the fuck I was going to do.

"But we'll be promoters Dad," he said with a completely straight face. "Are you joking, Joe?" I replied.

He wasn't.

Unfortunately.

Chapter Seventeen:

Calzaghe Promotions

I had so long to prepare for Joe's retirement that I should have been better adjusted by the time he came to make his decision. But I struggled to even put on a good poker face. I was starting to feel really low about how our stable had fallen to pieces.

Joe's official announcement of his retirement came in February 2009, after much deliberation. He had signed with the famed football agent Paul Stretford who is perhaps best known for working with Wayne Rooney, and Paul arranged for Joe to give an interview with the BBC. They reported his retirement on the six o'clock news and Joe did his column with the *South Wales Argus* straight afterwards. He explained that he felt he had nothing left to prove and owed it to his family to quit. He stated unequivocally that was that, done and dusted for good. Thirty years of his life dedicated to boxing and he signed off with two ten-minute interviews. Some TV highlight reels aired later in the week, tributes were written in the papers and then it was over with little fanfare.

I think Joe was quite heavily influenced by Lennox Lewis and the grace he showed in retirement. I know it's the natural reaction to dismiss a boxer retiring as being like a band leaving the stage when you know they'll be back for an encore. But with Joe it was different. He was committed to his decision. We talked long and hard about it and just as importantly, Joe really waited to assess exactly what options he had if he decided to fight on. Many people couldn't understand why he didn't want to chase Rocky Marciano's world record streak of 49-0. He could've done that easily in twelve to fifteen months. But he wasn't motivated by that record. If there had been four more quality fights for Joe, maybe, but the truth is there was no-one worth bothering with.

Mikkel Kessler wanted a rematch but we've never really gone in for rematches, it seems like a waste of time for everybody, especially the fans. There were people like Jermain Taylor and

Chad Dawson who were mouthing-off and of course Carl Froch who did nothing but call out Joe, but none of those fights was a motivation for us. I knew for three months that any day now Joe would be calling it a day, but I wanted things to stay as close as possible to normality, so I tried to put it out of my mind.

Four bums in a year and Joe would've had the greatest record in boxing history. He could've taken Carl Froch out at Wembley Stadium and what would it have meant? We just didn't see any potentially exciting match-ups. If Froch had been less brash, perhaps Joe would've been more agreeable to the prospect of facing him. In the past couple of years, thanks to the Super Six, Froch has shown himself to be world class. But at the time he was a mouth who couldn't back it up and we resented always having to talk about him.

In retrospect, and I'm sure Joe would acknowledge this, but since his retirement you can definitely make a case that Chad Dawson has proved he would've actually been a good option. Dawson has a great record, but I feel in his defeat to Jean Pascal we saw that he didn't quite have enough to be a legitimate threat to Joe. But that's the only fight that, in hindsight, I think maybe we should have considered more carefully.

I supported Joe's decision and thought he was doing the right thing. As his father I was thrilled and proud of him for showing such common sense and perspective on life. He was rich, had never been hurt and had achieved a phenomenal legacy in a dangerous sport. It was the right move. But as his trainer I was sad for myself. I knew how much I would miss working with and being with Joe every day and from that sense it was devastating. What now?

I still had Gavin Rees, Enzo Maccarinelli and Bradley Pryce and up-and-comers Kerry Hope and Hari Miles training with me. In addition, Mo Nasir had joined our stable and was a huge prospect. Mo was a local kid whose family came to South Wales from Yemen and I loved him instantly. He had been training in St Joseph's with Tony Borg and came to me after signing professionally with Frank Warren. He was an amateur star and a Commonwealth Games medallist and I had high hopes he could be my next world champion. He had lightning-fast hands and a relentless work rate and I felt his style was tailored perfectly to flourish under my watch. He was made for me.

Unfortunately it never worked out for Mo. A routine physical examination before his professional debut showed up an issue with a potential head injury and Mo was never granted a licence to box despite a two-year battle that saw him take medical test after test. I felt awful for the kid and it was a shame for Welsh boxing as he was a superb prospect, a potential world champion without question. Mo has now opened his own boxing and fitness gym in the centre of Newport and he conducts fitness sessions for all sections of society in the city, including some homeless people. He has lots of immigrants and street kids working out in his gym and has raised a lot of money for various charities. I am incredibly proud of him.

As far as possible, it needed to be business as usual after Joe retired. He was considering trying to be a promoter and had already obtained a US promoter's licence ahead of the Roy Jones fight. But in the immediacy he was preoccupied with his looming court case after his split with his promoter and that ended up taking a big toll on me too.

I had to give testimony in court and the timing couldn't have been worse, as both Enzo Maccarinelli and Bradley Pryce were set for action imminently on a big bill in London's Docklands, headlined by Amir Khan fighting Marco Antonio Barrera. Enzo's fight was for the interim WBO world title and it goes without saying that I was highly motivated to see him get back to world title level. But the truth is, for the last couple of weeks of his preparation, I simply wasn't around as much as I needed to be and need to hold my hands up to that fact.

Enzo was totally in control against Ola Afolabi, around five or six rounds clear on the judges' cards entering the ninth round. A couple of years before, Macca would have blasted Afolabi to Timbuktu but he hadn't been fighting as confidently since the defeat to David Haye. Enzo had become more and more preoccupied with his physique and developing muscle definition and it was to the detriment of his power and stamina. He was training in Swansea on the side and doing far too many weights and it changed him. Afolabi absolutely destroyed Enzo in that ninth round, a big shot and barrage leading to a brutal stoppage and I was heartbroken. It completed a thoroughly miserable night after Matthew Hall, a robust and powerful fighter who ended Kerry Hope's undefeated record, smashed seven shades of shit out of Bradley Pryce for six solid minutes, enough to take Brad's Commonwealth light middleweight title after six successful defences.

Both Enzo and everyone else laid the blame firmly at my door after the fight and I knew the writing was on the wall for our working relationship. Enzo wasn't going to be leaving Frank Warren, he had no reason to do so and he blamed me for losing a world title eliminator. I was toast as far as he was concerned. He announced that he had left our gym and what could I do? I sighed and got on with things. I didn't think Frank Warren would exactly be queuing up to offer Bradley a big fight after his quite pathetic performance and it dawned on me that it would be a long time until I was involved in a big boxing bill again. That was in March 2009 and I am still waiting to this day.

There were no obvious prospects for Gavin Rees and Bradley Pryce and both of them wanted to stay with me as their trainer and if we could get it off the ground, were happy to become Calzaghe Promotions fighters. They signed up with us after their release and Joe promised them he was serious about making it as a promoter.

In Paul Stretford, Joe had a high-profile name as a business partner and he had me to be his house trainer. He also had a lot of good will in South Wales to make a success of the venture and knowing that he needed someone with good organisation and a good business brain on board with him as well, we started working with Gary Lockett who was thinking seriously about going into boxing management. Brian Coleman was our matchmaker. On paper, we had as good a chance as anyone to make a good go of things with that team. We had a former world champion as our main fighter and both Bradley Pryce and Tony Doherty, as well as Kerry Hope from our stable plus a huge talent pool in Wales waiting for good opportunities.

It was an exciting period as the court case thankfully ended and everyone moved on ready to begin the next chapter. I was sad that

I was no longer working with Enzo Maccarinelli and Nathan Cleverly, but I completely understood why they opted to move on. If only we had done likewise. But plans were in place for Calzaghe Promotions and we called a press conference to announce our first show in Merthyr. Unfortunately, the only headline that came out of it was Bradley Pryce revealing he managed his weight for the Matthew Hall fight by becoming bulimic. I was embarrassed, mortified and ashamed this had happened on my watch, as it was a serious issue and thankfully one that he overcame. I really had taken my eye off the ball.

The show, to a degree, was a successful start for us in that all our punters enjoyed themselves. It was a good atmosphere and the action was spectacular. Sadly our headline fighter Kerry Hope lost very unfortunately after suffering a nasty cut against Taz Jones which was typical of his rotten luck. And while the fans enjoyed themselves, the show was amateur hour and very chaotic. We didn't have enough security staff and plenty of punters didn't pay to get in. We forgot about having any seats for the media boys and the journalists had to go to a storage cupboard at the Merthyr Leisure Centre to get foldaway chairs to sit on. Our ring announcer didn't turn up and several hundred posters disappeared too. We lost a shed load of money, over £20,000 on just one show. Welcome to promoting!

From then on we should have realised we were fucked, but stupidly Gary Lockett and I fought hard to keep going. I think reality set in for Joe on that very first show and he realised it wasn't for him, but pride meant we kept going even though we had nothing to offer.

Joe's involvement was becoming more and more half-hearted and I couldn't strike up a rapport with Paul Stretford. We argued constantly and that put Gary in an awkward position. We had no interest whatsoever from any television companies and that made us just another small-time operation. There are hundreds across the UK and our sloppy presentation meant we didn't stand out. I naively presumed the TV companies would queue up to support us because of Joe's name. I couldn't understand why they weren't offering to help and I wasted a lot of time trying to talk to TV executives on the phone.

It was quite a comedown from the heights of Vegas, Madison Square Garden and the Millennium Stadium to be squabbling over hundreds of pounds and negotiating six round fights in leisure centres. Ricky Hatton is a great example of how, if you were prepared to work hard, lose a lot of money initially and are passionate about what you are doing, it is possible to make a success of a new promotion company. But we didn't burn cash and that meant we were sunk from the start. Hatton Promotion shows looked the real deal and ours looked amateurish by comparison.

Unfortunately, Joe lacked the drive and passion for it and we weren't willing to invest serious money. We had to call off a show in Newport because ticket sales were abysmal and Joe's dedication to the cause lessened still when he agreed to sign up for BBC dancing show *Strictly Come Dancing,* after expressly writing in his autobiography that he never would!

It was understandable on his part as it was a good opportunity to raise his profile while he decided what he wanted to do with the rest of his life. It gave Joe a chance to be on a programme his mother would want to watch, doing something far removed from what he was known for. However, it was a full-on commitment with daily training and Joe's interest in Calzaghe Promotions diminished each day.

It was great in my mind that Joe was doing *Strictly* to try to maximise his earning potential. I had never understood his reluctance to do so in the past. Frank Warren presented Joe with potential earning opportunities several times over the years, but he turned them down flat. Marks and Spencer wanted Joe to do some modelling and he said no as he didn't want to be pictured in his underwear. He saw himself as a boxer, nothing more, nothing less, and didn't want the distractions of celebrity status. Now he was retired though, everything including our promotion company benefitted from him having an increased profile. Unfortunately, he didn't exactly take to dancing like a duck to water.

"I don't regret doing Strictly Come Dancing even though I promised I never would. What can I say? People change! It was actually a tremendous experience for me and since I retired, there

was probably never a time I was happier than when I did the programme. It gave my life structure and discipline like boxing did and I had missed that, having a purpose and discipline each and every day. I enjoyed rehearsals a lot and learning a new skill which I found challenging. But under the lights when the TV cameras were rolling? It was a totally different feeling. Each and every time I went out there I was shitting myself and didn't enjoy it one little bit. It became worse and worse as the weeks went on, I just couldn't get it together." Joe Calzaghe

It annoyed me that people who would never have the bottle to do something like that, absolutely slaughtered Joe with insults and jokes about how rubbish he was, but I was proud he gave it a go. And it wasn't all bad because he met his partner Kristina Rihanoff who had the unenviable task of dragging him around the studio every Saturday night. Kristina and Joe hit it off straight away and they have dated since.

We were planning on ending the year with a splash and putting on a Calzaghe Promotions show to make people stand up and take notice. We had the Newport Leisure Centre as the venue and a good undercard too. Lee Selby, now on his way to a world title was on the bill as was Hari Miles and a good kid named Jeff Evans who was one of the first fighters to sign as Gary Lockett embarked on a career as a boxing manager.

The top of the bill was the long-awaited return of Tony Doherty who had been inactive for absolutely ages as his weight ballooned and he picked up a facial injury fighting outside of the boxing ring. It wasn't exactly the return of the king, but we needed Tony back to his best if people were ever going to take us seriously. We weren't sure how likely it was that he could make it at welterweight, so we stuck him in with Geraint Harvey who was a light middleweight with a poor record of six wins in fifty one fights. We got it sanctioned as a Welsh title fight but that was irrelevant to us, we just needed Tony to look good in his inevitable victory to get tongues wagging.

Things did not pan out as we had hoped, to say the very least. Harvey fought for my matchmaker Brian Coleman and that was foolish for starters. Brian had such a vested interest it was unhealthy, just like when Kerry Hope fought Taz Jones, another boy from Brian's stable. Brian's boys kept beating mine! We had rushed Tony into action too quickly, his fitness was poor and even at light-middleweight he was totally drained. He'd lost something obscene like four stone to make weight and in retrospect we shouldn't have let him fight. After two very uninspiring rounds, Harvey hurt and then stopped Tony in the third which was a disaster. Geraint's fans went nuts in their celebrations at such a shock win and Tony's family and friends were absolutely horrified. Tempers were flaring and I was panicking about a full-on riot as the atmosphere suddenly got very dark. Luckily Gary Lockett talked some people into calming down and the security staff did their job to prevent a mass brawl, but Joe had fucked off out of there the second the fight ended. I never saw him move quicker! He hadn't enjoyed the show or being part of it and I knew for certain he wouldn't sink another penny into the venture.

We had deliberately kept Gavin Rees off the bill as he had taken a gamble and decided that he wanted to enter a relatively new format for British boxing called Prizefighter. Gavin was the boxing equivalent of a one-hit wonder after his short world title reign and he desperately needed a career shot in the arm. I am sad to say that meant by far and away his best option was Prizefighter.

At the time it was still a relatively new and exciting format and the boxing public had really embraced it. Personally speaking, I wasn't a fan and thought it absolutely ridiculous that a three round loss would count on your professional record and I have never changed my opinion on that. It's a fun format, but I don't give it much credence as a true measure of a fighter. But the situation was simple in that Gavin wanted to do it because the prize of £32,000 was lucrative and we would have done him a disservice if we denied him the chance. Gavin wasn't even entering at his natural weight. I'd have loved to have seen him concentrate on boxing at lightweight but he still lacked the understanding or desire to ensure his diet was suited to that of a professional sportsman.

Therefore we had no option but to get Gavin as well prepared as possible for a concept I still see as something of a crapshoot. Gavin was the thoroughbred in the field for the light-welter event, but with a strong calibre of competition there was no chance we could win it without Gavin showing the desire and commitment which led to him becoming a world champion.

Fortunately that was exactly the Gavin that we saw and it marked the beginning of a renaissance in his career. He was head-and-shoulders above the other contenders and I was extremely proud of him. Gavin dominated three exceptionally dangerous opponents in Ted Bami, Jason Cook and then Colin Lynes in the final. There were no stamina issues and the victory got people talking about Gavin again and that was exactly why he'd been so desperate to enter in the first place. I had been wrong in questioning his desire to participate as it was just what his career needed.

But where the fuck could we take him from there? No-one was saying it, but Calzaghe Promotions was dead as a dodo and with no prospect of getting things back on track. Poor Gary Lockett and Ian Bird who was doing our press were tearing their hair out by the end as everything fell to pieces. One boy signed for us called Chris Evangelou, a London lad who had previously been an actor. We unveiled him at a press conference, he had one session in the gym sparring with Gavin and Bradley and we never, ever saw him again. That about summed us up and our fighters risked being shut out in the cold for good.

I was letting the boys down. Suddenly all we were good for was six round fights on small bills for crap money and it felt shitty. I was becoming bitter about boxing, feeling like an outsider despite being praised and admired until Joe retired. I had utterly run out of motivation. That must have been getting through to the boys in the gym because they began talking about working with Gary Lockett as well who was ready to move on from Calzaghe Promotions and become a trainer/manager. I knew that with Gary the boys would have a far better chance of getting on bigger bills because their contracts with Calzaghe Promotions were turning out to be useless, whereas Gary had good relations with Matchroom Promotions and Matchroom had Sky Sports behind them. My boxers were asking questions I simply couldn't answer. When would I get them a fight? I had no idea. I felt like a washed, up trainer who no-one seemed to remember existed and I was holding the boys back.

In March 2010, I put a stop to everything. Everyone needed a change and I told my fighters to go to Gary Lockett with my blessing and that as far as I was concerned I would relinquish all financial commitments we had. As their manager, I was entitled to compensation, but that wouldn't have been fair. Tony Doherty, Gavin Rees and Bradley Pryce all left for a fresh start and I was ready to walk away. Hari Miles started training with Vince Cleverly and Kerry Hope went to America where it didn't work out and then to Bolton where thankfully it did. Kerry won the European middleweight title in 2012 in a huge upset and no-one was happier than me.

It was reported in the press that I was pretty much retired and at sixty years old I honestly believed it was all over. I should've been content with my lot, but I wasn't.

I was increasingly angry and felt more pissed off than proud. Boxing training had never been a calling for me. It was something I fell into. I lived perennially expecting Joe to leave at any minute and I'd never expected to have such a long and rewarding run. But when it was gone it hurt like hell and I couldn't fathom what I had done wrong to have everyone leave and walk out on me. I know that sounds melodramatic, but it was how I felt. Joe was splitting his time between home and London, so I was seeing him less and less and suddenly the gym was empty and silent. It tore at my heart. My home life with Jackie was wonderful and I got to see my daughters and grandchildren every day. That made me happy. But I'd been used to being Enzo the boxing trainer and suddenly that was gone.

Every single day, come rain or shine, I would get up, go running and then go to the gym. Nothing changed except I was no longer a trainer. I was still a bloke in a gym that used to house fighters, a man in his sixties with no idea whatsoever about how to fill his days or his time. Most of the time I just cleaned and swept the floors, still desperately clinging on to the glory days. I would ring journalists and bitch and moan about how unfair everything was, and before long a lot of the people who I had considered friends wouldn't even answer their phones anymore. I had become a bitter old geezer, and with nothing going on, I was becoming more and more engulfed in this cycle of misery and self-pity.

"I feel like a fucking ghost, Joe. I might as well be fucking dead," I told him now on more than one occasion. I'm becoming more used to the fact this is how it is, but my blood still boils four or five times a week when I get a phone call that never changes no matter who is on the line. It might be a producer for a boxing programme, a businessmen looking for an after-dinner speaker or a journalist looking for a line, but it's always the same conversation. An introduction, some small talk and then they ask me if Joe would be interested in this or that. I am his secretary to them, nothing more and nothing less.

I feel gutted every single time. Why has the boxing world turned its back on me? I just don't understand it. I've got the qualifications, haven't I? Have I not done enough for British boxing to be on the radio or the TV every now and again? Why am I a leper, seen as a useless old man who is good for nothing apart from being an answering service for Joe? Now that Joe isn't boxing, I don't exist. That pisses me off. People close to me say it's because the TV companies are probably worried I will burst out swearing and maybe they are right! But I never get asked for print interviews either.

It all got me down and there isn't really a way out of that until things change and largely speaking, you have to change them. But I was out of ideas and out of motivation. Boxing had become something I despised and that made me angry. Yet the more depressed and fed up I got, the more I obsessed about the sport and I would watch fights on television knowing I'd end up feeling miserable.

I had an especially hard time adjusting to watching Nathan Cleverly. Now I swear on my kids' lives, I have told you the complete truth when I explained that Nathan leaving the gym was cordial and done without animosity, but that didn't make it easier for me to cope.

As was natural, considering the way Joe and I parted the scene, Cleverly's promoters weren't shy in pointing out just what a super job Nathan's new training team were doing with him since he left the gym. There were quotes in the papers from Nathan saying how he'd moved on to a new level and that the Calzaghe gym was always more about Joe than anyone else. That fucking enraged me because it wasn't true. It also really struck me as being unnecessary.

There were also stories with quotes from Vince Cleverly in which he was playing down the role I had in Nathan's success and that hurt even more. I had always embraced Vince's presence in the gym even though Enzo Maccarinelli and Joe found him to be a pain in the arse at times. Vince sometimes said things before he engaged his brain and having given so much time and opportunity to him in our gym, I couldn't understand why he felt the need to degrade me.

That was then. I feel no resentment to Nathan or Vince and understand what was happening. Vince was trying to make a name for himself and legitimise himself in people's eyes as a genuine trainer of a future world champion. How could I, of all people, not understand that insecurity? Vince was Nathan's dad and until he proved otherwise, people would just assume he was along for the ride and lucky to be there. God knows, I had been there myself. And Nathan spoke to me a couple of times and made clear that things that were being said by him were to sell tickets, generate interest and only part of the smoke and mirrors of boxing. He never hid from Joe or I after he left the camp, and Nathan, from the day he arrived to today, has always treated me with respect and gratitude. In the boxing game it's not uncommon to find yourself making headlines for saying something you don't really mean. I can see the influence of the years he trained with me in the way he fights but I can't help but be impressed by the job Vince and Alan Davies have done with Nathan. While Gavin and Bradley were despairing as their careers stalled because they made the mistake of staying loyal to me, Nathan was flourishing. Frank Warren clearly had enormous faith in him and the very next fight after he appeared on the Hopkins bill in Las Vegas, he became a Commonwealth champion. After four successful defences he became the British champion too and a month before I walked away from boxing he won the European title.

Not only that, he was suddenly knocking people out left, right and centre. In 2011 Nathan went to the next level and won a world title. As I write this book he is undefeated, trained by his father and a world champion with the world at his feet. Naturally, he is compared to Joe in virtually every assessment and he copes wonderfully with such pressure.

Nathan fully credits Joe and me with the role we played in his success and Joe is Nathan's biggest supporter. The pair of them work-out together quite often and Joe is always the first to offer Nathan advice to go with the several hundreds of hours they've shared together in the ring during sparring sessions. I have no doubt whatsoever that when the time comes for Nathan to face a top calibre southpaw, Joe will happily pull on his gloves again and do some sparring in Bargoed if Nathan wants that. When Nathan beat Tommy Karpency in Cardiff in February 2012, I sat at ringside and I felt very, very proud of him.

While Nathan's career skyrocketed after he left us, it broke my heart watching Enzo Maccarinelli's career continue to flounder. It was very sad to see his slide continue. I knew in my heart that a lack of sparring and supervision wasn't the reason Enzo and Bradley Pryce lost their fights to Ola Afolabi and Matthew Hall respectively, and I worried for the pair of them. Bradley hadn't prepared properly and had dieted appallingly, and to my mind Enzo had never recovered from the Haye defeat and reacted in the wrong way by concentrating on the way he looked rather than the way he fought. He was rigid as a board because of all the weights he was doing.

Enzo's fortunes didn't change by leaving our gym and I wasn't surprised by that and it upset me to see him suffering. After he lost in a fight he should have won against Alexander Frenkel for a European title, and ended up with a broken jaw and a broken heart, everyone including me expected him to announce his retirement. But before all that happened I wanted him to know as a friend that he had my love and support and so I phoned him.

We chatted for quite a while and Enzo was at a low ebb. His heart was breaking, his jaw wired almost completely shut and he'd spent the past nine months commuting back and forth from Lancashire because of his training situation. Enzo knew I had effectively shut up shop and moved on, but he asked me if I would consider training him again.

That was genuinely a shock to me. I called him as a friend and I didn't have any ulterior motive about rekindling anything. But I liked the sound of it. I knew that if we started working together it would barely cause a ripple in the boxing ocean; we were both suddenly very small fish. I was a used-up trainer and Enzo a used up fighter and I felt like I wanted it, so I said yes. The more I thought about it, the more I realised how happy the thought of training a fighter five days a week made me. I was thrilled and Enzo and I have worked together for three fights and he won them all. We had a long heart-to-heart and the first thing I said was that I would insist on him becoming a light-heavyweight fighter. Enzo has always found it easy to control his weight and in retrospect it was a huge error to persist at cruiserweight after the Haye defeat. One of us should have spotted that fact sooner, but the problem was that Enzo's heavyweight power blinded us to that fact.

Unfortunately, following the death of his father Mario in 2012, who I considered a dear friend, Enzo returned to cruiserweight. Though he won a British title in tribute to his father, for me the fight against Shane McPhilbin emphasised why his future needs to be at light heavyweight. Enzo was put down and but for bad time-keeping, might have lost the fight. I hoped to continue his journey with him and remain his trainer but it wasn't to be after we had a few differences of opinion, including the fact I didn't want him to return to cruiserweight (for his own good). Enzo and I split for a second time in the summer of 2012. Hopefully he has one last big run in him and can get back to where he belongs.

But ever since that call with Enzo in early 2011, that has been my life again, training boxers on a daily basis with a few amateurs popping in from time to time. Chief among them is my grandson Joe and that means the world to me. Joe (senior) never, ever wanted his kids to box and Connor his youngest son has never shown the slightest bit of interest. But Joe Jr wanted to give it a crack and I enjoy working with him, and also his mate Cody who is the son of Kevin Davies, a great pal of Joe's who invented the Counterpunch boxing aid which we used in the gym, a device that measures how many punches you throw per second. It's very rewarding having the younger guys in, it's like going right back to the start of my career as a trainer. I've always got amateur fighters popping in now, I like it and consider it a compliment.

But that hasn't been all that has filled my days thankfully, because I never expect to be back among the elite in terms of British boxing trainers. I am no longer just focusing on boxing because frankly, I wouldn't know what the hell to do with myself for all those spare hours in the day. That is a problem for anyone moving away from professional sport, or going from full-time to part-time as I feel I have. Joe found it bloody difficult at first and the whole family endured the anger and shame when he hit the headlines after the *News of the World* set him up in a sting operation to admit he snorted cocaine. That was a lousy day and it still makes me angry to think about it. Firstly, there was no story. The *News of the World* went to great expense to set Joe up to admit that since he's retired from boxing, he had tried drugs, something he obviously didn't do in his teens or twenties, unlike most of his contemporaries.

Did it make us proud? Of course not, but by the same token Joe had been honest about things and it was nowhere near a big enough scandal, in my view, to justify the way they got the story. It was a fake sheikh sting operation and for what? To get a retired sportsman to admit he had tried recreational drugs. What is the purpose of that story? Probably about the same as some girl who was supposed to be Ricky Hatton's friend stitching him up in the same manner. It makes my blood boil. It's hardly like Joe or Ricky Hatton are publicity whores.

Joe needed direction after the promotion company hit the skids and his new relationship made the transition easier for him. He has been taking acting classes and doing bits and pieces on television and he seems content. He's back and forth from London and still sees his kids all the time. He's got things well worked out and that makes me happy.

I've kept myself busy too, but just occasionally things have happened that have simply blown me away. The first occasion was when our home town of Newbridge opened a brand new £3.2 million bridge that was named in our honour. It links the town centre to the outer sticks part of our community and that's an honour I can barely even express my gratitude for, not adequately anyway. Long after Joe and I are gone our names will live on in that bridge.

However, even that doesn't eclipse the elation and honour I felt when I was contacted to be told I was going to be awarded an MBE by Her Majesty the Queen. I have been proud to become so embraced by the British public over the years and this felt like the icing on the cake. I know some people are political and don't think much of these kind of titles, but to me it is a validation of your efforts and I was phenomenally excited.

They tell you to keep the news to yourself when they tip you the wink, awaiting a letter of confirmation, but it should come as little surprise that the whole of Newbridge and most of Wales, the boxing fraternity and a few random strangers knew pretty much as soon as I did. It was hard to not get emotional about the past when I heard the news. What would my mother have thought of me getting recognised by the Queen? I think it would've blown her mind. She so wanted me to make her proud and I hope that I have done. What greater validation of my life's work since residing in the United Kingdom? And as an Italian going to Buckingham Palace was almost as exciting as being awarded the medal, it was a dream.

But, not long after I got the letter, a phone call arrived, a game-changer. It was a very simple enquiry. Was I a British citizen?

Hand on heart, I had no idea if I was or not. I presumed so, as I was married to a Welsh girl and had lived in the UK on and off for fifty years, but I didn't know for sure. I promised to investigate, so did the Home Office and we both came to the same conclusion – no, I wasn't a British citizen. The upshot of that was that I would be unable to go to Buckingham Palace to receive my MBE.

I didn't really know what to say about that, but I was advised to discuss the matter with the Welsh Assembly, so I did. They were incredibly supportive and explained to me that I could go to Buckingham Palace to collect the MBE and take my wife as I dreamed, but only if I could pass the UK Citizenship Test. The what? I had no idea what they were talking about. But apparently if I paid thirty-five quid I could take an exam with twenty-four questions about the United Kingdom and if I passed I would become a British citizen. I had frankly never heard a bigger load of nonsense in my life, but I went along with it and even agreed to do some practice questions with some of the Welsh Assembly staff.

"Enzo do you know what a quango is?" they asked me.

"Of course I do, it's a song," I said, dead serious. They all cracked-up laughing and explained a quango is an acronym for quasi-autonomous non-governmental organisation. "I see, I see," I nodded along. I didn't have the heart to tell them I didn't understand a single word they had just said, including the word 'acronym'. What's a fucking acronym? I thought it was something you took when you had a headache?

But I went to Cardiff and took the test despite myself, and there wasn't a single person there who had lived in the UK for anywhere near as long as I had, so I was confident. Shortly after we finished, they started administering the results and everyone seemed very happy and relieved to be getting good news. I was the very last person called and I anticipated I'd been kept to the end because I was a little bit of a celebrity and they wanted to make a fuss of me.

"Pietro Calzaghe I presume," the man said. "I am very sorry to tell you that you've been unsuccessful."

I blew my lid. I couldn't believe that despite all my years of living in the UK I couldn't get citizenship because of a stupid test. They told me I could do it again, but I didn't see the point. I felt humiliated, I guess, and couldn't see any logic in the process. My sister Alba, bless her, hasn't lived in the UK a day since she was a little kid, but she is a British citizen. If you don't want me to be a citizen then fine, but don't make your decision based on some stupid test with out-dated questions. I'm angry even writing about it.

But unfortunately that failed test put an end to any hope of going to Buckingham Palace. Despite that disappointment it was still lovely to be recognised for services to boxing and being awarded the MBE at a reception in Wales was still a wonderful moment in my life.

But more and more, I am happy to be out of the sport in any significant sense. Boxing to me is the greatest sport on earth but there are certain things that niggled me for decades and still do.

Sometimes, when you are a boxing trainer, you feel you are treated like a dog. If a fighter loses, it's invariably the trainer who gets the blame from the promoter. If the promoter can't get a fighter the purse he wants, then the fighter will bitch and moan to the trainer. Trainers get a tiny, tiny percent of what a fighter earns and yet it is the fighter's prerogative to dump a trainer on a whim whenever he see fit. Similarly, many promoters would advise a boxer to change trainers irrespective of what is going on behind the scenes. We often feel like we're at the bottom of the barrel in boxing, yet without trainers, the sport couldn't exist. I would love to change that, though I have no idea how I could.

The chances are that I will never again stand in the corner for a top fight, will never again hear the roar from a capacity crowd. Slowly but surely, I've come to accept that fact. But my life has been full of adventure since moving to England as a toddler, I can't just sit down and do nothing. What's next?

Epilogue:

Smiling Again

As I said before, being idle simply isn't for me. My effective retirement from boxing can't just lead to a game of golf a week or a game of bridge because if I stand still, I am worried I will drop dead. Why not try and properly live in every moment?

I still have aims and ambitions for my life and passions, things I can do to make me happy. The hardest transition in my life was after Joe's retirement and the failure of Calzaghe Promotions. It made me a bitter person and slowly but surely I've accepted boxing and me are probably over and done with in terms of being a top level trainer. But I am not without ideas and plans.

I'd love to try and tackle the general obesity in the United Kingdom, particular, among young children. I think bringing boxing back into schools would be a wonderful idea and I would love to be involved in boxing at an amateur level. To have the chance to work with some future Olympic champions would be a dream, but I have no idea if it will come to fruition. My gym door is always open and the ring is still in use. We've put on some great amateur shows there for a few dozen people and I love it.

The obesity issue is something I can do my best to tackle here and now, though ,and I've already started. In 2012, I started the 'Calzaghe Challenge' which sees large groups of kids coming to my gym and doing a big workout session. It's amazingly rewarding. I have loved doing it and would love to make it a nationwide thing. We need to get kids off the PlayStation and into exercise. I've also done a bootcamp-style training session with Glamorgan County Cricket Club which was great fun and I'm thinking of allowing corporate companies to come and pay to do the same thing. It seems a good business idea.

My brother Sergio and I also made a fitness DVD called 'Rage against Obesity.' Again, this is aimed at kids. It's quite musical and all of the characters in it are computer animations, funny little characters that a friend of mine helped me to create. We play melodies and try and make the work-out fun and interactive. It was enjoyable to make. I've also started doing some after-dinner speaking. It doesn't come naturally, but I love meeting the boxing fans and talking about the great nights we had.

I still play music every day too. Sometimes Serge, Uccio and I get together and jam and it makes me feel twenty-one again. We've recorded a few tracks in the past few years and that is always a thrill.

Without a big stable of fighters to train, I have got involved in some other projects and have become fascinated with filming, ever since we were followed by a camera crew for a documentary on BBC Wales called the *Calzaghe Clan*. It followed our lives and mine in particular when we were trying to get Calzaghe Promotions off the ground. I enjoyed the experience and asked a million and one questions to the production team about the mechanics of what they were doing. Television is a funny format in a lot of ways. By way of example, the BBC insisted we had no more than seven instances of the word "fuck" per episode. I think the editors had their work cut out with me. Since making the show I've invested in some cameras of my own and we've had lots of things going on.

I filmed a tonne of footage recently in Sardinia and took a crew with me to do a documentary. Hopefully somewhere, someday it'll be seen by someone whose surname isn't Calzaghe. Sardinia is a beautiful place full of great stories and I want to show that. I love the documentary style and it is something I hope to try again.

I also decided to try and make a movie; and yes, I know that sounds crazy. I have absolutely no experience or expertise in that field, but I decided to make a film and I've had a helping hand from lots of people in Newbridge and the surrounding areas in making it a reality. We've filmed at the boxing gym, in the local pubs, the shops and let me tell you everyone in Newbridge is in the bloody thing. I've got a role, Sergio has a role, Enzo Maccarinelli is in it, my mate Kevin Davies, some local guy who pushes a trolley around the village called Dai Trolley – you name it, and they are in this film. It is a gangster film set in the backdrop of the boxing world – the *Godfather* meets *Rocky*. Now I will be honest here, I don't necessarily think that Steven Spielberg should shit his pants and give up on his career as a director. Something tells me that our debut film, which I have called *Stitched Up* although the title has changed about seventeen times since we started filming, isn't necessarily destined for the Oscars.

But what else am I going to do? Sit around doing nothing and become a couch potato watching Eastenders? No thanks. I have come to the realisation that the only way I can move on from the bitterness I feel about the end of the Team Calzaghe stable is to keep myself as active as possible.

But sometimes I realise all that stuff I find myself obsessing about isn't as important as I make it out to be. The boxing politics, the feeling of rejection from the sport, it isn't the be-all and end-all, and whenever I am feeling sorry for myself I try to remember how lucky I am.

For Father's Day last year Joe got the whole family round to his place. So that's Jackie and me, Sonia and Dave, her partner, and her four kids, Chris, Chloe, Elle and Louise, Melissa and her husband Tim plus Mel's kids Dylan, Jacques and her youngest, Alba. Kristina, as well as Joe's kids, Joe Jr and Connor, were also there and it was wonderful, all being together. We drank, we laughed, we ate lots and lots of food and then Sergio and the grandkids proceeded to throw me into Joe's swimming pool fully clothed! The kids obviously found this the most hysterical sight of their lives and within a few minutes virtually the whole family were in the pool too, and we were all splashing about and shouting our heads off. Even Jackie got chucked in fully clothed and she's the boss! But it was that sort of occasion. Laughter and love and all that a man my age could need to fill his heart.

I looked around me and realised this was as special and as perfect as life gets. Everything I've done and everything I plan to do means nothing at all without family to share it with. To my grandchildren I am just grandpa Enzo and with that title, how bad can things ever really get? I see my grandchildren every day and that's enough for any man to feel happy about. I can look forward to my grandchildren getting married, maybe even making me a great,granddad. What a privilege.

While I don't intend to retire gracefully and fade into the shadows, and I will always be on the lookout for the next adventure, I have made certain promises to myself. I am determined to no longer obsess about what I had and what I feel I am entitled to in boxing. As long as my family are by my side, I will be a happy man. I'll keep my enthusiasm for life and adventure and see where it takes me. But if I'm destined to fade from the spotlight and just be grandpa Enzo, I am ok with that. I've lived my dreams and I wouldn't change it for the world. It's been a beautiful ride.